AMERICAN VISTAS
1877 to the Present

American Vistas
1877 to the Present

Edited by **LEONARD DINNERSTEIN**
UNIVERSITY OF ARIZONA

AND **KENNETH T. JACKSON**
COLUMBIA UNIVERSITY

New York OXFORD UNIVERSITY PRESS
London   1971   Toronto

For
Barbara Jackson
and
Myra Dinnerstein

PREFACE

The last century of American history has been as exciting a period as any nation has ever known. In this time the United States emerged as the dominant industrial and military power in the world. At home there have been extremes of riches and poverty, and abroad glory and despair. American ideals have permeated global institutions, and American leaders have been both hallowed and vilified, but never ignored.

It is rewarding for students to study these past one hundred years because many contemporary concerns have evolved from events of this period. The notion that our present-day society is unique may indeed be true, but it is necessary to recognize that contemporary issues are deeply rooted in past problems and concerns. Certainly our search for panaceas is endless, but we must be informed in our attempted solutions by knowledge of past times, people, and places. Urban affairs and ecology, for example, constitute two of America's most serious domestic concerns, but the problems of slums, overcrowding, sanitation, fire, transportation, disease, prostitution, and clean air and water were as serious concerns in the last century as they are in this one. And venal city and state governments in the 1890's and early years of the twentieth century more than matched anything contemporary society possesses. Even "imperialistic wars" predate the contemporary era.

The sixteen essays included in this volume deal with the panorama of human experience through an examination of American heroes and myths, urban development, varying standards of morality, economic depression, and the proper use of American power on the world scene. Unfortunately, popular history has been a term with unsavory connotations because most works in this category are more popular than they are history. The essays within were selected on the basis of interest and readability, but they also represent the work of some of the most distinguished scholars in the United States. With this combination, it is hoped that *American Vistas* will offer to the student an exciting, rich, and intelligent sampling of this nation's past.

Because we assume that this anthology will be used chiefly in conjunction with a survey textbook, we have focused upon questions and events generally lightly treated in the basic classroom volume. This has meant a heavy emphasis upon urban, social, and minority history, and relatively slight treatment of the political aspects of our national development. And where we do deal with major political figures and events, such as Presidents Franklin D. Roosevelt and John F. Kennedy, or the United States in world affairs, we have selected essays which treat these subjects from perspectives different from those set forth in the standard texts.

In such a short volume the problem of proportion has been especially difficult. Obviously all of the major aspects in American history could not be encompassed, but we have attempted to maintain a rough chronological and geographical balance. Each article is preceded by a brief introduction which places the selection in context and points out some of the more important issues that the selection might raise. The complete citation is also included so that students seeking documentation may refer to the original source.

For aid in the selection of articles we wish to thank Professor William E. Leuchtenburg of Columbia University, and Professor William H. Hackett of Henry Ford Community College. Joseph A. Fineman and Christine Niklaus Sharp helped with the proofreading. It would be impossible to acknowledge adequately the substantial participation of Barbara Bruce Jackson at every stage of compilation. She represented the intelligent non-professional historian in our deliberations and worked as an equal partner to help make our anthology both scholarly and literate.

Leonard Dinnerstein
University of Arizona

Kenneth T. Jackson
Columbia University

December 1970

CONTENTS

I INDUSTRIAL DEMOCRACY
1877–1920

The Frontier Hero in History and Legend

KENT L. STECKMESSER

• Long before Frederick Jackson Turner gave his famous
1893 address on "The Significance of the Frontier in American History," the idea of the West was important to Americans. In a vast almost unexplored and unknown land the
men who first faced the wilderness were obvious candidates
for national hero-worship. Oral legends circulated about a
Tennessee backwoodsman named Davy Crockett even before he was dead; when he fell at the Alamo in 1836, his
place in folklore was assured. As Professor Kent L. Steckmesser observes in the following reading, Kit Carson, Wild
Bill Hickok, and Buffalo Bill were among the superhuman
heroes who shaped a national ideology of self-reliance, energy,
and optimism. Of course the image of the West did not
conform to reality; the average frontiersman did not kill wild
animals with his bare hands, and the streets of Dodge City
did not regularly run with the blood of high noon shoot-outs.
At no time did the "West" account for as much as 10 per
cent of the nation's population. Yet the images and the legends live on. Do television and motion picture stereotypes
of the western hero represent a continuation of a century-long
search for national heroes? Or does the popularity of "westerns" reflect the need of an urbanized people to look back
toward a seemingly more exciting albeit less complex and
troubled time?

The frontier hero personifies the westward movement in American
history. The characters and exploits of such type-figures as Daniel
Boone and Billy the Kid, Kit Carson and Buffalo Bill Cody are well

From *Wisconsin Magazine of History*, 83 (1963), 168–79. Reprinted
by permission of the author and the editor.

known to the American public which knows that Boone discovered Kentucky while looking for "elbow room"; that Carson was an Indian fighter; that Bonney killed twenty-one men before he died at twenty-one. Yet the popular narratives about these heroes are only partly historical. In fact, underlying the surface variations among the heroes is a common pattern of anecdote and characterization which is literary and folkloric rather than historical in nature. This pattern is most clearly revealed in four aspects of heroic legend: Genteel Qualities; Clever Traits; Prowess; and Epic Significance.

In 1835, at the fur trappers' summer rendezvous in Wyoming, Kit Carson fought a duel to the death with a French-Canadian bully named Shunan. Shunan had been riding up and down threatening to "take a switch to the Americans" in camp, and Carson challenged him. In his manuscript "Autobiography," Kit says he warned the bully that "if he made use of any more such expressions, I would rip his guts"—and we can be sure that his language was even stronger than that. But in the first Carson biography, published by DeWitt C. Peters in 1858, the speech is reported as follows: "Shunan, before you stands the humblest specimen of an American in this band of trappers, among whom, there are, to my certain knowledge, men who could easily chastise you; but being peaceably disposed, they keep aloof from you. At any rate, I assume the responsibility of ordering you to cease your threats, or I will be under the necessity of killing you."

This editing of Carson's language illustrates a significant feature of frontier legend. The reality of the hero's speech—as well as his character, philosophy, and appearance—are seldom recorded in popular narratives. Biographers, responding to literary conventions and metropolitan preconceptions, typically edit all these personal details. The result is often a stereotyped character who is both pretentious and genteel. The frontier hero's speech becomes exceedingly elegant in both diction and grammar. The coarseness of the mountain man's lingo, with its "hoss," "wuth it," and "wagh," which is accurately recorded in firsthand narratives such as those by Lewis Garrard and George Ruxton, is missing in the popular biographies. The language is purified, and the barbarisms are replaced by refined expressions. From a technical literary viewpoint, it is difficult for an author to write a biography or a novel using dialect only. Yet the end result of this purification of language is an inaccurate record of frontier life.

All frontier heroes are given this conventional, stilted language. Daniel Boone delivers grandiloquent speeches when he first discovers Kentucky: "No populous city, with all the varieties of commerce and stately structures, could afford so much pleasure to my mind, as the beauties of nature I found here." Boone was no ignoramus. He could write passable English, though he did spell "bear" as "bar." But such speeches were the handiwork of his first biographer, John Filson. Even in biographies of outlaw-heroes, where one would expect some earthy language, the weight of the literary convention is so great that these ferocious characters are assigned drawing-room diction. In one paperback volume (1881) which purports to be a biography of Billy the Kid, there is this dialogue:

He was riding along the road in an aimless manner, when he again came upon his friend and partner, Tom O'Fallaher.

"Well, Billy, what now?" asked Tom.

"Old Chisum an' I have had a row," replied the Kid.

"What, you and he split?"

"We have."

"He owes me, and won't pay."

"Why blast his mug, take cattle enough to pay you."

The idea had never struck the Kid before. It was capital, and just the thing.

"I'll do it," he said. "We will organize the old band again, and prey upon his cattle. The old scoundrel, after all we have done for him, to be thrown aside for some new favorite."

"The old band and the good old times. The dashing down on ranches and moonlight raids again; hip, hurrah for the jolly old band."

The hero's character, as well as his language, is altered to fit the genteel pattern. The hero must not smoke or drink. He must profess the Christian religion. He must have philosophical depth, and be self-conscious about his historical role in settling the West. One reason for this kind of purification is made clear in the preface to J. W. Buel's popular anthology, *Heroes of the Plains* (1882): "While this volume abounds with thrilling adventures, sanguinary encounters and personal combats of the most startling character, yet through every page there is observed a thread of wholesome justice, upon which is strung every deed recounted, preserving a forcible and moral influence beneficial to young and old alike." If the frontier hero is thus to become a model for "young and old alike," this purpose requires the excision of material which, though factual, may be of questionable moral quality.

The actual Kit Carson swore on occasion. In his youth he enjoyed the riotous, drunken brawls at the fandangos which the trappers held when they returned to Taos. He was indifferent to religion; his conversion to Catholicism at the age of thirty-four was merely expediential, being necessary for his marriage to a Spanish woman. But these facts have been carefully ignored by his biographers. John S. C. Abbott said in 1873: "Indeed Kit Carson was never a jolly man. He had no taste for revelry. As in every man of deep reflection and true greatness, the pensive element predominated in his character. . . . We can not doubt that Mr. Carson was in heart thoroughly a religious man. It is the element of religion alone, which, in the midst of such temptations, could form a character of such remarkable purity." This interpretation is not outdated, since Abbott's book was republished in 1901 and 1915, and is today the only Carson biography in many public libraries.

Other heroes go through a similar ritual purification by their biographers. Buffalo Bill Cody, for example, admitted in his own *Autobiography* that he had a fondness for the liquor bottle. In fact, the historical evidence for the location of many of his scouting parties on the plains are the piles of champagne and beer bottles which he left behind. Yet Cody biographers seldom refer to this character trait.

The hero is also required to have an elevated sense of his own mission, and to philosophize about his historical role. The Boone of history moved west because of economic desires, and left Kentucky not because he wanted "elbow room" but because his incompetence in legal and business affairs forced him to vacate his land claims. The Boone of legend, however, goes west because of an epic vision of his role in settling the wilderness. Biographer Filson gives the pioneer this speech: "I now live in peace and safety, enjoying the sweets of liberty, and the bountres [*sic*] of Providence, with my once fellow-sufferers, in this delightful country, which I have seen purchased with a vast expense of blood and treasure, delighting in the prospect of its being, in a short time, one of the most opulent and powerful states on the continent of North-America; which, with the love and gratitude of my country-men, I esteem a sufficient reward for all my toil and dangers." Reported John M. Peck in 1847: "He spoke feelingly, and with solemnity, of being a creature of Providence, ordained by Heaven as a pioneer in the wilderness, to advance the civilization and the extension of his country." Despite the evidence of innumerable biographies, however, it is safe to say that the frontier heroes of history were not philosophical types. The firsthand documents suggest that they were men of action who did not spend time pondering the deeper implications of their activities.

The legend also requires that the hero be of impressive physical stature and appearance. Thus writers who scarcely know their subjects describe Boone as "a tall man of powerful frame," while Carson is often compared with Hercules. Actually the epic frontiersmen were of small to medium build. Kit Carson was five feet six inches tall by one hundred and thirty-five pounds, and contemporaries describe him as "short and wiry." Nathan Boone described his father as "five feet eight inches high—broad shoulders and chest, and tapered down. His usual weight was about one hundred and seventy five pounds." Bill Cody was about five feet ten inches tall, and weighed around one hundred and seventy pounds. These are hardly Herculean statures, which means that the popular writers are creating their own heroes.

So the hero's speech, character, and appearance are altered to fit a preconceived ideal. The ideal is essentially metropolitan: the gentility, the elegance, and the moral virtue of the type-figure are superimposed upon the heroes by those not of the frontier. This is true even of frontier biographies written in the twentieth century. Although the Christian requirement has been removed, the moral purity is still insisted upon. Of course the actual Boone, Carson, and Cody were admirable men in many respects. But there is a yawning gap between the men revealed to us in historical documents, and the genteel paragons of legend.

Dime novels were important in the early deification of the frontier hero. Custer, Cody, Carson, and Hickok romped through hundreds of paperbacks in which they are cleansed of all vices. Carson's reply to a bully in Edward S. Ellis' *Carson the Guide* (1872) represents the type of language featured in these narratives: "Do you suppose that I would retract to such a miserable coward as you? Do you think I am afraid of you? I despise you as I do the greatest loafer in New Mexico. If you don't like what I say, do what you think best about it." These novels also propagated the idea that gunfights were chivalric affairs in which the participants observed a "code of the West." In Prentiss Ingraham's *Wild Bill, the Pistol Dead Shot* (1882), the *code duello* is punctilliously observed. Bill and his opponents wait politely for the signal before beginning to shoot. However, Wild Bill's own death at Deadwood is probably more typical of frontier shooting than the legendary duels of the dime novels. It is, of course, hard to tell how seriously the readers accepted these stories. But they were commonly subtitled as "authentic," "ever true," or "historically true." And utilization of a well-known name as the vehicle for a series of fictional adventures has a persuasive appeal that has been fully appreciated by the producers of our current television westerns.

A second major aspect of the legendary pattern is the assignment to the hero of "clever" traits. The hero invariably outwits his frontier adversaries, be they Indians or renegade whites. Illustrative anecdotes are gratuitously assigned to particular heroes as symbols of the necessary character trait. Most of these stories are significant as legend, although irrelevant as history. None of them meets the standard tests of historical documentation. The exploits are usually performed alone, so that no authentication is possible.

To this class belong the various cliff-jumping episodes in which the hero thwarts pursuing Indians. Daniel Boone is trapped on the precipitous heights above Dick's River in Kentucky by a band of Shawnees: "Fearful to trust himself in the clutches of the Indians, he unhesitatingly made the leap, and lighted, as he aimed, in the thick top of a small sugar maple, down which he slid to *terra firma*, and found himself, comparatively unhurt, some sixty feet below the elevation from which he had just taken his flight." Or Wild Bill Hickok is trapped by Cheyennes while prospecting in Wyoming. He jumps off a cliff into a frozen stream, being lucky enough to land in an airhole. The Indians give him up for dead, but Bill survives by breathing from a pocket of air under the ice.

Such tales make the hero more memorable, but they are clearly generic or traditional rather than historical. The story of Boone's leap, though recorded by Lyman C. Draper, a renowned collector of Boone documents, was denounced by Boone's son and other relatives. Equally important, the sixty-foot leap was a traditional tale in the Ohio River country, being assigned to numerous individuals. Morgan Neville, in his 1828 story, *The Last of the Boatmen*, reported an identical incident for a pioneer named Huling. A similar tale appearing in various newspapers in the 1820's and 1830's was called "Ulin's Leap." The story was simply assigned to Boone to symbolize his ability to outwit pursuers.

Another type of "clever" tale popular with biographers is represented by the Boone "tobacco story." Boone, reported biographer Peck in 1847, was once surprised by four Indians while working up on the scaffold of his tobacco shed. The Indians taunt him and gloat over their success. But Boone has been quietly gathering an armful of dry tobacco leaves. With the savages' faces all turned up toward him, he hurls the bundle down, blinding them with dust. The redskins choke and curse while Boone jumps down and races to the safety of his cabin. From the historian's viewpoint, however, there is one flaw in this story. Daniel Boone never raised tobacco.

This class of tales is not confined to outsmarting Indians. The gunfighting exploits of Wild Bill Hickok and the escapades of Jesse James also fit the pattern. On the streets of Hays City, Wild Bill suddenly encounters Jack Mulvey, a gunman who covers him with drawn pistols. It looks like the end for Wild Bill, but glancing behind Mulvey he calls out, "Boys, don't hit him." As the startled ruffian turns to face this threat, Hickok draws and puts two bullets through his slow-witted adversary. This story has a classic appeal, but unfortunately the Kansas census records for the year in which this episode is said to have occurred do not record the death of any such individual as "Jack Mulvey."

As a Union scout during the Civil War, Hickok outwits his Confederate opponents by disguising himself and assuming the dialect of an Arkansas hillbilly. Similarly, Jesse James plays the part of a rustic innocent, and joins up with a posse searching for Jesse James. Both these episodes were contributed to the James and Hickok legends by the same biographer, J. W. Buel. He used a tested device for personifying a universally admired trait.

Many of these tales are legendary by virtue of a distorted interpretation of the facts. One of the cleverest exploits in Western history was Billy the Kid's escape from the Lincoln County, New Mexico, jail in 1881. Somehow Bonney acquired a gun and killed his two guards, J. W. Bell and Bob Olinger. This exploit was greeted not with applause but with shock and horror by the local press. The Las Vegas *Optic* of May 4, 1881, said: "Two efficient officers, in the discharge of their duties, were cut down in the prime of rife manhood, and while death is ever sad, this picture of ruthless murder in a stronghold dedicated to justice, is sad beyond portrayal by our weak words. To this young demon . . . the drooping forms of widows and the tear-stained eyes of orphans, give no token of the anguish within."

The conversion of this event into a heroic feat took many years to accomplish, but it was finally consummated in Walter Noble Burns' quasi-historical *Saga of Billy the Kid* (1926). Olinger is expertly portrayed as a snarling, foul-mouthed bully. The reversal of roles is of course, required by the legend of a heroic Billy. In an article for *Everybody's* magazine in 1902, Emerson Hough had described Bell and Olinger as "worthy deputy sheriffs," who "treated their prisoner kindly and with a certain good fellowship." But in the *Saga*, Olinger "never ceased to revile the Kid in tirades of scurrility and billingsgate." He taunts the Kid to escape so that he can be potted like a rabbit. " 'Eighteen buckshot, Kid,' he snarled. 'Don't forget what I said. Make a break and you get 'em right between your shoulder blades.' " This dramatic writing enlists sympathy for the helpless Kid, and when Billy greets Olinger from over the sights of the bully's own shotgun, one exults to see the tables turned. For latter-day enthusiasts this has been one of the most satisfying episodes in the Bonney legend, thanks to Burns' revision.

In addition to his cleverness, the hero typifies exceptional ability in such frontier skills as trailing, marksmanship, and hand-to-hand combat with Indians and wild animals. So there is a body of generic tales which serve to illustrate the hero's prowess. In all these activities, identical feats are assigned to different individuals. Both Boone and Cody, for example, perform the "two-in-one shot." This type of story became popular in journals like the *Farmer's Almanac* early in the nineteenth century. A hunter goes out and fires at a deer, the bullet killing not only the deer but several quail, a fine rabbit, and some fish. A similar story was assigned to Daniel Boone by Lewis Collins in his *History of Kentucky.* Boone goes out into the woods and encounters two hostile Indians. "He determined to kill both at one shot, and bringing his gun to his shoulder aimed at the foremost and waited anxiously for the other to fall in range. He did so, and Boone fired, the ball passing through the head of one and lodging in the other's shoulder." Buffalo Bill Cody is riding in pursuit of two Indians who are mounted on the same horse. He fires and the bullet kills both of them.

A variant of this tale-type is symbolized by the legend of Wild Bill Hickok's ability to shoot forward and backward simultaneously. The legend took printed form in O. W. Coursey's *Wild Bill* (1924). Two gunmen had decided to kill Hickok by closing in on him from opposite ends of a restaurant. But a friendly waitress warns Bill of the scheme, and he is equal to the occasion: "Wild Bill, facing the desperate character who entered the front door, had shot him with a revolver in his left hand, while with his right hand he had thrown the other gun back over his left shoulder and shot the man coming from the rear. History does not record a more daredevil act, a more astute piece of gun-work, or a cleaner fight." One can only agree with Mr. Coursey that history does not record such a performance.

Another classic symbol of frontier prowess is the four-hundred-yard shot. Buffalo Bill shoots the Indian Tall Bull off a horse at this distance, which was a respectable one for the frontier rifle. Cody's exploit was printed in an anthology called *Story of the Wild West* (1888) which was widely distributed. So we are not surprised to find other writers assigning the four-hundred-yard shot to their own heroes. Thus in a magazine article appearing in 1896, Kit Carson shoots an Indian off a cliff at four hundred yards.

The hero of legend always overcomes tremendous odds. The Indian-fighting stories often involve ratios of ten to one, with the hero invariably triumphant. Wild Bill Hickok became a national figure by virtue of his singlehanded defeat of the whole McCanles gang. The historical facts of this episode were that on July 12, 1861, Hickok shot down three unarmed men from behind a curtain at the Rock Creek stage station in Nebraska. The only member of the "gang"

who managed to escape was twelve-year-old Monroe McCanles. Wild
Bill and his friends were arraigned for murder, but were acquitted
because the county lacked funds for a full-scale trial.

George Ward Nichols in his famous story for *Harper's Magazine* in
1867 made a heroic legend out of this unpromising episode by effect-
ing certain changes in the story. The number of the McCanles party
is increased from four to ten. McCanles becomes a Confederate
conspirator who attacks Wild Bill because of the latter's Union sym-
pathies. Hickok defeats the whole gang in face-to-face battle, rather
than from behind a curtain. This fable, reprinted with little change
by scores of biographers and journalists, made Hickok a celebrated
hero. Even today, when this legend has been sufficiently debunked, the
encyclopedias still refer to the McCanles "gang."

In many versions of this story, one of the villains escapes to spread
word of Wild Bill's prowess. Nine-out-of-ten and three-out-of-four
legends abound in frontier narratives. Hickok rides up to a saloon in
Nebraska, where four insolent cowboys insult him and jostle him
as he is about to drink. In the resulting gunfight, three of the four
rowdies are killed. The survivor lives in Kansas City, and willingly
tells the story of the fight to all inquiring journalists. Billy the Kid
rides up to the line camp of his enemy, John S. Chisum, and shoots
three of the four cowboys there. The survivor takes word of the Kid's
prowess back to his boss.

Dime novels contributed to the inflation of frontier narratives. In
fact, reading exaggerated accounts of the hero's exploits robs his authen-
ticated feats of any meaning. The actual Carson's Indian-fighting accomplishments seem tame compared with the account in *The Fighting
Trapper; or Kit Carson to the Rescue* (1879) of how Kit fights with a
knife in each hand, and "slays two of his enemies at two different times
by such devices." Boone's actual combats are less impressive than his
defeat, in Frederick Whittaker's *Boone the Hunter* (1873), of a European fencing-master in a sword duel. And Bill Cody's documented exploits appear pale in comparison with Prentiss Ingraham's story, in
Adventures of Buffalo Bill (1881), of how he acquired his nickname:
he escapes from the Indians by riding the back of a bull buffalo.

The frontiersman is required to prove his prowess in encounters with
wild animals. There is a complete American bestiary in frontier narratives, and hand-to-claw combats with buffaloes, bears, and mountain

lions are a standard fixture. This convention reflects in part tall-tale inflation of actual encounters which were, of course, part of frontier life. But such episodes are more often a gratuitous contribution of biographers, frequently being borrowed from earlier accounts.

Many of these tales appear to have been inspired by the Davy Crockett *Autobiography* and almanacs. Crockett typically out-grins bears and performs other comic exploits. Subsequent heroes do not win their victories in this comic manner, but there is evidence that these narratives served as a prototype. The Crockett *Autobiography* describes Davy's fight with a "Mexican lion" when he is on his way to the Alamo. "He seized hold of the outer part of my right thigh, which afforded him considerable amusement." An identical episode, with the comic overtones omitted, is assigned to Kit Carson in later narratives. Similarly, one of Boone's biographers in 1833 describes how the pioneer, armed with only a knife, fights a huge bear. The story resembles the Crockett tales being printed in the same period. Wild Bill Hickok also fights a bear using only a knife, and his shout of defiance is clearly drawn from the Crockett tradition: " 'Chew away, old lady, for this is the arm that does the work,' shouted Bill, as he again drove his knife to the hilt." In border anthologies, particularly, it is evident that these classic animal-encounter tales are assigned indiscriminately to every hero represented in the collection.

A fourth connecting link in the legendary pattern is the assignment of epic significance to the hero's career. Epic claims are a convention in frontier biography. Of Daniel Boone, renowned in legend as the discoverer and founder of Kentucky, Lewis Collins said: "As the founder of what may without impropriety be called a *new empire*, Greece and Rome would have erected statues of honor, if not temples of worship." Other writers compared his explorations with those of Christopher Columbus. Kit Carson was compared with Hercules, Bayard, and Hannibal. Writing in 1858, DeWitt C. Peters said that "we think a world will eventually regard this extraordinary man as one raised up by Providence to fulfill a destiny of His all-wise decree." Writing in 1928, Stanley Vestal said: "Kit Carson's endless journeys through the wilderness make the fabled Mediterranean wanderings of Odysseus seem week-end excursions of a stay-at-home; his humanity rivals Robin Hood's; in readiness to fight and in chivalry to women he rates a *siege* at the Round

Table; his courage and coolness against hopeless odds may be matched but not surpassed by the old Norse heroes; while his prowess in innumerable battles . . . makes Achilles look like a wash-out." General George A. Custer was to his biographer "one of the few really great men that America has produced." And Wild Bill Hickok was something more than the cowtown marshal of history. He "played his part in the reformation of pioneer society more effectively than any character in the annals of American history."

From the historian's point of view these epic claims are not justified. The heroes were less important in the over-all history of the westward movement than the legend-makers would have us believe. Daniel Boone did not discover Kentucky; in fact hundreds of white men had preceded him there. Carson was only one of John C. Frémont's many guides, and he was perhaps a great traveler rather than a great explorer. George Armstrong Custer looms large in folklore, but he is only a minor figure in American history. Whether Wild Bill was a help or a hindrance in the settlement of the plains frontier is still a matter of debate, but it is significant that the people of Abilene built a monument not to Hickok but to his predecessor, Tom Smith. Hickok and Cody did some valuable scouting for the Army during the Indian Wars, but their real significance lies in theatrical history and showmanship rather than in the actual settlement of the West.

The preoccupation with epic stature tends to lead the biographer into sins of omission. He will leave out of the Carson biography such episodes as Kit's cold-blooded execution of three unarmed Mexicans at San Rafael in 1846. Carson was acting under orders from Frémont, but the episode was carefully ignored by biographers. Not until Edwin L. Sabin's book appeared in 1914 did the general reader learn of it.

Or the biographer may refuse to concede that some of his hero's actions are controversial, as did William E. Connelley in his treatment of Hickok's role in the McCanles affair. Connelley viewed Hickok as the greatest of frontiersmen, because he braved danger to clear a path for civilization. Any criticism of this idealized figure, any challenge to the legend, provoked an emotional response. Thus when the *Nebraska History Magazine* in 1927 published documents which cast an unfavorable light on Hickok's exploit at Rock Creek, Connelley attacked the "preposterous account." He was so dazzled by the vision of an epic frontiersman that he could not tolerate any blemishes in his idol. Indeed, it takes a courageous biographer to peer into the dark shadows of a hero's life.

However, this body of heroic literature does constitute an epic, though not in the sense claimed by the biographers. The Western hero's career has become an American epic by virtue of the form and content of the legends, rather than because of the historical importance attaching to their activities. The biographer's ritualistic observance of what is essentially a world-wide legendary pattern, guarantees his man a place in the pantheon of American heroes. The "Clever Hero," for example, is a type which folklorists have found in all nations. Thus the biographer who incorporates anecdotes in which his subject cleverly outwits his enemies is working with a proven formula. Similarly, the type of prowess which the frontier hero exemplifies in his combats with Indians and wild animals is also universally admired. The editing of the hero's personal characteristics in response to cultural expectations and conventions is also part of the pattern. Thus it is conformance with an age-old formula which explains the heroes' popularity.

The proven appeal of the legends also explains why they continue to be incorporated into biographies and histories. If Daniel Boone did not jump off the cliff, or if Wild Bill did not outsmart Jack Mulvey, then each is so much less the hero. So the biographer will continue to include these episodes, even though they are unhistorical, because they serve to confirm the heroic stature of his subject. Many biographers are quite frank in stating that such legendary anecdotes are *illustrative* of their hero's abilities. This is the key to the whole process. As symbolization proceeds, as generic anecdotes and characterizations are added to the hero's biography, the actual individual who lies at the bottom of the legend tends to become irrelevant.

Many of these same patterns can be seen in movie and television representations of the hero. These two media have now become the prime agents in disseminating legends about the West. In some cases producers have based scripts upon the printed biographies, and have simply appropriated legends from this source with little change. But more frequently they have made wholesale revisions of history to fit the demands of a particular production. This leads not only to distortions of history, but also to contradictory legends. In one film, *They Died With Their Boots On* (1941), Custer is portrayed as being sympa-

thetic to the Indians he had to fight. In another, *Sitting Bull* (1954),
he is depicted as a violent Indian-hater opposed to all treaties. In neither
case does the viewer get a historically honest picture of the man involved.

The genteel tradition is still strong in Hollywood versions of the
frontier hero. The first Billy the Kid movie in 1930 featured Johnny
Mack Brown, All-American football player, as the clean-cut hero. He
was dressed in fancy clothing, spoke flawless English, and served a just
cause by pursuing the corrupt lawmen. One reviewer remarked that
the Kid "was shown as sort of a philanthropic Robin Hood who shot
only to avenge a wrong done to a friend." The script writers were so
enchanted by this paragon that they permitted him to escape with his
girl friend at the end of the story, contrary to all history. Subsequent
films (above twenty-five in all) have also treated Bonney in sentimental
fashion, and have starred such wholesome leading men as Robert Taylor.

Gary Cooper played the leading role in the film version of Wild Bill
Hickok's career, *The Plainsman* (1936). Hollywood's Hickok was clean-
shaven, virtuous, and involved in a romance with the beautiful Calamity Jane. The Wild Bill–Calamity Jane legend is rooted in her
presence at Deadwood during the last months of Hickok's life, in her
burial next to him, and in printed stories which linked the two ro-
mantically. An early example of the latter is "Calamity Jane, Queen of
the Plains," a serial printed in Street and Smith's *New York Weekly* in
1882, which featured tender love scenes between the two. However,
there is no documentary evidence to support this tradition. Hickok was
happily married to Mrs. Agnes Thatcher Lake at the time he was in
Deadwood, and even had he strayed from the path he would more than
likely have picked a handsomer woman than Calamity Jane. Yet the
film imprinted this romantic legend upon the minds of millions of
moviegoers in highly dramatic fashion. And Cooper's identification with
heroic roles guaranteed that Hickok would henceforth be viewed as a
demi-god, however questionable the representation from a historical
standpoint.

Carson, Hickok, and Bonney have all become television heroes. The
Hickok series was first on the scene, in 1953, and it became the model
for a number of other pseudo-biographical programs featuring such
characters as Wyatt Earp and Bat Masterson. The heroes all function
as virtuous do-gooders. The Kit Carson of television has no occupation,

but simply rides around the West apprehending outlaws. He is accompanied by a Mexican companion who functions as a Sancho Panza to Carson's Don Quixote. Hickok is also accompanied by a comic deputy, and had the real Hickok seen their performances in his own day he would undoubtedly have hurled his impersonator through the nearest pasteboard scenery. But the conversion of Billy the Kid into a television hero, in a series called *The Tall Man,* is probably one of the most astounding transfigurations in Western legendry. Portraying this horse thief and hired killer as an occasionally mischievous juvenile delinquent is one of the grossest misrepresentations ever practiced in the industry. But the program is simply the latest and most distorted form which commercial exploitation of the West has taken.

In fact, the television Westerns differ little in either plot or characterization from their predecessors, the dime novels of the post-Civil War period. In both cases the exploits are exaggerated, historical events are rearranged to make a more sensational story, and the characters seldom represent the actual men whose names have been appropriated. However, the standard apparatus of frontier legend has been expertly utilized in both forms. The television heroes, like their dime-novel predecessors, perform "clever" exploits similar to the Boone tobacco story or Hickok's defeat of Jack Mulvey. By smart use of his gold-headed cane, Bat Masterson overcomes the corrupt sheriff and walks jauntily away leaving the lawman behind bars. Billy the Kid outwits the villainous sheriff "Tolinger" and rides off to perform further generous acts. By drawing upon the classic frontier legends just as Prentiss Ingraham did, the television producers have gotten a firm grip on the public imagination.

The history-legend pattern of popular Western narrative has been remarkably uniform ever since John Filson's sketch of Daniel Boone appeared in 1784. The nineteenth-century biographer and the twentieth-century script writer have both worked from a pre-set formula in which history has been expertly manipulated. The formula is recognizable through certain fixed characteristics. There is editing of the hero's career to make it conform to metropolitan literary or commercial standards. Constant use is made of stock exploits which, regardless of their historical authenticity, have proven their popularity. Great feats which the hero may actually have performed at some point in his career are generalized into an expected norm of conduct for his entire life. Sensational exploits which may have occurred years apart are made to appear as everyday events when compressed into a ten-page dime novel or a thirty-minute television show. The end result of these operations is that what we know as frontier "history" is quite often nothing but the repetition of a well-worn stereotype.

Some of these stereotypes have had an amazing vitality, and have a history almost as long as that of the frontier hero tradition itself. Daniel Boone has long been regarded as an antisocial individual, whose most characteristic statement was: "Too crowded; Too crowded! I need elbow room." Most Americans, in the many years that Boone has been a national hero, have accepted this characterization as authentic. Boone himself protested about this legend, which was growing even in his own lifetime. As he told one traveler who visited him in Missouri: "Nothing embitters my old age but the circulation of the absurd and ridiculous stories that I retire as Civilization advances; that I shun the white man and seek the Indians." Yet James Fenimore Cooper and other literati asserted that Boone fled when humans settled within ten miles of him. The elbow-room statement itself was invented by Timothy Flint, the Parson Weems of the Boone legend. It first appeared in Flint's biography in 1833, thirteen years aften Boone's death and a good thirty-four years after he had presumably uttered it. Later writers adopted the statement, erroneously assuming that it was verifiable. It has since appeared in the whole range of media by which a legend is transmitted: biographies, dime novels, histories, newspapers. Its most recent repetition was in Walt Disney's television version of Boone's life (March 19, 1961).

The creators and exploiters of these frontier formulas continue to be the professional hero-makers: novelists, newspapermen, script writers, and popular biographers. They moved into a vacuum left by serious historians, and captured the Western field by default. Since Americans have generally learned about the frontier West from these popular interpreters, it is clear why their picture has not been a true one. But these writers have been adept at creating the kinds of legends that people want to believe about the frontier and its heroes. They have done their job so effectively that Americans now revere the legends more than the truths.

Thus it appears that the most characteristic form of the Western legend is a popular narrative which features a hero with a historical name, and which perhaps contains a skeletal framework of authentic biographical information. However, the body of the narrative commonly incorporates exploits, traits, and evaluations which are inflated and legendary. Even competent historians are seduced by the color and obvious symbolic appropriateness of materials which they know to be legendary. These legends appeal to the human imagination: if they did not occur, they should have occurred. So the heroic narratives, in whatever form they appear, are valuable as a record of American aspirations and traditions. They are also valuable as case studies in the legend-making process, perhaps more so than as sources of factual information about the westward movement.

The Myth of the Happy Yeoman

RICHARD HOFSTADTER

• Throughout the first three hundred years of its colonial and early national history, the United States was primarily a land of farmers. As late as 1900, almost 46 million persons were making their living in agriculture or in rural areas from trades largely sustained by farming. By 1970, however, only 5 per cent of American families worked on the land; and there were fewer than four million farms in the entire country. The journey from country to city, from farm to factory had been constant with the effect of technology and urbanization. Thomas Jefferson's idealistic image of the independent farmer who labored on his own soil had been dimmed by an increasingly mechanized and unionized economy.

Yet the stereotype of the farmer with his homespun philosophy, folk wisdom, and self-reliance has been persistent in American politics, economy, and literature. In many instances, he was almost a folk hero, and his way of life has been frequently elevated to a religion. In The Blithedale Romance, Nathaniel Hawthorne recalls the hopes of his new way of life as a yeoman in the experimental utopian Brook Farm; it was to be "the spiritualization of labor . . . our form of prayer and ceremonial of worship. Each stroke of the hoe was to uncover some aromatic root of wisdom, heretofore hidden from the sun." After a brief time behind the hoe, however, Hawthorne observes: "The clods of earth, which we so constantly belabored and turned over and over, were never etherealized into thought. Our thoughts, on the contrary, were fast becoming cloddish."

This more tragic reality of farm life was dealt with by American novelists. Hamlin Garland in his masterpiece Main-Travelled Roads (1891) was the first to portray rural

From American Heritage, April 1956. Copyright © 1956 by American Heritage Publishing Co., Inc. Reprinted by permission.

life without an idyllic glow. Conscious of the farmer's back-breaking work and small return, Garland wrote of the farmer as an automaton, caught in a grim set of circumstances that drained joy and ambition from his soul and left it spiritless and dry. The saga of man's being humbled by the soil was repeated in novels by Ole Rolvaag and Willa Cather.

Yet, even today we are more inclined to the romantic and sentimental images of the rural settings depicted in a Whittier poem or a Currier and Ives print. Political candidates even in our urbanized era have pointed with pride to their rural beginnings as a means of vote-getting, and the American people are still prone to think of the farmlands as not only the heart of the nation but as the backbone of our democracy.

Professor Richard Hofstadter traces the development and the effects of the myth surrounding the farmer in American history, and points out the contrast between the "verbal deference" and the real economic position he was in. Actually, Hofstadter shows that despite the glorification of the farmer by his observers the yeoman of old gradually changed into an ordinary businessman just trying to keep step with his times.

The United States was born in the country and has moved to the city. From the beginning its political values as well as ideas were of necessity shaped by country life. The early American politician, the country editor, who wished to address himself to the common man, had to draw upon a rhetoric that would touch the tillers of the soil; and even the spokesman of city people knew that his audience had been in very large part reared upon the farm.

But what the articulate people who talked and wrote about farmers and farming—the preachers, poets, philosophers, writers, and statesmen—liked about American farming was not, in every respect, what the typical working farmer liked. For the articulate people were drawn irresistibly to the noncommercial, non-pecuniary, self-sufficient aspect of American farm life. To them it was an ideal.

Writers like Thomas Jefferson and Hector St. John de Crèvecœur admired the yeoman farmer not for his capacity to exploit opportunities and make money but for his honest industry, his independence, his frank spirit of equality, his ability to produce and enjoy a simple abundance. The farmer himself, in most cases, was in fact inspired to make money, and such self-sufficiency as he actually had was usually forced upon him by a lack of transportation or markets, or by the necessity to save cash to expand his operations.

For while early American society was an agrarian society, it was fast becoming more commercial, and commercial goals made their way among its agricultural classes almost as rapidly as elsewhere. The more commercial this society became, however, the more reason it found to cling in imagination to the noncommercial agrarian values. The more farming as a self-sufficient way of life was abandoned for farming as a business, the more merit men found in what was being left behind. And the more rapidly the farmers' sons moved into the towns, the more nostalgic the whole culture became about its rural past. Throughout the nineteenth and even in the twentieth century, the American was taught that rural life and farming as a vocation were something sacred.

This sentimental attachment to the rural way of life is a kind of homage that Americans have paid to the fancied innocence of their origins. To call it a "myth" is not to imply that the idea is simply false. Rather the "myth" so effectively embodies men's values that it profoundly influences their way of perceiving reality and hence their behavior.

Like any complex of ideas, the agrarian myth cannot be defined in a phrase, but its component themes form a clear pattern. Its hero was the yeoman farmer, its central conception the notion that he is the ideal man and the ideal citizen. Unstinted praise of the special virtues of the farmer and the special values of rural life was coupled with the assertion that agriculture, as a calling uniquely productive and uniquely important to society, had a special right to the concern and protection of government. The yeoman, who owned a small farm and worked it with the aid of his family, was the incarnation of the simple, honest, independent, healthy, happy human being. Because he lived in close communion with beneficent nature, his life was believed to have a whole-someness and integrity impossible for the depraved populations of cities.

His well-being was not merely physical, it was moral: it was not merely personal, it was the central source of civic virtue; it was not merely secular but religious, for God had made the land and called man to cultivate it. Since the yeoman was believed to be both happy and honest, and since he had a secure propertied stake in society in the form of his own land, he was held to be the best and most reliable sort of citizen. To this conviction Jefferson appealed when he wrote: "The small land holders are the most precious part of a state."

In origin the agrarian myth was not a popular but a literary idea, a preoccupation of the upper classes, of those who enjoyed a classical education, read pastoral poetry, experimented with breeding stock, and owned plantations or country estates. It was clearly formulated and al-most universally accepted in America during the last half of the eighteenth century. As it took shape both in Europe and America, its promulgators drew heavily upon the authority and the rhetoric of classical writers—Hesiod, Xenophon, Cato, Cicero, Virgil, Horace, and others—whose works were the staples of a good education. A learned agricultural gentry, coming into conflict with the industrial classes, welcomed the moral strength that a rich classical ancestry brought to the praise of husbandry.

Chiefly through English experience, and from English and classical writers, the agrarian myth came to America, where, like so many other cultural importations, it eventually took on altogether new dimensions in its new setting. So appealing were the symbols of the myth that even an arch-opponent of the agrarian interest like Alexander Hamilton found it politic to concede in his *Report on Manufactures* that "the cultivation of the earth, as the primary and most certain source of national supply . . . has intrinsically a strong claim to pre-eminence over every other kind of industry." And Benjamin Franklin, urban cosmopolite though he was, once said that agriculture was "the only *honest way*" for a nation to acquire wealth, "wherein man receives a real increase of the seed thrown into the ground, a kind of continuous miracle, wrought by the hand of God in his favour, as a reward for his innocent life and virtuous industry."

Among the intellectual classes in the eighteenth century the agrarian myth had virtually universal appeal. Some writers used it to give simple, direct, and emotional expression to their feelings about life and nature; others linked agrarianism with a formal philosophy of natural rights. The application of the natural rights philosophy to land tenure became especially popular in America. Since the time of Locke it had been a standard argument that the land is the common stock of society to which every man has a right—what Jefferson called "the fundamental right to labour the earth"; that since the occupancy and use of land are the true criteria of valid ownership, labor expended in cultivating the earth confers title to it; that since government was created to protect property, the property of working landholders has a special claim to be fostered and protected by the state.

At first the agrarian myth was a notion of the educated classes, but by the early nineteenth century it had become a mass creed, a part of the country's political folklore and its nationalist ideology. The roots of this change may be found as far back as the American Revolution, which, appearing to many Americans as the victory of a band of embattled farmers over an empire, seemed to confirm the moral and civic superiority of the yeoman, made the farmer a symbol of the new nation, and wove the agrarian myth into his patriotic sentiments and idealism.

Still more important, the myth played a role in the first party battles under the Constitution. The Jeffersonians appealed again and again to the moral primacy of the yeoman farmer in their attacks on the Federalists. The family farm and American democracy became indissolubly connected in Jeffersonian thought, and by 1840 even the more conservative party, the Whigs, took over the rhetorical appeal to the common man, and elected a President in good part on the strength of the fiction that he lived in a log cabin.

The Jeffersonians, moreover, made the agrarian myth the basis of a strategy of continental development. Many of them expected that the great empty inland regions would guarantee the preponderance of the yeoman—and therefore the dominance of Jeffersonianism and the health of the state—for an unlimited future. The opening of the trans-Allegheny region, its protection from slavery, and the purchase of the Louisiana Territory were the first great steps in a continental strategy designed to establish an internal empire of small farms. Much later the Homestead Act was meant to carry to its completion the process of continental settlement by small homeowners. The failure of the Homestead Act "to enact by statute the fee-simple empire" was one of the original sources of Populist grievances, and one of the central points at which the agrarian myth was overrun by the commercial realities.

Above all, however, the myth was powerful because the United States in the first half of the nineteenth century consisted predominantly of literate and politically enfranchised farmers. Offering what seemed harmless flattery to this numerically dominant class, the myth suggested a standard vocabulary to rural editors and politicians. Although farmers may not have been much impressed by what was said about the merits of a noncommercial way of life, they could only enjoy learning about their special virtues and their unique services to the nation. Moreover, the editors and politicians who so flattered them need not in most cases have been insincere. More often than not they too were likely to have begun life in little villages or on farms, and what they had to say stirred in their own breasts, as it did in the breasts of a great many townspeople, nostalgia for their early years and perhaps relieved some residual feelings of guilt at having deserted parental homes and childhood attachments. They also had the satisfaction in the early days of knowing that in so far as it was based upon the life of the largely self-sufficient yeoman the agrarian myth was a depiction of reality as well as the assertion of an ideal.

Oddly enough, the agrarian myth came to be believed more widely and tenaciously as it became more fictional. At first it was propagated with a kind of genial candor, and only later did it acquire overtones of insincerity. There survives from the Jackson era a painting that shows Governor Joseph Ritner of Pennsylvania standing by a primitive plow at the end of a furrow. There is no pretense that the Governor has actually been plowing—he wears broadcloth pants and a silk vest, and his tall black beaver hat has been carefully laid in the grass beside him —but the picture is meant as a reminder of both his rustic origin and his present high station in life. By contrast, Calvin Coolidge posed almost a century later for a series of photographs that represented him as haying in Vermont. In one of them the President sits on the edge of a hay rig in a white shirt, collar detached, wearing highly polished black shoes and a fresh pair of overalls; in the background stands his Pierce Arrow, a secret service man on the running board, plainly waiting to hurry the President away from his bogus rural labors. That the second picture is so much more pretentious and disingenuous than the first is a measure of the increasing hollowness of the myth as it became more and more remote from the realities of agriculture.

Throughout the nineteenth century hundreds upon hundreds of thousands of farm-born youths sought their careers in the towns and cities. Particularly after 1840, which marked the beginning of a long cycle of heavy country-to-city migration, farm children repudiated their parents' way of life and took off for the cities where, in agrarian theory if not in fact, they were sure to succumb to vice and poverty.

When a correspondent of the *Prairie Farmer* in 1849 made the mistake of praising the luxuries, the "polished society," and the economic opportunities of the city, he was rebuked for overlooking the fact that city life "*crushes, enslaves,* and *ruins so many thousands of our young men* who are insensibly made the victims of *dissipation,* of *reckless speculation,* and of *ultimate crime.*" Such warnings, of course, were futile. "Thousands of young men," wrote the New York agriculturist Jesse Buel, "who annually forsake the plough, and the honest profession of their fathers, if not to win the fair, at least form an opinion, too often confirmed by mistaken parents, that agriculture is not the road to wealth, to honor, nor to happiness. And such will continue to be the case, until our agriculturists become qualified to assume that rank in society to which the importance of their calling, and their numbers, entitle them, and which intelligence and self-respect can alone give them."

Rank in society! That was close to the heart of the matter, for the farmer was beginning to realize acutely not merely that the best of the world's goods were to be had in the cities and that the urban middle and upper classes had much more of them than he did but also that he was losing in status and respect as compared with them. He became aware that the official respect paid to the farmer masked a certain disdain felt by many city people. "There has . . . a certain class of individuals grown up in our land," complained a farm writer in 1835, "who treat the cultivators of the soil as an inferior caste . . . whose utmost abilities are confined to the merit of being able to discuss a boiled potato and a rasher of bacon." The city was symbolized as the home of loan sharks, dandies, fops, and aristocrats with European ideas who despised farmers as hayseeds.

The growth of the urban market intensified this antagonism. In areas like colonial New England, where an intimate connection had existed between the small town and the adjacent countryside, where a community of interests and even of occupations cut across the town line, the rural-urban hostility had not developed so sharply as in the newer areas where the township plan was never instituted and where isolated farmsteads were more common. As settlement moved west, as urban markets grew, as self-sufficient farmers became rarer, as farmers pushed into commercial production for the cities they feared and distrusted, they quite correctly thought of themselves as a vocational and economic group rather than as members of a neighborhood. In the Populist era the city was totally alien territory to many farmers, and the primacy of agriculture as a source of wealth was reasserted with much bitterness. "The great cities rest upon our broad and fertile prairies," declared Bryan in his "Cross of Gold" speech. "Burn down your cities and leave our farms, and your cities will spring up again as if by magic; but destroy our farms, and the grass will grow in the streets of every city in the country." Out of the beliefs nourished by the agrarian myth there had arisen the notion that the city was a parasitical growth on the country. Bryan spoke for a people raised for generations on the idea that the farmer was a very special creature, blessed by God, and that in a country consisting largely of farmers the voice of the farmer was the voice of democracy and of virtue itself.

The agrarian myth encouraged farmers to believe that they were not themselves an organic part of the whole order of business enterprise and speculation that flourished in the city, partaking of its character and sharing in its risks, but rather the innocent pastoral victims of a conspiracy hatched in the distance. The notion of an innocent and victimized populace colors the whole history of agrarian controversy.

For the farmer it was bewildering, and irritating too, to think of the great contrast between the verbal deference paid him by almost everyone and the real economic position in which he found himself. Improving his economic position was always possible, though this was often done too little and too late; but it was not within anyone's power

to stem the decline in the rural values and pieties, the gradual rejection
of the moral commitments that had been expressed in the early exalta-
tions of agrarianism.

It was the fate of the farmer himself to contribute to this decline.
Like almost all good Americans he had innocently sought progress from
the very beginning, and thus hastened the decline of many of his own
values. Elsewhere the rural classes had usually looked to the past, had
been bearers of tradition and upholders of stability. The American
farmer looked to the future alone, and the story of the American land
became a study in futures.

In the very hours of its birth as a nation Crèvecœur had congratulated America for having, in effect, no feudal past and no industrial
present, for having no royal, aristocratic, ecclesiastical, or monarchial
power, and no manufacturing class, and had rapturously concluded:
"We are the most perfect society now existing in the world." Here
was the irony from which the farmer suffered above all others: the
United States was the only country in the world that began with per-
fection and aspired to progress.

To what extent was the agrarian myth actually false? During the
colonial period, and even well down into the nineteenth century, there
were in fact large numbers of farmers who were very much like the yeomen idealized in the myth. They were independent and self-sufficient,
and they bequeathed to their children a strong love of craftsmanlike
improvisation and a firm tradition of household industry. These yeomen were all too often yeomen by force of circumstance. They could
not become commercial farmers because they were too far from the
rivers or the towns, because the roads were too poor for bulky traffic,
because the domestic market for agricultural produce was too small
and the overseas markets were out of reach. At the beginning of the
nineteenth century, when the American population was still living
largely in the forests and most of it was east of the Appalachians, the
yeoman farmer did exist in large numbers, living much as the theorists
of the agrarian myth portrayed him.

But when the yeoman practiced the self-sufficient economy that was
expected of him, he usually did so not because he wanted to stay out
of the market but because he wanted to get into it. "My farm," said a
farmer of Jefferson's time, "gave me and my family a good living on

the produce of it; and left me, one year with another, one hundred and fifty dollars, for I have never spent more than ten dollars a year, which was for salt, nails, and the like. Nothing to wear, eat, or drink was purchased, as my farm provided all. With this saving, I put money to interest, bought cattle, fatted and sold them, and made great profit." Great profit! Here was the significance of self-sufficiency for the characteristic family farmer. Commercialism had already begun to enter the American Arcadia.

For, whatever the spokesman of the agrarian myth might have told him, the farmer almost anywhere in early America knew that all around him there were examples of commercial success in agriculture—the tobacco, rice, and indigo, and later the cotton planters of the South, the grain, meat, and cattle exporters of the middle states.

The farmer knew that without cash he could never rise above the hardships and squalor of pioneering and log-cabin life. So the savings from his self-sufficiency went into improvements—into the purchase of more land, of herds and flocks, of better tools; they went into the building of barns and silos and better dwellings. Self-sufficiency, in short, was adopted for a time in order that it would eventually be unnecessary.

Between 1815 and 1860 the character of American agriculture was transformed. The rise of native industry created a home market for agriculture, while demands arose abroad for American cotton and foodstuffs, and a great network of turnpikes, canals, and railroads helped link the planter and the advancing western farmer to the new markets. As the farmer moved out of the forests onto the flat, rich prairies, he found possibilities for machinery that did not exist in the forest. Before long he was cultivating the prairies with horse-drawn mechanical reapers, steel plows, wheat and corn drills, and threshers.

The farmer was still a hardworking man, and he still owned his own land in the old tradition. But no longer did he grow or manufacture almost everything he needed. He concentrated on the cash crop, bought more and more of his supplies from the country store. To take full advantage of the possibilities of mechanization, he engrossed as much land as he could and borrowed money for his land and machinery. The shift from self-sufficient to commercial farming varied in time through-

out the West and cannot be dated with precision, but it was complete
in Ohio by about 1830 and twenty years later in Indiana, Illinois, and
Michigan. All through the great Northwest, farmers whose fathers
might have lived in isolation and self-sufficiency were surrounded by
jobbers, banks, stores, middlemen, horses, and machinery.

This transformation affected not only what the farmer did but how
he felt. The ideals of the agrarian myth were competing in his breast,
and gradually losing ground, to another, even stronger ideal, the notion of opportunity, of career, of the self-made man. Agrarian sentiment sanctified labor in the soil and the simple life; but the prevailing
Calvinist atmosphere of rural life implied that virtue was rewarded with
success and material goods. Even farm boys were taught to strive for
achievement in one form or another, and when this did not take them
away from the farms altogether, it impelled them to follow farming not
as a way of life but as a *career*—that is, as a way of achieving substantial
success.

The sheer abundance of the land—that very internal empire that
had been expected to insure the predominance of the yeoman in American life for centuries—gave the *coup de grâce* to the yeomanlike way
of life. For it made of the farmer a speculator. Cheap land invited extensive and careless cultivation. Rising land values in areas of new settlement tempted early liquidation and frequent moves. Frequent and
sensational rises in land values bred a boom psychology in the American farmer and caused him to rely for his margin of profit more on the
appreciation in the value of his land than on the sale of crops. It took
a strong man to resist the temptation to ride skyward on lands that
might easily triple or quadruple their value in one decade and then
double in the next.

What developed in America, then, was an agricultural society whose
real attachment was not, like the yeoman's, to the land but to land
values. The characteristic product of American rural society, as it developed on the prairies and the plains, was not a yeoman or a villager,
but a harassed little country businessman who worked very hard, moved
all too often, gambled with his land, and made his way alone.

While the farmer had long since ceased to act like a yeoman, he
was somewhat slower in ceasing to think like one. He became a businessman in fact long before he began to regard himself in this light. As
the nineteenth century drew to a close, however, various things were

changing him. He was becoming increasingly an employer of labor, and though he still worked with his hands, he began to look with suspicion upon the working classes of the cities, especially those organized in trade unions, as he had once done upon the urban fops and aristocrats. Moreover, when good times returned after the Populist revolt of the 1890's, businessmen and bankers and the agricultural colleges began to woo the farmer, to make efforts to persuade him to take the business-like view of himself that was warranted by the nature of his farm operations. "The object of farming," declared a writer in the *Cornell Countryman* in 1904, "is not primarily to make a living, but it is to make money. To this end it is to be conducted on the same business basis as any other producing industry."

The final change, which came only with a succession of changes in the twentieth century, wiped out the last traces of the yeoman of old, as the coming first of good roads and rural free delivery, and mail order catalogues, then the telephone, the automobile, and the tractor, and at length radio, movies, and television largely eliminated the difference between urban and rural experience in so many important areas of life. The city luxuries, once so derided by farmers, are now what they aspire to give to their wives and daughters.

In 1860 a farm journal satirized the imagined refinements and affectations of a city girl in the following picture:

> Slowly she rises from her couch. . . . Languidly she gains her feet, and oh! what vision of human perfection appears before us: Skinny, bony, sickly, hipless, thighless, formless, hairless, teethless. What a radiant belle! . . . The ceremony of enrobing commences. In goes the dentist's naturalization efforts; next the witching curls are fashioned to her "classically molded head." Then the womanly proportions are properly adjusted; hoops, bustles, and so forth, follow in succession, then a profuse quantity of whitewash, together with a "permanent rose tint" is applied to a sallow complexion; and lastly the "killing" wrapper is arranged on her systematical and matchless form.

But compare this with these beauty hints for farmers' wives from the *Idaho Farmer*, April, 1935:

> Hands should be soft enough to flatter the most delicate of the new fabrics. They must be carefully manicured, with none of the

hot, brilliant shades of nail polish. The lighter and more delicate tones are in keeping with the spirit of freshness. Keep the tint of your fingertips friendly to the red of your lips, and check both your powder and your rouge to see that they best suit the tone of your skin in the bold light of summer.

Nothing can tell us with greater finality of the passing of the yeoman ideal than these light and delicate tones of nail polish.

The Lower East Side

MOSES RISCHIN

• Inscribed in bronze on the pedestal of the Statue of Liberty are the celebrated lines of Emma Lazarus's "New Colossus":

> . . . Give me your tired, your poor
> Your huddled masses yearning to breathe free
> The wretched refuse of your teeming shore.
> Send these, the homeless, tempest-tost to me
> I lift my lamp beside the golden door.

Yet not far from New York harbor, the cry was "gibt mir luft,"—give me air, for between 1870 and 1914, a million and a half Jews left their Eastern European ghettos for the promised land of America, and most of them streamed into the twenty-block section of New York's Lower East Side. The highest degree of residential congestion the world had yet known was the result.

The teeming and noisy streets were wretched and demoralizing, but the passion to push ahead and move out was never extinguished. Overworked and underpaid, garment workers and pushcart peddlers managed nevertheless to see their children or grandchildren enter the American middle class. Thousands of attorneys, physicians, professors, and suburban housewives, along with such twentieth-century luminaries as composer Irving Berlin, United States Senator Jacob Javits, and Yale Law School Dean Abraham Goldstein can trace their origins to the Lower East Side. As Harry Golden has said: "The second generation came along and soon the sons took the old folks away, out to Brooklyn, or up to the Bronx, and thus they made room for new immigrants. America gave them all hope and life, and they repaid America. There has never been a more even trade."

From *The Promised City: New York's Jews, 1870–1914*, Cambridge, Mass.: Harvard University Press. Copyright © 1962, by the President and Fellows of Harvard College. Reprinted by permission.

In the past half-century, the Jews of the Lower East Side
have been largely replaced by Puerto Ricans, blacks, hippies,
and other minority groups. But visitors to New York can still
find vestiges of the old Yiddish tradition. Every Sunday
morning, along Delancey, Orchard, and Essex streets, the
colorful life of the sidewalk vendor and merchant is re-
created along the curbs and narrow walks of one of the nation's most storied neighborhoods. How would you compare
the old Jewish ghetto with the ghettos of the second half
of the twentieth century? Is there reason to believe that the
same avenues for success are open to today's ghetto dwellers?

From their homes they come rosy-cheeked and with health and
Spring. They have had little fish, little meat, little bread, and it
is to get more that they come hither. But they have had air and
light. . . . Air and light, and water have been from all time the
heritage of man and even of the animals.

Evening Journal (1903)

By the first decade of the twentieth century, the Lower East Side had
become an immigrant Jewish cosmopolis. Five major varieties of Jews
lived there, "a seething human sea, fed by streams, streamlets, and rills
of immigration flowing from all the Yiddish-speaking centers of Europe." Clustered in their separate Jewries, they were set side by side
in a pattern suggesting the cultural, if not the physical, geography of
the Old World. Hungarians were settled in the northernmost portion
above Houston Street, along the numbered streets between Avenue B
and the East River, once indisputably *Kleindeutschland*. Galicians
lived to the south, between Houston and Broome, east of Clinton, on
Attorney, Ridge, Pitt, Willett, and the cross streets. To the west lay
the most congested Rumanian quarter, "in the very thick of the battle
for breath," on Chrystie, Forsyth, Eldridge, and Allen streets, flanked
by Houston Street to the north and Grand Street to the south, with
the Bowery gridironed by the overhead elevated to the west. After 1907
Levantines, last on the scene and even stranger than the rest, for they
were alien to Yiddish, settled between Allen and Chrystie streets
among the Rumanians with whom they seemed to have the closest

31 Labor Temple
32 Rand School
33 Hebrew Charities Building
34 Metropolitan Life Building
35 Madison Square Garden
36 City College

BOUNDARIES OF SUB-ETHNIC DISTRICTS
•••••• Hungarian
—+— Galician
•–•–• Rumanian
⌃⌃⌃⌃ Levantine
– – – Russian

Shaded blocks indicate Tenth Ward

0   MILE   ¼

THE LOWER EAST SIDE

1 Newspaper Row
2 World Building
3 Chatham Sq. Library
4 Beth Israel Hospital
5 Israel Elchanan Yeshiva
6 Seward Park Library
7 Forward Building on Yiddish Newspaper Row
8 Educational Alliance
9 Henry St. Settlement and Clinton Hall
10 Machzike Talmud Torah
11 Hebrew Sheltering House
12 Hebrew Technical School for Girls
13 Home for Aged
14 Jewish Maternity Hospital
15 Young Men's Benevolent Association
16 Camp Huddleston Hospital Ship School
17 Beth Hamedrash Hagadol
18 Pro-Cathedral Mission
19 University Settlement
20 Grand Theater
21 Yiddish Rialto
22 Thalia Theater
23 People's Bath
24 Police Headquarters
25 Public School 63
26 Music School Settlement
27 Asch Building
28 Astor Library
29 Cooper Union
30 Hebrew Technical School for Boys

City plan: The Lower East Side

affinity. The remainder of the great Jewish quarter, from Grand Street
reaching south to Monroe, was the preserve of the Russians—those
from Russian Poland, Lithuania, Byelorussia, and the Ukraine—the
most numerous and heterogeneous of the Jewries of Eastern Europe.

The leading streets of the Lower East Side reflected this immigrant
transformation. Its most fashionable thoroughfare, East Broadway, bi-
sected the district. To the north lay crammed tenements, business, and
industry. To the south lay less crowded quarters where private dwellings, front courtyards, and a scattering of shade trees recalled a time
when Henry, Madison, Rutgers, and Jefferson street addresses were
stylish.

The Russian intelligentsia, for whom the Lower East Side was New
York, fancied East Broadway as New York's Nevsky Prospect, St.
Petersburg's grand boulevard. In addition to the physicians and den-
tists who occupied the comfortable brownstone fronts that lined its
shaded curbs, an ever-growing number of public and communal buildings came to endow it with a magisterial air. By the second decade of
the twentieth century, the ten-story edifice of the *Jewish Daily Forward*,
set off by Seward Park on Yiddish Newspaper Row, loomed command-
ingly over the two Carnegie-built libraries, the Educational Alliance,
the Home for the Aged, the Jewish Maternity Hospital, the Machzike
Talmud Torah, the Hebrew Sheltering House, the Young Men's Benevolent Association, and a host of lesser institutions.

Only second to East Broadway was Grand Street. Long a leading
traffic artery and a major retail shopping center of lower New York,
Grand Street fell into eclipse after the turn of the century with the
widening of the Delancey Street approach to the Williamsburg Bridge
and the comparative decline in ferry traffic. Grand Street's popular
department stores, Lord and Taylor's, Lichtenstein's, and O'Neill's,
moved uptown, and Ridley's closed, leaving the way open for conquest
by the newcomers. Bustling Delancey Street, lined with naphtha-lit stalls
crammed with tubs of fish; Hester Street, with its agents on their way
to becoming bankers after the example of Jarmulowsky's passage and
exchange office; and the Bowery, with the largest savings bank in the
world, symbolized the district's new retail character.

Only after 1870 did the Lower East Side begin to acquire an immigrant Jewish cast. In the early years of the century a small colony
of Jewish immigrants had lived there. Dutch, German, and Polish

Jews had settled on Bayard, Baxter, Mott, and Chatham streets in the 1830's and 1840's. Shortly thereafter, German and Bohemian Jews took up quarters in the Grand Street area to the northeast and subsequently Jews of the great German migration augmented their numbers. Except for highly visible store fronts, Jews made little impress on the dominantly German and Irish neighborhood. But practically all East European immigrants arriving after 1870 initially found their way to the Lower East Side. Virtually penniless upon their arrival in the city, they were directed to the Jewish districts by representatives of the immigrant aid societies, or came at the behest of friends, relatives, or employers.

The changes brought about by the great Jewish migration forced the district's middle-class Germans and Irish, living in predominantly two- and two-and-one-half story dwellings, to retreat to less crowded quarters. By 1890 the Lower East Side bristled with Jews. The tenth ward (loosely coinciding with the Eighth Assembly District), closest to the central factory area, was the most crowded with 523.6 inhabitants per acre; the adjacent wards, the thirteenth and seventh, numbered 428.6 and 289.7 persons per acre respectively. Exceeding 700 persons per acre by 1900, the tenth ward was the most densely settled spot in the city; residential block density was even more appalling as factories and shops crowded tenements. In 1896 a private census counted 60 cigar shops, 172 garment shops, 65 factories, and 34 laundries in the tenth ward. In 1906, of fifty-one blocks in the city with over 3000 inhabitants each, thirty-seven were on the Lower East Side. On Rivington Street, Arnold Bennett remarked, "the architecture seemed to sweat humanity at every window and door." Hardy, older, or improvident remnants of the region's earlier Irish residents and a floating seafaring population still clung to the river edges along Cherry and Water streets; at the turn of the century, Italian immigrants crossed the Bowery on Stanton and East Houston streets and crowded into the lower reaches of East Broadway. But in the second decade of the new century, the Lower East Side, from the Bowery to within a stone's throw of the East River, and from Market Street to 14th Street, had become a mass settlement of Jews, the most densely packed quarter in the city. In 1914 one sixth of the city's population was domiciled below 14th Street upon one eighty-second of the city's land area; most of New York's office buildings, and factories that employed over one half of the city's industrial workers were located in this district.

Once the immigrants had come to rest on the Lower East Side, there was little incentive to venture further. Knowing no English and with few resources, they were dependent upon the apparel industries, the tobacco and cigar trades, and other light industrial employments that sprang up in the area or that were located in the adjacent factory district. Long hours, small wages, seasonal employment, and the complexity of their religious and social needs rooted them to the spot. It was essential to husband energies, earnings, and time. Lodgings of a sort, coffee morning and evening, and laundry service were available to single men for three dollars a month. Bread at two and three cents a pound, milk at four cents a quart, a herring for a penny or two, and apples at from one to five for a cent, depending on quality, were to be had. Accustomed to a slim diet, an immigrant could save much even with meager earnings and still treat himself to a bracing three-course Sabbath dinner (for fifteen cents). Thrift and hard work would, he hoped, enable him in time to search out more congenial and independent employment. Until new sections of the city were developed at the turn of the century only country peddlers were to stray permanently beyond the familiar immigrant quarters.

There was a compelling purpose to the pinched living. Virtually all immigrants saved to purchase steamship tickets for loved ones and many regularly mailed clothing and food parcels to dependent parents, wives, and children overseas. The power of home ties buoyed up the spirits of immigrants wedded to the sweatshop and peddler's pack, whose precious pennies mounted to sums that would unite divided families. Among the early comers women were relatively few, but the imbalance between the sexes soon was remedied. In 1890 an investigation by the Baron de Hirsch Society into the condition of 111,690 of an estimated 135,000 Jews on the Lower East Side counted 60,313 children and 22,647 wage-earners, with 28,730 unspecified, mostly women. Undoubtedly, the proportion of women and children in New York was far greater than it was elsewhere. In 1910 women exceeded men among Hungarians and Rumanians, were equal among Austrians, and made up 47 per cent of the Russians. As non-Jews from these countries were heavily male, Jewish women clearly outnumbered men, accentuating the group's domesticity. Among the major ethnic groups of New York, only the Irish, 58 per cent female, exceeded the Jewish ratio.

A nondescript colony of Jews in the 1870's swelled into a center of Jewish life by the turn of the century, the drama of whose fortunes and passions was closely followed by fellow immigrants throughout the country as well as by those in the lands they left behind. A highly visible knot of Jews "huddled up together" around Baxter and Chatham streets had been engulfed by an influx that saturated the whole region with its flavor and institutions.

THE TENEMENT BOOM

Ever since the 1830's New York's housing problem had been acute. Manhattan's space limitations exacerbated all the evils inherent in overcrowding, and refinements in the use of precious ground only emphasized the triumph of material necessities over human considerations. New York's division of city lots into standard rectangular plots, 25 feet wide by 100 feet deep, made decent human accommodations impossible. In order to secure proper light and ventilation for tenement dwellers twice the space was needed, a prohibitive sacrifice considering real estate values. No opportunity was overlooked to facilitate the most economical and compact housing of the immigrant population. To the improvised tenements that had been carved out of private dwellings were added the front and rear tenements and, finally, the dumbbell-style tenement of 1879.

With the heavy Jewish migration of the early 1890's, the Lower East Side, still relatively undeveloped compared to the Lower West Side, became the special domain of the new dumbbell tenements, so called because of their shape. The six- to seven-story dumbbell usually included four apartments to the floor, two on either side of the separating corridor. The front apartments generally contained four rooms each, the rear apartments three. Only one room in each apartment received direct light and air from the street or from the ten feet of required yard space in the rear. On the ground floor two stores generally were to be found; the living quarters behind each had windows only on the air shaft. The air shaft, less than five feet in width and from fifty to sixty feet in length, separated the tenement

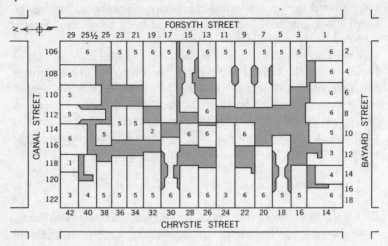

A tenement block: smaller numbers indicate number of stories.

buildings. In the narrow hallways were located that special improve-
ment, common water closets. In 1888 a leading magazine described
typical dumbbell tenements on Ridge, Eldridge, and Allen streets.

>   They were great prison-like structures of brick, with narrow
> doors and windows, cramped passages and steep rickety stairs.
> They are built through from one street to the other with a
> somewhat narrower building connecting them . . . The narrow
> court-yard . . . in the middle is a damp foul-smelling place,
> supposed to do duty as an airshaft; had the foul fiend designed
> these great barracks they could not have been more villainously
> arranged to avoid any chance of ventilation . . . In case of fire
> they would be perfect death-traps, for it would be impossible
> for the occupants of the crowded rooms to escape by the narrow
> stairways, and the flimsy fire-escapes which the owners of the
> tenements were compelled to put up a few years ago are so laden
> with broken furniture, bales and boxes that they would be
> worse than useless. In the hot summer months . . . these fire-
> escape balconies are used as sleeping-rooms by the poor wretches
> who are fortunate enough to have windows opening upon them.
> The drainage is horrible, and even the Croton as it flows from
> the tap in the noisome courtyard, seemed to be contaminated
> by its surroundings and have a fetid smell.

As if the tenement abuses were not degrading enough, the absence of public toilet facilities in so crowded a district added to the wretched sanitation. It was reported that "in the evening every dray or wagon becomes a private and public lavatory, and the odor and stench . . . is perfectly horrible."

Conditions became almost unendurable in the summer months. Bred in colder and dryer climates, tenement inhabitants writhed in the dull heat. Added to the relentless sun were the emanations from coal stoves, the flat flame gas jets in lamps, and the power-producing steam boilers. Inevitably, roofs, fire escapes, and sidewalks were converted into sleeping quarters, while the grassed enclosure dividing Delancey Street and Seward Park supplied additional dormitory space. Late July and early August of 1896 were especially savage. Between August 5 and 13, 420 New Yorkers perished from the continuous heat, "the absolute stagnation of the air, and the oppressive humidity," noted Daniel Van Pelt, although the temperature averaged 90.7 degrees and never reached 100.

Fire and the possibilities of fire brought added terror to the inhabitants of overcrowded tenements. "Remember that you live in a tenement house," warned insurance agents. In 1903, 15 per cent of the tenements in the district still were without fire escapes. Of 257 fatalities in Manhattan fires between 1902 and 1909, 99 or 38 per cent were on the Lower East Side, all victims of old-law tenements.

Few families could afford the privacy of a three- or four-room flat. Only with the aid of lodgers or boarders could the $10 to $20 monthly rental be sustained. The extent of overcrowding in the tenements, reported a witness before the United States Immigration Commission, was never fully known.

A typical dumbell tenement

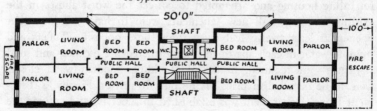

At the hour of retiring, cots or folded beds and in many
instances simply mattresses are spread about the floor, re-
sembling very much a lot of bunks in the steerage of an ocean
steamer . . . The only way to properly determine the census of
one of these tenements, would be by a midnight visit, and should
this take place between the months of June and September, the
roof of the building should not be omitted.

However trying tenement living proved to be for adults, for children
it was stultifying, concluded a settlement worker. "The earlier years
of the child are spent in an atmosphere which . . . is best described
by a little girl, 'a place so dark it seemed as if there weren't no sky.' "

Evictions for nonpayment of rent and rent strikes were perennial.
Uncertainty of employment, nonpayment of wages, unexpected obli-
gations, dependents, and adversities contributed to the high incidence
of evictions. In the year 1891–1892 alone, in two judicial districts
of the Lower East Side, 11,550 dispossess warrants were issued by the
presiding magistrates. In 1900 the absence of mass evictions was
regarded as a mark of unexampled well-being.

Earlier residents of the Lower East Side and hereditary property
owners profited from the overcrowding. The rise in real estate values,
exorbitant rents, and the low upkeep provided tenement owners with
ample returns upon their investments. Even allowing for losses due
to nonpayment of rent and an average occupancy of ten months in
the year, landlords earned ten per cent. By more studied neglect, a
resourceful agent might reap even higher returns. The Lower East
Side tenements soon came to be recognized as the most lucrative
investment in the city. Nowhere else did the speculator's market in
tenement properties flourish as luxuriantly as it did here, where earlier
immigrants had learned to exploit the misery of later comers.

In 1901 the further construction of dumbbell tenements was prohibited. The Tenement House Law of that year set new standards
for future housing and attempted to correct the worst abuses in the
existing buildings. All new tenements were to have windows that
opened at least twelve feet away from those opposite. Toilets and
running water in each apartment, unobstructed fire escapes, and solid
staircases were required. In the old buildings modern water closets
were to be installed in place of the outside privies. Finally, a Tenement House Department was established to supervise and enforce the

provisions of the law. While the law never was effectively enforced, its initial achievements proved encouraging.

Many new tenements were quickly built according to the new specifications. In the fiscal year ending July 1, 1903, 43 per cent of New York's new tenements were located on the Lower East Side. Its inhabitants eagerly welcomed the brightly lighted rooms, bathtubs, and other improvements. At first, landlords on the Lower East Side were more prompt to make alterations in old-law tenements than landlords elsewhere in the city, for the heavy pressure of population made even remodeled properties attractive. The years 1905 to 1909 saw an unparalleled boom throughout the city with houses to fit every taste, from tenements to palatial mansions for chance customers, at unprecedented prices ranging up to $500,000. "It is doubtful if New York City, or in fact any other city of the world, ever before witnessed the expenditure of so many millions of dollars in the construction of tenement houses during a similar period."

While new housing was on the rise, the fast developing clothing trades also were relocating and building. As the heavy settlement of East Europeans decisively affected the housing of the city's earlier residents, so the new growth of the apparel industry, manned by Lower East Side Jews, helped to transform the city's business districts. Once legislation and the advent of electric power combined to reduce Lower East Side sweatshops, thousands of garment shops and factories pushed up the axial thoroughfares of Lower Manhattan. By 1910 the continued march uptown found the garment industry intruding upon once fashionable Madison Square, the site of New York's tallest skyscrapers. Brownstones and brick residences were razed to be displaced by 16- to 20-story steel-girdered loft buildings trimmed with granite and marble and housing scores of clothing shops. In the course of this displacement, the city's central retailing district and its theater and hotel district were forced northward. The main retailing center, at 14th Street in 1880 and at 23rd Street in 1900, became anchored at 34th Street by 1910.

DISEASE AND CRIME

Superficially, East European Jews seemed ill-prepared to contend with the demands that tenement living thrust upon them. "Their average stature is from five feet one inch to five feet three inches, which means that they are the most stunted of the Europeans, with the exception of the Hungarian Magyars." Shortest were the Galicians, tallest and sturdiest, the Rumanians. Undersized and narrow-chested, a high proportion were described as "physical wrecks." Centuries of confinement, habituation to mental occupations, chronic under-nourishment, and a deprecation of the physical virtues ill-fitted them for heavy labor. Between 1887 and 1890 nearly five thousand immi-grants were returned to Europe labeled physically "unfit for work." Seemingly helpless and emaciated, they were to exhibit exceptional capacity for regeneration; traditional moral and religious disciplines were to serve them in good stead.

Despite the trying conditions under which the immigrants lived, they showed a remarkable resistance to disease. With the highest average density of tenants per house in the city, the tenth ward had one of the lowest death rates. Indeed only a business ward and a suburban ward surpassed it in healthfulness. Dr. Annie Daniel, a pioneer in public health, volunteered her interpretation of this before the Tenement House Committee:

> "The rules of life which orthodox Hebrews so unflinchingly obey as laid down in the Mosaic code . . . are designed to main-tain health. These rules are applied to the daily life of the indi-viduals as no other sanitary laws can be . . . Food must be cooked properly, and hence the avenues through which the germs of disease may enter are destroyed. Meat must be "kosher," and this means that it must be perfectly healthy. Personal cleanliness is at times strictly compelled, at least one day in the week the habitation must be thoroughly cleaned."

True, only some 8 per cent of Russian Jewish families had baths, ac-cording to a study of 1902, and these often without hot water. Yet the proliferation of privately owned bathhouses in the city was attributable largely to the Jewish tenement population. "I cannot get along without a 'sweat' (Russian bath) at least once a week," insisted a newcomer. In 1880, one or two of New York's twenty-two bath-houses were Jewish; by 1897, over half of the city's sixty-two bathhouses (including Russian, Turkish, swimming, vapor, and medicated bath-houses) were Jewish. If standards of cleanliness were not as faith-fully maintained as precept required, the strict regimen of orthodoxy, even when weakened, contributed to the immigrant's general well-being.

Nevertheless, close crowding and unsanitary conditions made all communicable diseases potentially contagious. Despite great apprehension between 1892 and 1894, Jewish immigrants did not carry to New York the cholera and typhus epidemics raging at the European ports of embarkation. But in 1899 the United Hebrew Charities became alarmed by the Board of Health's report of the mounting incidence of tuberculosis in the city. That Jewish immigrants might become easy victims of the "White Plague" was hardly to be doubted. "As many as 119 Jewish families have lived in one tenement house on Lewis Street within the past five years." Hundreds of flats had been occupied by fifteen successive families within a brief period. "Many of these houses are known to be hotbeds of the disease, the very walls reeking with it." Increasingly, the dread disease with its cough and crimson spittle took its toll. Ernest Poole, an investigator, frequently heard the plea of the afflicted. "Luft, gibt mir luft—Air, give me air." Especially susceptible were the intellectuals, whose often shattered spirits, overwrought minds, and undernourished bodies fell prey to the killer. Yet so great was the immigrant's concern for health that the mortality rate from tuberculosis was lower on the East Side than in the city's prosperous districts. Venereal diseases, previously almost unknown among Jews in Eastern Europe, became progressively more common among young men, as restraints were weakened by exposure to new temptations.

Alcoholism, a prime contributor to poverty, ill-health, and mortality among other national groups, was unusual among Jewish immigrants. As Jews replaced the earlier inhabitants, the many saloons of the Lower East Side, trimmed with shields that proclaimed them "the workman's friend," declined. Those that survived drew few clients from a neighborhood addicted to soda water, "the life-giving drink"; they depended on the throng of transients that passed through the district. Jews did not abstain from drink. Yet only upon religious festivals and during the Sabbath ritual when the Kiddush cup was emptied did alcohol appear in the diet of most immigrants. In 1908, $1.50 a year for holiday and ritual wine seemed adequate for a family of six. "The Day of Rejoicing of the Law and the Day of Purim are the only two days in the year when an orthodox Jew may be intoxi-

cated. It is virtuous on these days to drink too much, but the sobriety
of the Jew is so great that he sometimes cheats his friends and himself
by shamming drunkenness," Hutchins Hapgood noted. Jews habitually
imbibed milder beverages. Russians were notorious tea drinkers.
Hungarians were addicted to coffee. The less austere Galicians and
Rumanians tippled mead and wine respectively. But in the New
World all fell victim to the craze for seltzer or soda water with its
purported health-giving powers. In his long experience, reported the
president of the United Hebrew Charities in 1892, he had known
only three chronic Jewish drunkards.

Neurasthenia and hysteria, however, took a heavy toll of victims.
Their sickness was the result of a history of continual persecution
and insecurity, intensified by the strains of settlement in unfamiliar
surroundings. Diabetes, associated with perpetual nervous strain, was
common. Suicide, rarely recorded among the small-town Jews of
Eastern Europe, also found its victims in the tenements of New York.
Despair, poverty, and the fears generated in the imagination led some
immigrants to take their own lives. "Genumen di gez" (took gas)
was not an uncommon headline in the Yiddish press. Yet in the late
1880's only the city's Irish showed a lower suicide rate than did
Russian Jews.

However desperate the straits in which Jewish immigrants found
themselves, confirmed paupers among them were few. The rarity
of alcoholism, the pervasiveness of the charitable impulse, the strength
of ties to family and *lanslite*, and a deep current of optimism preserved
the individual from such degradation.

Prior to the 1880's only the Rubinstein murder case spotted the
record of New York's Jews. Upon the testimony of doubtful witnesses,
Rubinstein was sentenced to death for the slaying of his girl cousin,
but cheated the hangman by taking his own life. The first crime of
violence attributed to a Jew in the city's annals, its very novelty gave
rise to the popular street song, "My name is Pesach Rubinstein." So
unassailable was the peaceful reputation of the Jewish districts that
it was a matter for continual commendation. In 1878 Jews numbered
7 in a workhouse population of 1178; 8 among 485 prison inmates;
and 12 among 1110 house-of-correction inmates.

The obloquy attached to the strident Jews of Baxter and Chatham
Streets; to the Canal Street clothing shop puller-in and the Division

Street millinery shop pulleress; to Michael Kurtz, better known as "Sheeney Mike," reputedly the "champion burglar of America"; and to "Marm" Mandelbaum, unmatched receiver of stolen goods, did not detract from the high repute of the city's Jews. The two dozen Bowery pawnshops were owned by Americans or earlier immigrants who catered to the needs of a heterogeneous population and were not part of the immigrant community.

The major crime and violence in the area did not stem from the immigrants. They were its victims. The Lower East Side had always attracted much of the city's criminal element to its margins. By the last decades of the nineteenth century, it had shed the ferocity of earlier years when the "Bowery B'hoys" and the "Dead Rabbits" terrorized the area. But Mayor Hewitt's reform drive in 1887 inadvertently reinforced the district's frailties by forcing criminals and prostitutes from their accustomed uptown resorts into the less conspicuous tenements of the tenth ward, where they remained, undisturbed even by the Parkhurst crusade. The Raines Law, which provided that only hotels could serve liquor on Sundays, worsened the situation. In 1896, of 236 saloons in the tenth ward, 118 were Raines Law hotels, while 18 were outright houses of prostitution. In the first decade of the twentieth century, crusading District Attorney William Travers Jerome kept open house in his special office on Rutgers Street, at the hub of the Lower East Side, and the most salient features of criminality were forced underground. By 1905 the "peripatetic sisterhood" had been driven from the Bowery, and Captain Godard's Anti-Policy Society's campaign banished gambling from the thoroughfare. But the criminal elements soon returned.

Crime was endemic to the Lower East Side. The close collaboration between police officers, politicians, and criminals, revealed in detail in the Lexow and Mazet investigations of the 1890's, had turned the district into a Klondike that replaced the uptown Tenderloin as a center of graft and illicit business. Invariably the culprits in these activities were not immigrants, but Americanized Jews learned in street-corner ways and shorn of the restraints of the immigrant generation. "It is not until they have become Americanized, have adapted themselves to the environment of the district and adopted its ways and vices, that they become full-fledged wretches," commented Dr. I. L. Nascher. In the early years of the twentieth century the effect of such

conditions upon the young deeply disturbed those anxious for the
public weal. In 1909 some 3000 Jewish children were brought before
Juvenile Court and in the next few years Jewish criminals regularly
made newspaper headlines. The appearance of an ungovernable youth
after the turn of the century was undeniable and excited apprehension.

The violations of the law that characterized the immigrant community differed from the crimes of the sons of the immigrants. The
former were an outgrowth of occupational overcrowding, poverty, and
religious habits. Straitened circumstances contributed to the large
number of cases of family desertion and nonsupport. Concentrated in
marginal commerce and industry, Jews were prone to transgress the
codes of commercial law. "The prevalence of a spirit of enterprise out
of proportion to the capital of the community" gave rise to a high
incidence of felonious larceny, forgery, and failure to pay wages.
Peddlers and petty shopkeepers were especially vulnerable to police
oppression for evading informal levies as well as formal licensing
requirements. Legislation controlling business on Sunday found
Jewish immigrants natural victims. In so congested a district, the
breaking of corporation ordinances was unavoidable and the slaughter-
ing of chickens in tenements in violation of the sanitary code proved
to be a distinctly Jewish infraction.

The Bowery, way-station of derelicts, transients, and unsuspecting
immigrants, attracted the less stable and wary of the immigrant girls.
The dancing academies that sprang to popularity in the first decade
of the twentieth century snared impetuous, friendless young women.
Lured by promises of marriages, they soon were trapped by procurers
for the notorious Max Hochstim Association and other white slavers
who preyed upon the innocent and the unsuspecting. The appearance
of prostitution, previously rare among Jewesses, alarmed the East Side.

The Lower East Side, girded by the Bowery with its unsavory
establishments and Water Street with its resorts of ill-fame that
catered to the seafaring trade, was surrounded by violence. Bearded
Jews often were viciously assaulted by young hoodlums, both non-
Jews and Jews, the area adjacent to the waterfront being especially
dangerous. In 1898 and 1899, the newly organized American Hebrew
League of Brooklyn protested a rash of outrages in the wake of the
Dreyfus affair. Nevertheless there was only one instance of mass
violence: the riot of July 30, 1902 at the funeral of Rabbi Jacob
Joseph. This incident, the only one of its kind, can be attributed to

the stored-up resentment of the Irish who were being forced out of the area by the incursion of Jews.

SIGNS OF CHANGE

Gradually the miseries and trials of adjustment were left behind. For those who had inhabited the hungry villages of Eastern Europe, the hovels of Berditchev, and the crammed purlieus of Vilna and Kovno, the factories and sweatshops of New York provided a livelihood and possible stepping-stone. Despite unsteady and underpaid employment, tenement overcrowding and filth, immigrants felt themselves ineluctably being transformed. The Lower East Side, with its purposeful vitality, found no analogue in the "leprous-looking ghetto familiar in Europe," commented the visiting Abbé Félix Klein. Physical surroundings, however sordid, could be transcended. Optimism and hope engulfed every aspect of immigrant life. For a people who had risen superior to the oppressions of medieval proscriptions, the New York slums acted as a new-found challenge. Each passing year brought improvements that could be measured and appraised. Cramped quarters did not constrict aspirations. "In a large proportion of the tenements of the East Side . . . pianos are to be seen in the dingy rooms." And soon the phonograph was everywhere. "Excepting among the recent arrivals, most of the Jewish tenement dwellers have fair and even good furniture in their homes."

The East Europeans began to venture beyond the boundaries of the Lower East Side into other areas where employment was available on terms compatible with religious habits. Brooklyn's German Williamsburg district, directly across the East River, where Central European Jews had been established for some decades, was settled early. In the late 1880's a few clothing contractors set up sweatshops in the languid Scottish settlement of Brownsville, south and east of Williamsburg. The depression delayed further expansion for a decade despite the extension of the Fulton Street El in 1889. Then the tide could not be stemmed. Between 1899 and 1904 Brownsville's population rose from ten thousand to sixty thousand. Land values soared as immigrants came at the rate of one thousand per week. Lots selling for two hundred dollars in 1899 brought five to ten thousand dollars five years later. As the real estate boom revolutionized land values, many a former tailor was suddenly transformed into a substantial landlord or realtor who disdained all contact with shears and needles of bitter memory.

The mass dispersion of Jews from the Lower East Side to other parts of the city was in full swing in the early 1890's, as the more prosperous pioneers hastened to settle among their German coreligionists in Yorkville between 72nd and 100th streets, east of Lexington Avenue. For many a rising immigrant family in this period of swift change, it was judged to be a ten-year trek from Hester Street to Lexington Avenue.

The unprecedented flow of immigrants into the old central quarter, exorbitant rents, and the demolition of old tenements incidental to the building of parks, schools, and bridge approaches drastically reduced the area's absorptive capacity and spurred the search for new quarters. The construction of the Delancey Street approach to the Williamsburg Bridge in 1903 displaced 10,000 persons alone. The consolidation of the city and the growth and extension of rapid transit facilities connected what were once remote districts with the central downtown business quarters. In the new developments, cheaper land made possible lower rents that compensated for the time and expense of commuting. On Manhattan Island, the construction of underground transit opened to mass settlement the Dyckman tract in Washington Heights and the Harlem flats. The new subway also opened the East Bronx to extensive housing development. In Brooklyn, in addition to the heavy concentrations in Brownsville, Williamsburg, and South Brooklyn, Boro Park with "tropical gardens" and "parks" became increasingly accessible. Even distant Coney Island was brought into range by improved transit facilities.

With 542,061 inhabitants in 1910, the Lower East Side reached peak congestion. Thereafter, a decline set in. By 1916 only 23 per cent of the city's Jews lived in the once primary area of Jewish settlement, compared to 50 per cent in 1903 and 75 per cent in 1892. By the close of the first decade of the twentieth century the Lower East Side had lost much of its picturesqueness. In tone and color, the ghetto was perceptibly merging with the surrounding city. East European Jews had scattered to many sections of the city and were swiftly becoming an integral, if not as yet a fully accepted, element in the life of the community.

In 1870 the Jews of New York were estimated at 80,000, or less than 9 per cent of the city's inhabitants. By 1915 they totaled close to 1,400,000 persons (nearly 28 per cent), a number larger than the city's total population in 1870. Before 1880 the Jews of the city were hardly more than a subject for idle curiosity. But thereafter, the flow of East European Jews quickened the city's industrial life, helped to transform its physical shape, and contributed a varied and malleable people to the metropolis. Despite poverty and great numbers, these immigrants created no new problems. But their presence accentuated New York's shortcomings in the face of unprecedented demands upon its imagination and resources. In the early years of the new century, their voice would be heard. The problems of industrial relations and urban living accentuated on the Lower East Side were to become the focus for major reforms.

The Age of the Bosses

WILLIAM V. SHANNON

• The traditional stereotype of the city boss is that of a corrupt, ruthless, and self-seeking tyrant determined to perpet-
uate himself in power and to frustrate the public interest.
There is of course some truth to the charge. Urban machines
often required kickbacks from government contractors, and
regular contributions from municipal employees. Jobs and
favors were granted to "friends," and harassment, and occasionally violence, were reserved for political opponents. Municipal elections were often frauds; ballot-box stuffing and
the use of "repeaters" were typical tactics. The prize was
control of city budgets, which were far larger than those of
the state governments.

To focus only on the negative aspects of the urban machine, however, would be to obscure its unique role in our
political system. To millions of penniless, inner-city immigrants the local political machine was not a monster, but a
welcome friend in a strange and hostile environment. The
city boss, and the often more powerful ward boss, must be
viewed against the rapid growth of large cities and the tenement situation of many residents. Men like "Big Tim" Sulli-
van and George Washington Plunkitt of New York City
and "Bathhouse John" Coughlan and "Hinky Dink" Kenna
in Chicago maintained power for decades because they performed a service for poor people which no other institution
could effectively undertake. Food, clothing, shelter, employment, even protection from the police, were not abstract
needs but everyday concerns with which the boss was pecu-
liarly equipped to deal. Underprivileged citizens saw nothing
unusual or wrong in repaying their debt by voting according
to the dictates of the political organization.

From American Heritage, June 1969. Copyright © 1969 by American
Heritage Publishing Co., Inc. Reprinted by permission.

In the following essay William V. Shannon catches some of the color and excitement of the "Age of the Bosses." Whether the urban machines were of ultimate benefit to their constituents is a matter of individual judgment. But, as Shannon suggests, the boss system was a significant aspect in American political development.

The big city and the political boss grew up together in America. Bossism, with all its color and corruption and human drama, was a natural and perhaps necessary accompaniment to the rapid development of cities. The new urban communities did not grow slowly and according to plan; on the contrary, huge conglomerations of people from all over the world and from widely varying backgrounds came together suddenly, and in an unplanned, unorganized fashion fumbled their way toward communal relationships and a common identity. The political bosses emerged to cope with this chaotic change and growth. Acting out of greed, a ruthless will for mastery, and an imperfect understanding of what they were about, the bosses imposed upon these conglomerations called cities a certain feudal order and direction.

By 1890 virtually every sizable city had a political boss or was in the process of developing one. By 1950, sixty years later, almost every urban political machine was in an advanced state of obsolescence and its boss in trouble. The reason is not hard to find. Some of the cities kept growing and all of them kept changing, but the bosses, natural products of a specific era, could not grow or change beyond a certain point. The cities became essentially different, and as they did, the old-style organizations, like all organisms which cannot adapt, began to die. The dates vary from city to city. The system began earlier and died sooner in New York. Here or there, an old-timer made one last comeback. In Chicago, the organization and its boss still survive. But exceptions aside, the late nineteenth century saw the beginning, and the middle twentieth, the end, of the Age of the Bosses. What follows is a brief history of how it began, flourished, and passed away.

Soft-spoken Irish farmers from County Mayo and bearded Jews from Poland, country boys from Ohio and sturdy peasants from Calabria, gangling Swedes from near the Arctic Circle and Chinese from Canton, laconic Yankees from Vermont villages and Negro freedmen putting distance between themselves and the old plantation —all these and many other varieties of human beings from every national and religious and cultural tradition poured into America's cities in the decades after the Civil War.

Rome and Alexandria in the ancient world had probably been as polyglot, but in modern times the diversity of American cities was unique. Everywhere in the Western world, cities were growing rapidly in the late nineteenth century; but the Germans from the countryside who migrated to Hamburg and Berlin, the English who moved to Birmingham and London, and the French who flocked to Paris stayed among fellow nationals. They might be mocked as country bumpkins and their clothes might be unfashionable, but everyone they met spoke the same language as themselves, observed the same religious and secular holidays, ate the same kind of food, voted—if they had the franchise at all—in the same elections, and shared the same sentiments and expectations. To move from farm or village to a big European city was an adventure, but one still remained within the reassuring circle of the known and the familiar.

In American cities, however, the newcomers had nothing in common with one another except their poverty and their hopes. They were truly "the up-rooted." The foreign-born, unless they came from the British Isles, could not speak the language of their new homeland. The food, the customs, the holidays, the politics, were alien. Native Americans migrating to the cities from the countryside experienced their own kind of cultural shock: they found themselves competing not with other Americans but with recently arrived foreigners, so that despite their native birth they, too, felt displaced, strangers in their own country.

It was natural for members of each group to come together to try to find human warmth and protection in Little Italy or Cork Hill or Chinatown or Harlem. These feelings of clannish solidarity were one basis of strength for the political bosses. A man will more readily give his vote to a candidate because he is a neighbor from the old country or has some easily identifiable relationship, if only a similar name or the same religion, than because of agreement on some impersonal issue. Voters can take vicarious satisfaction from his success: "One of our boys is making good."

With so many different races and nationalities living together, however, mutual antagonisms were present, and the opportunity for hostility to flare into open violence was never far away. Ambitious, unscrupulous politicians could have exploited these antagonisms for their own political advantage, but the bosses and the political organizations which they developed did not function that way. If a man could vote and would "vote right," he was accepted, and that was the end of the matter. What lasting profit was there in attacking his religion or deriding his background?

Tammany early set the pattern of cultivating every bloc and faction and making an appeal as broad-based as possible. Of one precinct captain on the Lower East Side it was said: "He eats corned beef and kosher meat with equal nonchalance, and it's all the same to him whether he takes off his hat in the church or pulls it down over his ears in the synagogue."

Bosses elsewhere instinctively followed the same practice. George B. Cox, the turn-of-the-century Republican boss of Cincinnati, pasted together a coalition of Germans, Negroes, and old families like the Tafts and the Longworths. James M. Curley, who was mayor of Boston on and off for thirty-six years and was its closest approximation to a political boss, ran as well in the Lithuanian neighborhood of South Boston and the Italian section of East Boston as he did in the working-class Irish wards. In his last term in City Hall, he conferred minor patronage on the growing Negro community and joined the N.A.A.C.P.

The bosses organized neighborhoods, smoothed out antagonisms, arranged ethnically balanced tickets, and distributed patronage in accordance with voting strength as part of their effort to win and hold power. They blurred divisive issues and buried racial and religious hostility with blarney and buncombe. They were not aware that they were actually performing a mediating, pacifying function. They did not realize that by trying to please as many people as possible they were helping to hold raw new cities together, providing for inexperienced citizens a common meeting ground in politics and an experience in working together that would not have been available if the cities had been governed by apolitical bureaucracies. Bossism was usually corrupt and was decidedly inefficient, but in the 1960's, when antipoverty planners try to stimulate "community action organizations" to break through the apathy and disorganization of the slums, we can appreciate that the old-style machines had their usefulness.

When William Marcy Tweed, the first and most famous of the big-city bosses, died in jail in 1878, several hundred workingmen showed up for his funeral. The *Nation* wrote the following week:

> Let us remember that he fell without loss of reputation among the bulk of his supporters. The bulk of the poorer voters of this city today revere his memory, and look on him as the victim of rich men's malice; as, in short, a friend of the needy who applied the public funds, with as little waste as was possible under the circumstances, to the purposes to which they ought to be applied —and that is to the making of work for the working man. The odium heaped on him in the pulpits last Sunday does not exist in the lower stratum of New York society.

This split in attitude toward political bosses between the impoverished many and the prosperous middle classes lingers today and still colors historical writing. To respectable people, the boss was an exotic, even grotesque figure. They found it hard to understand why anyone would vote for him or what the sources of his popularity were. To the urban poor, those sources were self-evident. The boss ran a kind of ramshackle welfare state. He helped the unemployed find jobs, interceded in court for boys in trouble, wrote letters home to the old country for the illiterate; he provided free coal and baskets of food to tide a widow over an emergency, and organized parades, excursions to the beach, and other forms of free entertainment. Some bosses, such as Frank Hague in Jersey City and Curley in Boston, were energetic patrons of their respective city hospitals, spending public funds lavishly on new construction, providing maternity and children's clinics, and arranging medical care for the indigent. In an era when social security, Blue Cross, unemployment compensation, and other public and private arrangements to cushion life's shocks did not exist, these benefactions from a political boss were important.

In every city, the boss had his base in the poorer, older, shabbier section of town. Historians have dubbed this section the "walking city" because it developed in the eighteenth and early nineteenth centuries, when houses and businesses were jumbled together, usually near the waterfront, and businessmen and laborers alike had to live within walking distance of their work. As transportation improved, people were able to live farther and farther from their place of work. Population dispersed in rough concentric circles: the financially most successful lived in the outer ring, where land was plentiful and the air was clean; the middle classes lived in intermediate neighborhoods; and the poorest and the latest arrivals from Europe crowded into the now-rundown neighborhoods in the center, where rents were lowest. Politics in most cities reflected a struggle between the old, boss-run wards downtown and the more prosperous neighborhoods farther out, which did not need a boss's services and which championed reform. The more skilled workingmen and the white-collar workers who lived in the intermediate neighborhoods generally held the balance of power between the machine and the reformers. A skillful boss could hold enough of these swing voters on the basis of ethnic loyalty or shared support of a particular issue. At times, he might work out alliances with business leaders who found that an understanding with a boss was literally more businesslike than dependence upon the vagaries of reform.

But always it was the poorest and most insecure who provided the boss with the base of his political power. Their only strength, as Professor Richard C. Wade of the University of Chicago has observed, was in their numbers.

> These numbers were in most cases a curse; housing never caught up with demand, the job market was always flooded, the breadwinner had too many mouths to feed. Yet in politics such a liability could be turned into an asset. If the residents could be mobilized, their combined strength would be able to do what none could do alone. Soon the "boss" and the "machine" arose to organize this potential. The boss system was simply the political expression of inner city life.

At a time when many newcomers to the city were seeking unskilled work, and when many families had a precarious economic footing, the ability to dispense jobs was crucial to the bosses. First, there were jobs to be filled on the city payroll. Just as vital, and far more numerous, were jobs on municipal construction projects. When the machine controlled a city, public funds were always being spent for more schools, hospitals, libraries, courthouses, and orphanages. The growing cities had to have more sewer lines, gas lines, and water-works, more paved streets and trolley tracks. Even if these utilities were privately owned, the managers needed the goodwill of city hall and were responsive to suggestions about whom to hire.

The payrolls of these public works projects were often padded, but to those seeking a job, it was better to be on a padded payroll than on no payroll. By contrast, the municipal reformers usually cut back on public spending, stopped projects to investigate for graft, and pruned payrolls. Middle- and upper-income taxpayers welcomed these reforms, but they were distinctly unpopular in working-class wards.

Another issue that strengthened the bosses was the regulation of the sale of liquor. Most women in the nineteenth century did not drink, and with their backing, the movement to ban entirely the manufacture and sale of liquor grew steadily stronger. It had its greatest support among Protestants with a rural or small-town back-ground. To them the cities, with their saloons, dance halls, cheap theatres, and red-light districts, were becoming latter-day versions of Sodom and Gomorrah.

Many of the European immigrants in the cities, however, had en-tirely different values. Quite respectable Germans took their wives to beer gardens on Sundays. In the eyes of the Irish, keeping a "public house" was an honorable occupation. Some Irish women drank beer and saw no harm in going to the saloon or sending an older child for a bucketful—"rushing the growler," they called it. Poles, Czechs, Italians, and others also failed to share the rage of the Prohibitionists against saloons. Unable to entertain in their cramped tenements, they liked to congregate in neighborhood bars.

The machine also appealed successfully on the liquor issue to many middle-class ethnic voters who had no need of the machine's economic assistance. Thus, in New York in 1897, Tammany scored a sweeping victory over an incumbent reform administration that had tried to enforce a state law permitting only hotels to sell liquor on Sundays. As one of the city's three police commissioners, Theodore Roosevelt became famous prowling the tougher neighborhoods on the hunt for saloon violations, but on the vaudeville stage the singers were giving forth with the hit song, "I Want What I Want When I Want It!" As a character in Alfred Henry Lewis' novel *The Boss* explained it, the reformers had made a serious mistake: "They got between the people and its beer!"

In 1902, Lincoln Steffens, the muckraker who made a name for himself writing about political bossism, visited St. Louis to interview Joseph W. Folk, a crusading district attorney. "It is good businessmen that are corrupting our bad politicians," Folk told him. "It is good business that causes bad government in St. Louis." Thirty-five years later, Boss Tom Pendergast was running the entire state of Missouri on that same reciprocal relationship.

Although many factory owners could be indifferent to politics, other businessmen were dependent upon the goodwill and the efficiency of the municipal government. The railroads that wanted to build their freight terminals and extend their lines into the cities, the contractors who erected the office buildings, the banks that held mortgages on the land and loaned money for the construction, the utility and transit companies, and the department stores were all in need of licenses, franchises, rights of way, or favorable rulings from city inspectors and agencies. These were the businesses that made the big pay-offs to political bosses in cash, blocks of stock, or tips on land about to be developed.

In another sense, profound, impersonal, and not corrupt, the business community needed the boss. Because the Industrial Revolution hit this country when it was still thinly populated and most of its cities were overgrown towns, American cities expanded with astonishing speed. For example, in the single decade from 1880 to 1890, Chicago's population more than doubled, from a half million to over a million. The twin cities of Minneapolis and St. Paul tripled in size. New York City increased from a million to a million and a half; Detroit, Milwaukee, Columbus, and Cleveland grew by sixty to eighty per cent.

Municipal governments, however, were unprepared for this astonishing growth. Planning and budgeting were unknown arts. City charters
had restrictive provisions envisaged for much smaller, simpler communities. The mayor and the important commissioners were usually
amateurs serving a term or two as a civic duty. Authority was dispersed
among numerous boards and special agencies. A typical city would have
a board of police commissioners, a board of health, a board of tax as-
sessors, a water board, and many others. The ostensible governing body
was a city council or board of aldermen which might have thirty, fifty,
or even a hundred members. Under these circumstances, it was difficult
to get a prompt decision, harder still to co-ordinate decisions taken by
different bodies acting on different premises, and easy for delays and
anomalies to develop.

In theory, the cities could have met their need for increased services
by municipal socialism, but the conventional wisdom condemned that
as too radical, although here and there a city did experiment with publicly owned utilities. In theory also, the cities could have financed
public buildings and huge projects such as water and sewer systems by
frankly raising taxes or floating bonds. But both taxes and debt were
no more popular then than they are now. Moreover, the laissez-faire
doctrine which holds that "that government is best which governs
least" was enshrined orthodoxy in America from the 1870's down to
the 1930's.

As men clung to such orthodox philosophies, the structures of government became obsolete; they strained to meet unexpected demands as
a swelling number of citizens in every class clamored for more services.
In this climate the bosses emerged. They had no scruples about taking
shortcuts through old procedures or manipulating independent boards
and agencies in ways that the original city fathers had never intended.
They had no inhibiting commitment to any theory of limited government. They were willing to spend, tax, and build—and to take the
opprobrium along with the graft. Sometimes, like Hague in Jersey City,
Curley in Boston, and Big Bill Thompson in Chicago, they got themselves elected mayor and openly assumed responsibility. More often,
like Pendergast in Kansas City, Cox in Cincinnati, the leaders of Tammany, and the successive Republican bosses of Philadelphia, they held
minor offices or none, stayed out of the limelight, and ran city govern-

ment through their iron control of the party organization. In ruling Memphis for forty years, Ed Crump followed one pattern and then the other. Impeached on a technicality after being elected three times as mayor, Crump retreated to the back rooms and became even more powerful as the city's political boss.

What manner of men became political bosses? They were men of little education and no social background, often of immigrant parentage. A college-educated boss like Edward Flynn of The Bronx was a rarity. Bosses often began as saloonkeepers, because the saloon was a natural meeting place in poorer neighborhoods in the days before Prohibition. They were physically strong and no strangers to violence. Seventy-five years ago, most men made their living with brawn rather than brain, and a man who expected to be a leader of men had to be tough as well as shrewd. Open violence used to be common at polling places on Election Day, and gangs of repeaters roamed from one precinct to another. Although the typical boss made his way up through that roughneck system, the logic of his career led him to suppress violence. Bloody heads make bad publicity, and it is hard for any political organization to maintain a monopoly on violence. Bosses grew to prefer quieter, more lawful, less dangerous methods of control. Ballot-box stuffing and overt intimidation never disappeared entirely, but gradually they receded to the status of weapons of last resort.

Political bosses varied in their idiosyncrasies and styles. A few, like Curley, became polished orators; others, like the legendary Charles Murphy of Tammany Hall, never made speeches. They were temperate, businesslike types; among them a drunk was as rare as a Phi Beta Kappa. If they had a generic failing it was for horses and gambling. Essentially they were hardheaded men of executive temper and genuine organizing talents; many, in other circumstances and with more education, might have become successful businessmen.

They have disappeared now, most of them. Education has produced a more sophisticated electorate; it has also encouraged potential bosses to turn away from politics toward more secure, prestigious, and profitable careers. A young man who had the energy, persistence, and skill in 1899 to become a successful political boss would in 1969 go to colleg and end up in an executive suite.

The urban population has also changed. The great flood of be-wildered foreigners has dwindled to a trickle. In place of the European immigrants of the past, today's cities receive an influx of Negroes from the rural South, Puerto Ricans, Mexicans, and the white poor from Appalachia. As they overcome the language barrier and widen their experience, the Puerto Ricans are making themselves felt in urban politics. New York City, where they are most heavily concentrated, may have a Puerto Rican mayor in the not too distant future.

But the other groups are too isolated from the rest of the community to put together a winning political coalition of have-nots. The Mexi-cans and the ex-hillbillies from Appalachia are isolated by their unique cultural backgrounds, the Negroes by the giant fact of their race. In-asmuch as they make up a quarter to a third of the population in many cities, are a cohesive group, and still have a high proportion of poor who have to look to government for direct help, the Negroes might have produced several bosses and functioning political machines had they been of white European ancestry. But until Negroes attain a clear numerical majority, they find it difficult to take political power in any city because various white factions are reluctant to coalesce them.

Regardless of the race or background of the voters, however, there are factors which work against the old-style machines. Civil service regulations make it harder to create a job or pad a payroll. Federal in-come taxes and federal accounting requirements make it more difficult to hide the rewards of graft. Television, public relations, and polling have created a whole new set of political techniques and undermined the personal ties and neighborhood loyalties on which the old organiza-tions depended.

The new political style has brought an increase in municipal govern-ment efficiency and probably some decline in political corruption and misrule. But the politics of the television age puts a premium on hy-pocrisy. Candor has gone out the window with the spoils system. There is still a lot of self-seeking in politics and always will be. But gone are the days of Tammany's Boss Richard Croker, who when asked by an investigating committee if he was "working for his own pocket," shot back: "All the time—same as you." Today's politicians are so busy tending their images that they have become incapable of even a mildly derogatory remark such as Jim Curley's: "The term 'codfish aristocracy' is a reflection on the fish."

Curley entitled his memoirs *I'd Do It Again*. But the rough-and-tumble days when two-fisted, rough-tongued politicians came roaring out of the slums to take charge of America's young cities are not to come again.

A Compulsory Heaven at Pullman

RAY GINGER

• Although the concept of the company town was not introduced in Pullman, Illinois, first the yellow-bricked planned
community for sleeping car workers on the fringes of Chicago attracted national and international attention in the
1880's. Industrial giant George M. Pullman viewed with paternal pride the comfortable homes, the parks, the library,
the band, the church, and the shopping center and confi-
dently expected that his controlled environment would improve the performance of his workers, and at the same time
yield a 6 per cent return on the company's capital investment.

When the company reduced wages but not rents, the
brainchild became rebellious toward its Puritanical father,
however, and in 1894 this pleasant model town touched off
the most famous strike in American history. It tied up the
nation's rail system and pitted crusading labor leader Eugene
V. Debs against the proud George Pullman and Illinois Governor John Peter Altgeld against the President of the United
States.

The town of Pullman is memorable for another reason,
however. That the experiment was conducted in a relatively
isolated environment well outside the boundaries of a booming metropolis was not accidental. George Pullman realized
that his factories needed to be located reasonably near the
rail network of a great city. But he also believed that saloons,
prostitutes, bright lights, and crowded residential districts
were not conducive to industrial efficiency or moral strength,
and like many people in our own time, he felt that the best
answer to urban problems was to escape them. Pullman
failed, but generations of suburbanites have followed his

panacea and fully planned communities are now operative in Reston, Virginia, and Columbia, Maryland, to name only the most recent examples. Do these communities offer a viable alternative to the problems of modern life? Was the fate of Pullman, Illinois, merely an isolated case of the failure of one man's attempts to be a benevolent dictator or does it indicate the inevitable outcome of all utopias?

In so far as philanthropists . . . are cut off from the great moral life springing from our common experiences, so long as they are "good to people" rather than "with them," they are bound to accomplish a large amount of harm.

JANE ADDAMS

I

George Mortimer Pullman was one of the great industrialists of the age, not just one of the most successful, but also one of the most creative. Inventor, strategist, executive, he was the perfect businessman. More than that, he recognized that the lives of his employees did not end when they left the shop at night. He had a vision of a richer existence for his labor force, and out of it he built the first model town in industrial America. It was a showplace. Visitors come from all over the world to admire it. Here was the solution to the labor question. But as the years passed, George Pullman's vision proved to be both more complicated and simpler than it had seemed at first. And in May, 1894, his heaven exploded.

Pullman was born in 1831 in a small town in upstate New York, one of the ten children of a general mechanic. He quit school early to be a cabinetmaker, then became a street contractor. His work took him to Chicago, where he quickly found a chance to show his resourcefulness. In 1858 the Tremont House, a downtown hotel, seemed to be settling into a bottomless pit of mud. Although the structure was four stories tall and made of brick, Pullman vowed that he could raise it without breaking a single pane of glass or awakening a single guest. He put 5,000 jackscrews in the basement and assembled twelve hundred men. At a signal, each man gave a half-turn to his four jackscrews. Inch by inch the building was plucked out of the morass.

Pullman began to tinker around at building a sleeping car for the Chicago & Alton Railroad. But when it was finished, the railroads were loath to adopt it; so he wandered out to the newly opened mining fields in Colorado and ran a store. By 1863 he was back to Chicago and working in earnest on his invention. His basic design, the key to which was the hinged upper berth, was just like the modern Pullman. But he decorated the car lavishly: other sleeping cars were built for about $5,000; Pullman spent $20,000 on his. In order to accommodate the berths properly, he made the car a foot wider and 2½ feet higher than ordinary railroad cars. Any railroad that wanted to use Pullmans would have to alter its bridges and its station platforms. Pullman didn't care; he was going to build his car right. He focused on one thing: maximum comfort for the passenger.

And he won out. By 1867 orders were pouring in. On every hand railroads were altering stations, bridges, culverts. The Pullman Palace Car Company was incorporated in Illinois, and gradually plants were built from New York to California. Pullman made other inventions: the restaurant car, the dining car, the chair car. He made railroad cars on contract for the railroads themselves. But his sleeping cars he would not sell. His company operated the cars itself; the railroads simply hauled them around the country. Pullman paid his stockholders a straight 8 percent dividend each year, and the rest of the profits he kept in the firm as surplus. Shares in the Pullman Company rose to twice their par value.

More manufacturing facilities were needed. And George Pullman had his vision. Other companies were frequently beset by labor troubles. Strikes occurred at crucial times and crippled production. Men got drunk and stayed home to recover. Workers strayed off to other jobs as soon as they had acquired the skill you needed. But if you gave them a really decent place to live, you could get a better class of workmen, labor turnover could be reduced, unrest would turn into contentment. Above all, if you owned the entire town, you could insulate your employees from corrupting influences. The environment could be kept as controlled and sterile as an incubator, a church, or a prison.

Some of the Pullman directors objected to using corporate funds for such a purpose. Their business, they said, was manufacturing and operating railroad cars, not real estate. But George Pullman overrode them. A perfect site for the new shops was the prairie twelve miles south of the business district of Chicago. Here was the railroad hub of the United States, accessible to more major railroads than any other spot in the country. But it was a relatively isolated spot, far from the residential areas of the working class. The only way to get a labor force was to build the housing.

But George Pullman never thought of the town solely in terms of its indirect benefits to the company. He also thought about its direct commercial value. Every dollar invested in the town was expected to yield a 6 percent return.

In 1880 the Pullman Company quietly bought a solid tract of four thousand acres, nearly seven square miles, on the west shore of Lake Calumet. It was in the town of Hyde Park, a sprawling congeries of settled areas and huge vacant stretches which adjoined Chicago. The town of Pullman was erected on three hundred acres, surrounded by an empty *cordon sanitaire*. The little community was a beautiful place, especially when compared to the filthy industrial giant just to its north. One tenth of the area of Pullman was taken by its parks. A miniature lake was created for boating and swimming. An island in the lake was used for many types of athletics.

Every street in town was paved with macadam. The sidewalks were paved too, usually with wood, and were lined with shade trees. The front lawn of every house in town was landscaped by the company. The buildings were nearly all yellow brick, made in Pullman itself of clay dredged from the bottom of Lake Calumet. By 1885 the town had fourteen hundred dwelling units. Most of them had five rooms, and they were built as row-houses. The company kept them in good repair. There were occasional complaints in cases where two families had to use a single toilet, but in Chicago few tenements had any indoor plumbing at all. In other respects, too, health conditions in Pullman were excellent. Sanitation was outstanding, the company even furnishing garbage receptacles and emptying them daily.

Pullman had a higher tax assessment for school purposes than any other area in Hyde Park. The term lasted for two hundred days, which was incredibly generous for that time. Schooling was free through the eighth grade, the only condition being that all students had to be vaccinated for smallpox. Another pioneering feature was the kindergarten

for children between the ages of four and six. An evening school taught
such commercial subjects as bookkeeping and stenography.

The cultural life of the town was quite varied. Besides the extensive
athletic program, there was a theater with one thousand seats, where
the foremost actors and musicians of the time performed during the
1880's. The library, luxurious with its Wilton carpets and plush chairs,
was opened in 1883 with an initial gift of five thousand volumes from
George Pullman. The eighty-piece Military Band, good enough one
year to win the statewide competition, was composed entirely of men
who worked for the company. During the summer it gave free weekly
concerts.

This industrial Arcadia grew year by year. It hit its peak in 1893,
just before the depression struck, when the population of the town was
12,600. At that time, employment in the Pullman shops was 5,500,
with many of the workers living in surrounding towns. The town grew
in value too. The land had cost $800,000 in 1880. Twelve years later,
George Pullman estimated that it was worth $5 million. He had rea-
son to congratulate himself.

But he had his problems with the town. The most serious was that
it never earned the return that he had expected from it. For years it
paid only about 4.5 percent. In 1892 and 1893 the return further declined to 3.82 percent.

Even to get that much, Pullman had to fight a continuing war
against the town of Hyde Park about his tax rates. He took no interest
in civic affairs outside his own town, but his business brought him into
politics anyway. In order to keep foreign competition away, he was a
high-tariff man, and that prompted him to contribute heavily to the
national Republican party. And his desires to keep his taxes down
and to be left alone to run his town as he saw fit—together they carried
him deep into local politics.

Foremen at the Pullman shops openly solicited votes for the
company-approved candidates in elections. Workers were discharged
because they persisted in running for public office contrary to the orders
of their superiors. When John P. Hopkins, a prosperous storekeeper
in Pullman, organized voters for Grover Cleveland in 1888, his landlord made life so difficult for him that he had to move his store to
nearby Kensington. The Pullman Company maneuvered and manipulated and coerced for years to prevent Hyde Park from becoming part

of Chicago, but in 1889 it lost that fight, and thereafter George Pullman had to go into Chicago politics to keep his taxes low.

He was an irascible, pompous man who could never see any viewpoint but his own. He thought that liquor was bad, so he banned it
from the town. He thought that prostitution was bad, so he banned that
too. He kept his eye on everything. He had informers in every lodge,
in every social group; sometimes it seemed that he had them in every
parlor on Saturday night. He wanted to know everything that happened. The town was his, and he would run it his way. He believed in
thrift, and hard work and sobriety. He believed in individual responsibility and the other Puritan virtues.

But many of his workers came from other traditions. As early as
1884 more than half of the residents were foreign-born. Eight years
later, 72 percent were, including 23 percent Scandinavian, 12 percent
British, the same proportion of Germans, 10 percent Dutch, 5 percent
Irish. Many of them could see no harm in a pint of beer. Many of
them wanted to worship in their own faith.

George Pullman had his ideas about that too. There was one church
building in town. Pullman owned it, just as he owned everything else.
He was a Universalist who didn't care about doctrinal niceties, but the
church was nonsectarian. It was part of the business; it too had to pay
its way. The rent set on it by Pullman was so high that no congregation in town could afford to pay it. The Presbyterians tried it for a few
years and went bankrupt. The resultant bitterness was summed up by
one Presbyterian minister: "I preached once in the Pullman church,
but by the help of God I will never preach there again. The word
monopoly seems to be written in black letters over the pulpit and the
pews." George Pullman didn't care.

From the very beginning, Pullman's high-handed ways aroused opposition. Prior to 1882 the shops had been expanded more rapidly than
the housing facilities. Many employees were still living in Chicago,
and they had to pay a round-trip fare of 20 cents a day on the Illinois
Central to get back and forth to work. The company paid this fare.
Then it announced that it would pay only half. A thousand men struck.
The strike was broken; the ringleaders fired.

In March, 1884, a group of 150 men in the freight-car department
struck against a wage cut. That strike was broken too. Then the company learned a new technique. In October, 1885, it instituted a wage

cut of 10 percent. But the reduction was introduced first in one department, then in another; the workers were never unified against it. So a strike did not come until the following spring, when an estimated fourteen hundred workers at Pullman were members of the Knights of Labor. They joined in the general movement for an eight-hour day that was sweeping through Chicago, and to the general demand they added their own—a 10 percent pay increase, to recoup what they had lost. The company refused; the workers struck; within ten days the shops were reopened under guard.

George Pullman wanted no truck with trade unions—and for the next eight years there was no effort at organization in his plant. Small strikes occurred in 1888 and 1891, but they were hardly serious enough to be annoying. In 1893 the company could announce smugly: "During the eleven years the town has been in existence, the Pullman workingman has developed into a distinctive type—distinct in appearance, in dress, in fact, in all the external indications of self-respect. . . ." A typical group of Pullman employees, said the statement, was "40 percent better in evidence of thrift and refinement and in all the outward indications of a wholesome way of life" than any comparable group in America.

The "outward indications"—Pullman could usually control those. But he could not legislate against the bitterness within. As one man protested: "We are born in a Pullman house, fed from the Pullman shop, taught in the Pullman school, catechized in the Pullman church, and when we die we shall be buried in the Pullman cemetery and go to the Pullman hell."

A year after the Company had congratulated itself, the inward bitterness of its employees burst forth in action, and the "distinctive type" of workingman proved that, if goaded hard enough, he could be an unruly ingrate like anybody else.

II

The financial policies of the Pullman Palace Car Company throughout its history had been so sound that the firm was in excellent position to meet the depression in 1893; usual dividends could have been maintained for years out of the undivided surplus that had been accumulated. But businessmen care about current income as well as about liquidity, and the gross receipts of the Pullman Company fell drastically in 1893. Income from operating its sleeping and dining cars held up well, but much of the firm's manufacturing activity consisted in filling orders from other firms for various types of railroad cars. These outside orders now dried up almost entirely; no railroad adds new equipment when much of what it has is idle.

George Pullman was not a man to stand quietly with his hands in his pockets while his money seeped away. He responded vigorously with a program of lay-offs, reduced hours, wage cuts. In July, 1893, the shops at Pullman employed 5,500 men; the following May, only 3,300. Wage rates were slashed an average of 25 percent, but the pay cuts were far from uniform: machinists in the street-car department claimed that their wages had been reduced more than 70 percent. At a time when painters in Chicago—those lucky enough to be employed—were getting 35 cents an hour, the painters at Pullman were paid 23 cents an hour.

These policies were superbly effective, as the company's accountants had reason to know:

Year ending July 31	Wages	Dividends
1893	$7,223,719	$2,520,000
1894	4,471,701	2,880,000

The outlay for wages had been reduced 38 percent in a single year; but dividends were actually increased. And the company had an undistributed surplus for the year 1893–1894 of $2,320,000!

During all this time, rental charges for housing in Pullman were not reduced. Renting houses was one thing; employing workmen was another; the two had no connection. And so long as the capital invested in the housing remained the same, why should rents be reduced? In regard to this, a Federal commission later concluded: "If we exclude the aesthetic and sanitary features at Pullman, the rents there are from 20 to 25 percent higher than rents in Chicago or surrounding towns for similar accommodations. The aesthetic features are admired by visitors, but have little money value to employees, especially when they lack bread."

As early as December, 1893, the Pullman Company felt constrained to issue a statement denying that extreme distress existed among the residents of Pullman. So the winter dragged on, and the workers and their families suffered. Since George Pullman had always managed the town arbitrarily, its institutions of local government were anemic. The town had no mechanisms for public relief, which was contrary to the owner's ideas of individual self-help. But the typical worker was hesitant to move away even after he had been laid off by the shops. House rents in Pullman were higher than elsewhere, but unemployment was everywhere, and the workers believed that residents of Pullman would be the first to be rehired. So destitution became unbearable; yet there was nothing to do except bear it. In some homes the children lacked the shoes and coats needed to go to school in the severe Illinois winter; in others they were kept in bed all day because there was no coal in the house.

And then came a voice of hope. A dim hope—yes, but still it was something. The previous spring, June, 1893, just as the depression was beginning, fifty railroad workers had met in Chicago to form the American Railway Union. Prior to that time the only trade unions on the railroads had been the various Brotherhoods, a separate one for each of the main occupations in railroading. The Brotherhoods of skilled workers, such as the Engineers, were the strongest and best organized, and they tended always to sneer at their fellow workers in the less skilled crafts—the switchmen, the brakemen, even the locomotive firemen—and they hardly recognized the existence of the men who worked on the railroads but had nothing to do with operating trains, such as the section hands.

The utter lack of cooperation, verging often on civil war, among the various Brotherhoods made it impossible for the unskilled crafts to bargain effectively with the railroads, and even the Engineers achieved many of their gains by ruthlessly sacrificing the interests of other crafts. Beginning about 1885, a movement developed in each of the Brotherhoods that aimed at bringing about joint action among them. Finally in 1889 the Supreme Council of the United Orders of Railway Employes was formed, consisting of the officers of several of the Brotherhoods. The organization for a time seemed to be working well, and it appeared that the other Brotherhoods would join and even that ultimately they might all merge into one big Brotherhood of railroad workers—one industrial union rather than many craft unions. But within less than two years, one of the member Brotherhoods conspired with the Chicago & Northwestern Railroad to destroy another of the member Brotherhoods. The Supreme Council collapsed.

The episode caused some of the more radical officials in the Brotherhoods to despair of their conservative fellows, who seemed determined to seek their own selfish ends and to block any moves toward unification of the different organizations. Chief among these dissidents was Eugene Victor Debs, secretary-treasurer of the Brotherhood of Locomotive Firemen since 1880 and editor of its magazine. When Debs took these jobs, the order was small and moribund, with sixty inactive lodges and a substantial debt. Twelve years later it was out of debt, had twenty thousand members, and was solidly established. Much of this progress was due to Debs personally: to his zeal, his dedication, his relentless drive, above all to his concern for the welfare of the poor.

Thirty-eight years old in 1893, he was a man of awesome vigor. His life was one perpetual organizing trip. Every day, day after day, he could travel two or three hundred miles, give a half-dozen speeches, and have energy left for a good deal of sociable drinking. His stamina welled outward from a tall, austere frame and a copious spirit. Debs was a visionary. He pictured a land from which poverty, whether of the body or of the heart, had disappeared, a land where violence was not even a bad memory, an America where everybody treated his fellows generously of his own will, because he could do no other, an America where everybody smiled and everybody sang.

But he knew that no man can smile with another's face or sing in a foreign language. Debs was no George Pullman, carrying a prefabricated Utopia around in his vest pocket. He spoke of the evils of this world and of the possibility of a better one. About the evils he was explicit: poverty, arbitrary power, treating men solely in terms of their cash value, one man imposing his will on another. But he never spelled out the details of the better life he was always talking about. He exhorted men to love one another; beyond that, they would have to find their own way. Men cannot be driven at all; and they cannot be led down a narrow and fenced road to a waiting corral. The job of leadership is to point a general direction and to awaken in men the hope that they can move in that direction. Debs could do this. When he talked,

men came to life, and they moved. He was an agitator. To agitate, all
that he needed was to feel sure himself of the general direction that
men should go.

In 1892 he was sure. He was fed up with the internecine warfare of
the Brotherhoods, which saw each of them cut the throat of the others
for some selfish and short-term gain. He was gagging on the smug ar-
rogance of the Brotherhood of Locomotive Engineers. He wanted to
see an organization that would really protect the railroaders, all of
them, against the tyranny and exploitation of the corporations. But
when he declined to stand for reelection as secretary-treasurer of the
Firemen in 1892, his plans were very general: "It has been my life's
desire to unify railroad employees and to eliminate the aristocracy of
labor, which unfortunately exists, and organize them so all will be on
an equality." The following spring Debs was one of the founders of
the American Railway Union, and became its president.

The ARU started its first local lodge on August 17, 1893. Thereafter
a flash flood of members threatened to drown Debs and the two other
full-time organizers. Within twenty days, thirty-four lodges had been
chartered. Members were joining at the rate of two hundred to four
hundred men a day. Entire lodges of Railway Carmen and Switchmen
changed their affiliation to the ARU. Conductors, firemen, even engineers, joined the new industrial union. But most of the applicants
were previously unorganized men in the less skilled crafts who had been
excluded from the Brotherhoods. These were the engine wipers, the
section hands, the most exploited and worst paid men on the railroads,
who had formerly been left to suffer in isolation. Now they rushed
toward the organization that had opened its ranks to them, rushed so
eagerly that the ARU had eighty-seven local lodges by mid-November:
for three months, a new lodge every day. The surge continued over
the winter, and in the spring of 1894 it was vastly accelerated when
the ARU won the first strike that any union had ever won against a
major railroad.

James J. Hill's Great Northern Railroad stretched westward from
Minneapolis clear to the Pacific. When its employees went on strike
in April, direction of the walk-out quickly passed into the hands of
Debs and his colleagues. After the entire line had been closed down
nearly a fortnight, the St. Paul Chamber of Commerce demanded that

Hill and the union should submit the dispute to arbitration. They did so. The award gave the strikers 97½ percent of their demands, an aggregate wage increase of $1,752,000 a year.

Although this victory was won in the Twin Cities, it was widely publicized in Chicago, where the ARU centered in many ways. Its national headquarters were there. Most of its local lodges were on roads running from Chicago westward. And it was there that Debs gave a fervent speech at the Columbian Exposition. It was in the autumn of 1893, before the dreadful winter at Pullman, and Debs did not mention George Pullman by name, but his speech contained an unqualified attack on Pullman's type of paternalism:

> The time is coming, fortunately, when we are hearing less of that old paternal Pharisaism: "What can we do for labor?" It is the old, old query repeated all along the centuries, heard wherever a master wielded a whip above the bowed forms of the slaves . . . We hear it yet, occasionally, along lines of transportation, in mines and shops, but our ears are regaled by a more manly query, . . . which is, "What can labor do for itself?" The answer is not difficult. Labor can organize, it can unify, it can consolidate its forces. This done, it can demand and command.

And in the spring of 1894, at the time of the victory over the Great Northern, the workers in the Pullman shops began to take Debs's advice. They were eligible for membership in the ARU because the Pullman Company operated a few miles of railroad leading to its shops, and, man by man, they joined. Their money was gone, and their patience with it. One blacksmith, when he worked six hours and was paid 45 cents, said that if he had to starve, he saw no reason why he should wear out his clothes at Pullman's anvil at the same time.

The workers went to the vice-president of the company and presented their demands. The official promised to investigate. The grievance committee held a meeting. Even though the top officials of the ARU urged delay, the committee voted a strike. Of the 3,300 workers in the factory, more than 90 percent walked out together on May 11. The company promptly laid off the others. Three days later, Eugene Debs was in Pullman. He had advised against the strike. But after walking through the town, hearing the stories, seeing the paychecks, he realized that it had been an act of desperation. Even the local leader of the strike said that they did not expect to win. They just didn't know what else to do.

The strike dragged along until June 12, when the first national convention of the American Railway Union met in Chicago. In one year, the organization had enrolled 150,000 members. The total membership of all the Brotherhoods was 90,000. But success had not gone to Debs's head. He knew that the union was loosely organized, that it was largely uncoordinated, that it had little money, that it was scanted for experienced leaders, especially in the farflung local lodges. The ARU had won its battle against the Great Northern; Debs was not sure it could win another against an equally powerful corporation.

A committee from Pullman appeared before the convention and made a plea: "We struck because we were without hope. We joined the American Railway Union because it gave us a glimmer of hope. . . . We will make you proud of us, brothers, if you will give us the • hand we need. Help us make our country better and more wholesome." A seamstress at Pullman, thin and tired, came to tell how, when her father died, she had been forced to repay $60 back rent that he owed the company.

The sentimental delegates were swept by indignation. One suggested that the convention declare a boycott of Pullman cars. Debs, who was presiding, refused to entertain the motion. Using every recourse available to a chairman to thwart actions that he disapproves, Debs suggested a committee from the convention to confer with the Pullman Company. Twelve men, including six strikers, were chosen to go to the company and propose arbitration of the wage dispute.

The committee returned next day to the convention, to report that the Pullman Company had refused to confer with any members of the ARU. Again a boycott was proposed. Again Debs blocked it. A second committee, consisting solely of strikers, was sent to the company with a request for arbitration. The company said that there was "nothing to arbitrate." After voting relief funds for the strikers at Pullman, the convention set up another committee to recommend a plan of action. When the recommendation came on June 22, it was direct: Unless the Pullman Company agreed, not to a settlement, but merely to begin negotiations within four days, the American Railway Union should

refuse to handle Pullman cars. Again Debs urged caution. But the delegates, in no humor for pussyfooting, adopted the committee's report.

Then the committee was sent back to Pullman for a final effort.
The firm would concede nothing. Nothing. Its position was that wages
and working conditions should be determined by management, with
no interference by labor. So the ARU convention unanimously voted
the boycott. Debs, his hand forced, devised the tactic: switchmen in
the ARU would refuse to switch any Pullman cars onto trains. If the
switchmen were discharged or disciplined for this refusal, all ARU
members on the line would cease work at once.

III

The boycott began at noon on June 26. At once the union was
opposed by the railroads, which took an active hand in the conflict.
Here was their chance to cut the ARU down to size. Unified by the
General Managers Association, the twenty-four railroads running out
of Chicago—with a combined capital of $818 million, with 221,000
employees—declared that their contracts with Pullman were sacred
and that they would operate no trains without Pullman cars.

Deadlock. By June 29, twenty railroads were tied up. An estimated
125,000 men had quit work. Agents of the General Managers were
busy in Eastern cities hiring unemployed railroaders as strikebreakers.
Leaders of the Railroad Brotherhoods were denouncing the ARU.
Eugene Debs was sending telegrams all over the Great Plains advising
his members to use no violence and to stop no trains forcibly; they
should simply refuse to handle Pullmans. But the Illinois Central
claimed that its property at Cairo, Illinois, was in danger, so Governor
Altgeld, with the permission of the local authorities, sent three companies of the state militia there. A crowd stopped a train at Hammond,
Indiana, and forced the crew to detach two Pullmans. Two other trains
were temporarily stopped by mobs in Chicago. But there were no
major riots. No mail had accumulated in Chicago. As late as July 5,
total strike damages to railroad property were less than $6,000.

But the facts were being misrepresented. The Federal district at-

torney in Chicago wired Washington on June 29 that conditions
there were so bad that special deputies were needed. The newspapers
were hysterical, with headlines like "Mob Is In Control" and "Law Is
Trampled On." The real cause of concern was stated by the Chicago
Herald: "If the strike should be successful the owners of the railroad
property . . . would have to surrender its future control to the class
of labor agitators and strike conspirators who have formed the Debs
Railway Union." It became common for the press to refer to "Dictator Debs."

Then the Federal government took a hand. On June 30 the General
Managers telegraphed Richard B. Olney, Attorney General of the
United States, urging him to appoint Edwin Walker as special Federal
attorney to handle the strike situation. Walker had been since 1870,
and was, at the time of the strike, attorney for a railroad that belonged
to the General Managers. But Olney didn't even pause to consult the
Federal district attorney on the spot before making the appointment.

Olney, a man as tyrannical as George Pullman, also sent Walker
some pointed advice: that the best way to cope with conditions was
"by a force which is overwhelming and prevents any attempt at resistance." Olney believed that a national railroad strike was illegal by
definition, and that the local and state officials in Illinois could not be
trusted to handle matters. In his judgment, the strikers were impeding
interstate commerce and the movement of the United States mails.
On either score President Cleveland could have used the Federal army
to remove the obstructions. But Olney doubted that Cleveland would
act except to enforce the order of a Federal court. So the thing to do
was to get such an order.

On July 2 in Chicago, Edwin Walker and the Federal district attorney drafted an application for an injunction against the strike
leaders. They were aided in its revision, before court opened, by Judges
Peter Grosscup and William A. Woods. Satisfied at last, the two
judges ascended their impartial bench and granted the application.
The breadth of their order was breathtaking: the strike leaders were
enjoined from any deed to encourage the boycott. They could not send
telegrams about it, or talk about it, or write about it.

If the ARU leaders obeyed the injunction, the boycott would collapse; central coordination was essential. But if they did not obey it,

all strikers would be in active opposition to the Federal government, and the leaders might well go to jail for contempt of court. Debs and his colleagues decided to ignore the writ. Debs declared bitterly, "The crime of the American Railway Union was the practical exhibition of sympathy for the Pullman employees." Sympathy was Christian, but practical sympathy was dangerous.

The Attorney General's plan worked out well. If the injunction was sweeping, enforcement of it was more so. An ARU official later testified: "Men have been arrested in Chicago because they refused to turn switches when told to; they were arrested when they refused to get on an engine and fire an engine." So by interpretation, the injunction forbade action by an individual as well as by the group, and required action in addition to forbidding it.

Olney hit a snag when he first proposed sending Federal troops to Chicago: the Secretary of War and the Army Chief of Staff both opposed it. But on July 3 he received a telegram saying that no agency but the army could protect the mails. There was no proof of the statement, but the telegram was signed by Judge Grosscup, Edwin Walker, and the Federal district attorney in Chicago. Now Grover Cleveland was ready to move. On the morning of Independence Day, by his orders, the entire command from Fort Sheridan turned out for active duty in Chicago.

The ARU was incensed. So was Governor Altgeld. The Constitution gives the President power to send the army into a state "on Application of the Legislature, or of the Executive (when the Legislature cannot be convened)" in order to protect the state "against domestic Violence." Altgeld protested to the President that neither he nor the legislature had asked for help. Three regiments of state militia in Chicago could be mustered into active service, but "nobody in Cook county, whether official or private citizen," had asked for their help. The local and state authorities were adequate to what little violence had occurred. "At present some of our railroads are paralyzed," Altgeld told the President, "not by reason of obstruction, but because they cannot get men to operate their trains. . . . The newspaper accounts have in many cases been pure fabrications, and in others wild exaggerations." Lastly, Altgeld protested that "local self-government is a fundamental principle of our Constitution. Each community shall govern itself so long as it can and is ready and able to enforce the law."

The President's reply was brief. He wired back that the postal authorities had asked for the removal of obstructions to the mails, that Judge Grosscup had asked for help in enforcing the injunction, and that there was "competent proof that conspiracies existed against commerce between the states." Any of these conditions, Cleveland contended, was ample to give him power to order Federal troops into Illinois.

Altgeld reasserted his position forcibly and at length. The President closed the discussion curtly: "While I am still persuaded that I have neither transcended my authority nor duty in the emergency that confronts us, it seems to me that in this hour of danger and public distress, discussion may well give way to active efforts on the part of all in authority to restore obedience to law and to protect life and property."

Although Governor Altgeld had to yield to the power of the army, similar protests were made by the governors of four other states. And the dispute between state and Federal officials served to underscore an issue that was not merely constitutional; it was political and ethical also. Even assuming that the President had properly enforced the law as it existed at the time, his action seemed grossly partisan. The full thrust of Federal power was exerted to break the boycott, while nothing was done—nothing was said—to incline George Pullman or the railroads toward a peaceful settlement. Eugene Debs spoke for a sizable group when he telegraphed the President that a "deep-seated conviction is fast becoming prevalent that this Government is soon to be declared a military despotism." This issue of public policy could be resolved only at the ballot boxes and in the convention halls, and in 1896 John Peter Altgeld was to get his revenge against Grover Cleveland.

But for the time the army ruled—along with five thousand special Federal deputy marshals. Since these temporary jobs were unattractive to most men, they were filled by petty criminals, labor spies, riff-raff generally. Local officials told of special deputies who fired without reason into crowds, wantonly killed bystanders, stole property from railroad cars, cut fire hoses while cars burned. The result was chaos.

On July 5, the day after the army reached Chicago, violence there was more serious than before. The next day it reached its peak; railroad tracks were blocked, dozens of railroad cars were burned—a crime for which nobody was ever indicted. Total damage in the one day was $340,000, although on no other day was it more than $4,000. If the army and special deputies were meant to keep the peace, their immediate effect was just the opposite.

Eugene Debs, continuing his efforts to prevent violence, again told the strikers: "Our men have the right to quit, but their right ends there. Other men have the right to take their places, whatever the opinion of the propriety of so doing may be. Keep away from railroad yards, or right of way, or other places where large crowds congregate. A safe plan is to remain away entirely from places where there is any likelihood of an outbreak." Debs repeatedly argued that the rioting was being done by hooligans, not by strikers. During the entire boycott, not a single ARU number in Chicago was killed or wounded by the law-enforcement authorities.

The outbreak of violence was distressing; the propaganda about it was chilling. In Chicago, headlines read:

Unparalleled Scenes of Riot, Terror and Pillage
Anarchy is Rampant
THIRSTY FOR BLOOD
Frenzied Mob Still Bent on Death and Destruction
Violence on Every Hand

Newspapers and ministers charged that Debs was a dipsomaniac. A Brooklyn cleric declared: "The soldiers must use their guns. They must shoot to kill." One of the most prominent religious leaders in the country revived the themes of a year earlier by calling Governor Altgeld the "crowned hero and worshiped deity of the Anarchists of the Northwest."

On July 10, with the boycott obviously on its last legs, a Federal grand jury in Chicago delivered another blow by indicting Debs and three of his colleagues for conspiracy to obstruct a mail train on the Rock Island Railroad. Arrested at once, the four men were released on bail within a few hours, but their freedom made little

practical difference. The next day trains were moving even in California, where the boycott had been most effective. The mayors
of Chicago and Detroit made a futile call on the vice-president of the
Pullman Company to again request arbitration. They found him un-
yielding. "The issue at question, which was simply that of reopening
the shops at Pullman, and carrying them on at a ruinous loss, was
not a proper subject for arbitration," he was reported to have said.

The boycott dragged along another week, while at Pullman the
leader of the original strikers announced that they were being starved
into submission. Then, on July 17, Debs and his associates were again
arrested, this time for violating the July 2 injunction. They refused
to post bail and were imprisoned. Twenty-four hours later a notice
was put up on the gates of the Pullman shops: "These gates will be
opened as soon as the number of operatives is sufficient to make a
working force in all departments." It was the end.

Of the men now hired at Pullman, one of every four had not worked
there before the strike. Every applicant was forced to sign a pledge
that he would not join any union. A thousand former employees
were left destitute. Governor Altgeld appealed to the Pullman Company to help them. He got no reply. Altgeld then called upon the
public for a relief fund. Even the Chicago *Tribune* cooperated in raising it.

In January, 1895, the ARU leaders were brought to trial on the
conspiracy charges. For nearly a month their lawyers, Clarence
Darrow and S. S. Gregory, used the proceedings as a forum to indict
the prosecution. Eugene Debs, seeming very much a benign and
immaculate businessman, testified at length about his career on the
railroads. Leaders of the General Managers were called to the stand,
where they could "not remember" what had happened at their meetings. Then a juror became ill. After four days Judge Grosscup discharged the jury and continued the case until May. It was never
reopened.

But Debs went to jail anyway, for six months, for having violated
the injunction. The case went all the way to the United States Supreme Court, where the union leaders were represented by Darrow,
Gregory, and the aging Lyman Trumbull. The Court decision virtually
ignored the Sherman Act, on which the injunction had been based.

Instead the Court unanimously ruled that the equity powers of Federal courts could be used to prevent interference with the mails and with interstate commerce. An injunction, regardless of the validity of its provisions, must be obeyed. Violation could be punished by a jail sentence. And it was.

IV

The end of the boycott did not end the shouting and pondering about what it had meant. President Samuel Gompers of the American Federation of Labor, in sending Debs a contribution to his legal defense, said the money was intended "as a protest against the exercise of class justice, and as a further protest against the violation of rights guaranteed by the Constitution and the Declaration of Independence." In opposition to this was the New York *Tribune*, which charged that Debs was a self-seeking dictator and warned the working people against "surrendering their liberty and prosperity into the hands of a single individual."

A Federal investigating commission appointed by President Cleveland, after hearing testimony from railroad officials, strikers, union leaders, public servants, denounced Pullman's refusal to arbitrate the dispute. The report urged compulsory arbitration as insurance against future strikes on the railroads. Ultimate responsibility for the Pullman boycott, said the commission, "rests with the people themselves and with the government for not adequately controlling monopolies and corporations, and for failing to reasonably protect the rights of labor and redress its wrongs."

Four years later another governmental body, the supreme court of Illinois, passed judgment on one element in the situation that had led to the Pullman strike. Holding that the corporation had no right under its charter to construct the town of Pullman, the court ordered the Pullman Company to dispose of all property not required for its manufacturing activities. Company towns such as this, said the court, were "opposed to good public policy and incompatible with the theory and spirit of our institutions."

The poet Eugene Field, a Chicago newspaperman during the strike, was concerned with the characters of the men involved: "If ye be ill,

or poor, or starving, or oppressed, or in grief, your chances for sympathy and for succor from E. V. Debs are 100 where your chances
with G. M. Pullman would be the little end of nothing whittled
down."

But it was left for Jane Addams, in a speech before the Chicago
Woman's Club, to give the most searching interpretation of "the
shocking experiences of that summer, the barbaric instinct to kill,
roused on both sides, the sharp division into class lines with the
resultant distrust and bitterness." All this, she declared, could be
endured only if it resulted in some "great ethical lesson."

Like Eugene Field, she was impressed by "the manifestation of
moral power" in the efforts of the American Railway Union to aid
the strikers at Pullman, men who had done nothing to help the
union but were helped by it. Here was evidence that the workingmen
were beginning to act on new watchwords: "brotherhood, sacrifice,
the subordination of individual and trade interests to the good of the
working class." Nor was George Pullman open to indiscriminate condemnation. His standard for treatment of his employees, "exception-
ally liberal in many of its aspects," had been close to the ideal of "the
best of the present employers." Pullman had manifested that ideal
more fully than the others. "He alone gave his men so model a town,
such perfect surroundings." His policies, in fact, had seemed to
many businessmen a case of intemperate sympathy for the lower
classes.

But Pullman had been utterly blind to the "touch of nobility" in
the ARU sympathetic boycott. He could recognize nothing as virtuous
except the individualism that he had learned in his youth, the ruthless self-reliance that had brought him to the top of the heap. And
ironically, he had actually succeeded in teaching part of that morality
to his employees at Pullman, so that throughout the strike they were
"self-controlled and destroyed no property."

Pullman's failure, then, was the failure of an ideal. The magnitude
of his indulgence was watched by the magnitude of the disaster it
engendered. He was—and here Jane Addams took her title—"A
Modern Lear." King Lear too was lavish in his gifts. Only he had
kingdoms to give, and he gave them. But he demanded from everybody the acknowledgment that all gifts flowed from him. He insisted
on his right to do things for people, and denied them the right to do

things for themselves. He demanded the right for his will to impose itself on others.

Similarly George Pullman, insisting on his right to be a benefactor, had grown away from "the power of attaining a simple human relationship with his employees, that of frank equality with them." Pullman had ceased to be a part of "the great moral life springing from our common experiences," and by setting himself above the common run of men he had done an immense amount of harm. He had failed to sense "that the social passion of the age is directed toward the emancipation of the wage-worker; that a great accumulation of moral force is overmastering men and making for this emancipation as in another time it made for the emancipation of the slave; that nothing will satisfy the aroused conscience of men short of the complete participation of the working classes in the spiritual, intellectual and material inheritance of the human race."

But in this noble effort the workingmen must not become selfish or vindictive. The story of King Lear holds a lesson for them, too. At the beginning of the play Cordelia seeks her salvation alone. She demands her right to be herself, but her vision is not broad enough to include her father. By the time her conscience has reached out to enfold the blinded Lear, "the cruelty and wrath" had become "objective and tragic." Only then, on their way to prison and probable death, do Lear and Cordelia find salvation together. The Pullman strike should be a warning that "the emancipation of the working people will have to be inclusive of the employer from the first or it will encounter many failures, cruelties and reactions."

Jane Addams called on all would-be philanthropists to remember "the old definition of greatness: that it consists in the possession of the largest share of the common human qualities and experiences, not in the acquirements of peculiarities and excessive virtues." The greatest of all Americans was the man who had gathered to himself "the largest amount of American experience": Abraham Lincoln. Seeking to draw out the vital center of Lincoln's life, Jane Addams concluded:

> The man who insists upon consent, who moves with the people, is bound to consult the feasible right as well as the absolute right. He is often obliged to attain only Mr. Lincoln's "best possible," and often have the sickening sense of compromising with his best convictions. He has to move along with

those whom he rules toward a goal that neither he nor they see very clearly until they come to it. He has to discover what people really want, and then "provide the channels in which the growing moral force of their lives shall flow." What he does attain, however, is not the result of his individual striving, as a solitary mountain climber beyond the sight of the valley multitude, but it is underpinned and upheld by the sentiments and aspirations of many others. Progress has been slower perpendicularly, but incomparably greater because lateral.

Prostitution, the Alien Woman and the
Progressive Imagination, 1910–1915

EGAL FELDMAN

• Virginity for the unwed female ranks high in the galaxy
of American values. Generation after generation has deplored
the loosening of moral codes in society, and fearful predictions have been made about the consequences of degeneration. In the Progressive era, however, many conscientious
citizens became particularly alarmed about the incidence of
white slavery—the women kept as prisoners in houses of ill
repute and used to satisfy the lustful desires of predatory
males—and set out to do something about it by establishing
homes and protective associations for girls without friends
or relatives in the cities. Sparked by the energies of social
workers like Jane Addams and Lillian Wald, among others,
they managed also to have Congress pass the Mann Act in
1910 which prohibited the transportation of females across
state lines for immoral purposes.

A number of American nativists—and it is important to
remember that this group included some of the most upright
Progressives—associated the increase of prostitution with the
numbers of foreigners entering the country and used this as
a basis to call for immigration restriction. Others, however,
recognized that innocent girls without friends or knowledge
of American customs could be kidnapped or deceived by
wily entrepreneurs. And this of course did happen. At one
point some New York employment agencies were accused
of selling girls for prices of up to fifty dollars after luring
them in by notices of good jobs available.

In the following selection Egal Feldman discusses the
concern Progressives showed for the alien woman who might

From *American Quarterly*, Vol. XIX, no. 2 part 1, pp. 192–206 (1967).
Reprinted by permission of the journal, the author, and the University
of Pennsylvania, publisher. Copyright © 1967 by the Trustees of the
University of Pennsylvania.

be seduced and kept against her will as an employee for one of the alleged international vice rings. Feldman also emphasizes the double task facing those reformers who tried to alert the public to the need for protecting young women while at the same time attempting to dispel the notion that rising rates of immigration were directly responsible for the increased numbers of prostitutes.

In no period of American history did the custodians of American morality direct more serious attention to the eradication of prostitution than they did in the few years preceding World War I. With the passage of the Mann Act in 1910 their efforts also embraced the interests of the national government. Ministers, social workers, men and women of medicine, science and letters all joined in the unusually massive assault. Their united determination to eradicate white slavery reminds one of the previous crusade against black servitude. In both cases its participants first pressed for international and interstate regulation of the traffic. Rescue homes in bleak urban areas suggest memories of the underground railroad; while an abundant literature designed to expose the intricate, sinister workings of the institution leave the impression of another chapter in the writings of abolitionism.

The energetic outburst against sexual immorality, however, grew out of a relatively new presumption; it was predicated upon the conviction that society's and man's behavior can be controlled and regulated; that man and his environment are both perfectible. Edward A. Ross' *Social Control* (1901), or Ellen H. Richards' *Euthenics: the Science of Controllable Environment* (1910), are examples of books which periodically re-enforced such hopes, infusing progressive uplifters with the confidence that success would be theirs. "Whatever one may hold as to ultimate dealings with the subject," remarked the prominent physician Abraham Flexner, in 1914, "it is clear that prostitution is at any rate a modifiable phenomenon." Commissioned in 1912 by the New York Bureau of Social Hygiene to investigate European prostitution, Flexner grew confident that within man's reach was the power, if not to eradicate totally, certainly to minimize the age-old custom of commercialized sexual pleasure. "Civilization," wrote Flexner with a militant optimism so characteristic of his generation,

> has stripped for a life-and-death wrestle with tuberculosis, alcohol and other plagues. It is on the verge of a similar struggle with the crasser forms of commercialized vice. Sooner or later, it must fling down the gauntlet to the whole horrible thing. This will be the real contest—a contest that will tax the courage, the self-denial, the faith, the resources of humanity to their utmost.

The Flexner report on vice, published in 1914, drove forward another point, that prostitution was an urban problem whose precise character was largely dependent upon the size of the town. The belief that temptations of modern urban living could easily overwhelm the virtuous was, in fact, a somewhat old but typical notion of the age. "Thrilled by the mere propinquity of city excitements and eager to share" in them, observed the Head Worker, Jane Addams, the young and innocent found it enormously difficult to "keep to the gray and monotonous path of regular work." This particular observation was meant for the benefit of rustic maidens who found themselves in the big metropolis, alone and unattended by family or friends for the first time. "From the point of view of the traffickers in white slaves," Miss Addams noticed, "it is much cheaper and safer to procure country girls . . . because they are much more easily secreted than girls from the city. A country girl entering a vicious life quickly feels the disgrace and soon becomes too broken-spirited and discouraged to make any effort to escape."

Yet it was the condition of the unemployed, friendless immigrant girl that seemed to worry her most. "Loneliness and detachment which the city tends to breed in its inhabitants is easily intensified in such a girl into isolation and a desolating feeling of belonging nowhere," warned Miss Addams. "At such moments a black oppression, the instinctive fear of solitude, will send a lonely girl restlessly to walk the streets even when she is 'too tired to stand,' and where her desire for companionship in itself constitutes a grave danger."

To many Americans, less sensitive, less insightful than Jane Addams, the discovery of a thriving existence of commercialized prostitution in the midst of American cities became the basis for a blanket indictment of urban living. "What forces are there, hidden in American cities, which are dragging them . . . into a state of semibarbarism?" queried a leading popularizer of urban mismanagement and vice in 1907. To many the city emerged as a monster, a veritable house of ill repute. "If I lived in the country and had a young daughter I would go to any length of hardship and privation myself rather than allow her to go into the city to work or to study" was a typical reaction. "The best and the surest way for parents of girls in the country to protect them from the clutches of the 'white slaver' is to keep them in the country." That the city was an illusive trap set carefully for country virgins was a notion strongly endorsed in these years by numerous respected educators, clerics and lawyers. But what is of greater consequence here was the prevalent notion that behind the scenes of urban vice were found the nation's newcomers. Surely it was the foreigner, a good many upright Americans were convinced, who was organizing, supporting and thriving upon the lucrative traffic of prostitution. One might say that there was a nativist assault on prostitution which envisioned well-organized networks of vice connecting European and American cities; export-import syndicates thriving on the trade of loose women, diabolical agencies forever searching for new opportunities in the American metropolis.

Southern Italians and Russian Jews came under special attack by those who dreamed of a purer America. Behind men like Paul Kelly and Jimmie Kelly "and other Italians masquerading under Irish names" were detected the networks of international vice. Serious discussions of procuring and pimping inevitably led to an anti-Semitic rhetoric. "It is an absolute fact that corrupt Jews are now the backbone of the loathsome traffic in New York and Chicago," wrote one irate puritan with dogmatic certainty. It was "the Jewish dealer in women, a product of New York politics, who has vitiated, more than any other single agency, the moral life of the great cities of America in the past ten years," wrote George Kibbe Turner in the respectable and widely read *McClure's Magazine* in 1909. Turner's influential articles, appearing regularly in this popular organ of muckrakers, had for years contained a sharp nativist ring, and his animosity was aimed most directly at New York's Jewry. The traffic in women, wrote Turner, was lodged solidly in the hands of "a large number of criminals," most of whom were "Austrian, Russian, and Hungarian Jews." Well guarded by corrupt Tammany politicians, the lewd enterprise had centered its headquarters in New York City, under the guise of a "Jewish society that goes under the name of the New York Independent Benevolent Association." This organization, explained Turner,

> was started in 1896 by a party of dealers who were returning from attendance at the funeral of Sam Engel, a brother of Martin Engel, the Tammany leader of the red-light assembly district. In the usual post-funeral discussion of the frailty of human life, the fact was brought out that the sentiment of the Jews of the East Side against men of their profession barred them generally from societies giving death benefits, and even caused discrimination against them in the purchase of burial-places in the cemetery. A society was quickly incorporated under the laws of New York, and a burial-plot secured and enclosed in Washington cemetery in Brooklyn.

Through the good offices of the Benevolent Association, houses of prostitution in numerous American cities were amply supplied. Focusing less upon any one particular nationality or ethnic group one commentator accused all aliens at once, and warned that

> unless we make energetic and successful war upon the red light districts . . . we shall have Oriental brothel slavery thrust upon us . . . with all its unnatural and abnormal practices, established among us by the French traders. Jew traders, too, will people our "levees" with Polish Jewesses and any others who will make money for them. Shall we defend our American civilization, or lower our flag to the most despicable foreigners— French, Irish, Italians, Jews and Mongolians? . . . On both coasts and throughout all our cities, only an awakening of the whole Christian conscience and intelligence can save us from the importation of Parisian and Polish pollution, which is already corrupting the manhood and youth of every large city in the nation.

The link between prostitution and the alien was solidified in the public imagination when confirmed by government investigators. The subject of prostitution served as fodder for the more nativistic passages of the United States Immigration report of 1911 and left the impression, at times, that vice followed immigration as night does day. "A very

large proportion of the pimps living in the United States are foreigners," reported the federal investigators, making special note of the
fact that "Egyptian, French, Chinese, Belgian, Spanish, Japanese,
Greek, Slavic, Hungarian, Italian, and Russian" were the nationalities
involved most frequently in the traffic of women. Failing to uncover
any evidence of an international "monopolistic corporation whose
business it is to import and exploit these unfortunate women," the
commissioners were, nevertheless, convinced that there were gentlemen's agreements among foreign procurers, singling out the French
and Jews for special attention. "There are large numbers of Jews
scattered throughout the United States," they wrote, "who seduce
and keep girls. Some of them are engaged in importation, but apparently they prey rather upon young girls whom they find on the
street, in the dance halls, and similar places, and whom, by the
methods already indicated—love-making and pretenses of marriage—
they deceive and ruin." The Italian panderer, they noted, was "vicious
and criminal," and was more "feared by their women than are the
pimps of other nationalities."

The nativist assault on prostitution proved awkward and somewhat embarrassing to the liberal friends of aliens who were equally
swept up by the desire to eradicate commercialized vice. American
Jews, for example, were stunned by Turner's revelations, resenting
especially his blanket indictment of an entire immigrant group, the
Eastern European Jew. Yet subsequent investigations proved that a
considerable number of Jews were involved in the business of commercialized vice. The prominent rabbinical figure, Dr. Emil G. Hirsch,
preached a special sermon at the Sinai Temple in Chicago on
September 25, 1909, when he learned that the President of a neighboring congregation was deeply implicated. "Over on the West Side,"
thundered Rabbi Hirsch, "the worst thing has occurred that has
ever happened to our race. The name of God and Jew has been
profaned as never before." In the wake of this revelation, Jews of
Chicago, led by Adolf Kraus, President of the local B'nai B'rith
Chapter, and Clifford G. Roe, a distinguished attorney, laid plans
to combat the scourge of white slavery in their midst.

There were, in fact, two separate campaigns during these years, a
nativistic attack on prostitution with all its ugly xenophobic overtones
paralleled by an anti-nativist outburst. Whereas the former crusade

was irrational, evangelical, uncompromising and completely divorced from the humanitarianism of the early twentieth century, the latter was closely associated with the temper of the social gospel, the social settlement and the more rational humanitarian ambitions of progressivism. The latter's task was more complex, for not only did the anti-nativist assume the responsibility of scientifically searching for the true causes of the disease, but hoped also to clear the fog of prejudice which engulfed the entire issue. In short, he hoped to explain the causes and discover solutions for the problem of prosti- ·tution and at the same time to disassociate the reputation of the immigrant from commercialized vice.

Obviously the attack on prostitution was not always polarized between the friends and enemies of aliens. Many of its participants fell somewhere between the two extremes. Nevertheless, in order to appreciate fully the precise nature of the crusade, one should be aware of its emotional extremities.

That the immigrant was a victim as well as a cause was conceded by many. If the tentacles of the "syndicate" stretched across the ocean, the first victim, it was noticed, was usually an innocent unprotected young immigrant. "In other words," explained one investigator, the "watchers for human prey scan the immigrants as they come down the gang plank of a vessel which has just arrived and 'spot' the girls who are unaccompanied by fathers, mothers, brothers or relatives to protect them." Once detected, the victim was approached "by a man who speaks her language." Tempting "promises of an easy time, plenty of money, fine clothes and the usual stock of allurements—or a fake marriage" follow. "In some instances the hunters really marry the victims." If this cultivated approach proved ineffective, "intoxication and drugging" were applied to reduce the victim to a state of helplessness and total servitude.

> Once a white slave is sold and landed in a house or dive she becomes a prisoner . . . [in]a room having but one door, to which the keeper holds the key. . . . What mockery it is to have in our harbor in New York the Statue of Liberty with outstretched arms welcoming the foreign girl to the land of the free! How she must sneer at it and rebuke the country with such an emblematic monument at its very gate when she finds here a slavery whose chains bind the captive more securely than those in the country from which she has come!

This tendency to bewail the innocence of the alien female threatened
by the predatory desire of her male counterpart revealed an ambivalent
strain in the American attack upon vice. It was also echoed by the
United States Immigration Commission's investigations and reports,
so frequently referred to by contemporary journalists writing on the
subject of white slavery. Attributing the cause of prostitution to the
coming of the New Immigration, federal investigators, nevertheless,
oozed compassion and concern over the fate of the immigrant female.
"The alien woman is ignorant of the language of the country, knows
nothing beyond a few blocks of the city where she lives, has usually
no money, and no knowledge of the rescue homes and institutions
which might help her," they reported in 1910. Even then nativist
Turner waxed "melancholy" over the discovery of "little Italian
peasant girls, taken from various dens, where they lay, shivering and
afraid, under the lighted candles and crucifixes in their bedrooms."

That the immigrant girl was the major casualty of commercialized
vice was, in fact, underscored by a number of investigations conducted independently by private agencies during these years. One,
launched in Chicago in 1910 by a Church Federation meeting "composed of clergy representing six hundred congregations," requested
the Mayor of Chicago to "appoint a commission made up of men and
women who command the respect and confidence of the public at
large." The Mayor complied, and in March 1910 appointed a Vice
Commission consisting of medical and legal experts, Protestant,
Catholic and Jewish clergy, leading businessmen and sociologists. The
final draft of the Commission's report conceded that "the immigrant
woman furnishes a large supply to the demand," but it placed the
blame on the lack of protection offered to her by government and
private agencies. "Generally virtuous when she comes to this country,"
it explained, "she is ruined and exploited because there is no adequate
protection and assistance given her after she reaches the United
States." It was for this reason that Jane Addams and her Hull House
staff insisted so strongly upon the need for governmental protective
machinery to guard the "foreign girl who speaks no English, who
has not the remotest idea in which part of the city her fellow-
countrymen live, who does not know the police station or any agency
to which she may apply" during the first days following her arrival.
It was at this vulnerable juncture, Chicago's social workers warned,

that the young immigrant was "as valuable to a white trafficker as a girl imported directly for the trade." Indeed, a New York City investigation in 1913 indicated some surprise that, given the deplorable conditions of immigrant life, the involvement of the alien women in prostitution was not larger. Conducted by Katherine Bement Davis, Superintendent of the State Reformatory for Women at Bedford Hills, New York, the study was based upon the records of a few thousand prostitutes committed to state reformatories. It was mostly concerned with the relationship of prostitution to the city's heterogeneous population, and concluded that American-born women contributed overwhelmingly more than their proportion to New York prostitution. But even here the immigrant was not handed a total clearance, for the sins of his children devolved upon him. If the foreign-born contributed less than their expected quota, the group that contributed "out of proportion to its percentage in the population" was their American-born daughters. Miss Davis admitted, of course, that there was a reasonable explanation for this.

> When we remember that here we have a group in which the fathers and mothers belong to a civilization with speech, tradition and habits different from those of the country in which they are living, the children, native-born Americans with American companions and American schooling, adopt ideals often not of the highest and are very apt, even when quite young, to feel that they know more than their parents.

America's discovery of prostitution and its growing conviction that its roots were European gave rise to a demand, advocated especially by nativists, that immigrant ladies of doubtful behavior be immediately deported; but a number of reformers, friends of aliens, counseled differently. "Certainly the immigration laws might do better than to send a girl back to her parents, diseased and disgraced, because America had failed to safeguard her virtue from the machinations of well-known but unrestrained criminals," warned one of the nation's leading social workers. "Certainly no one will doubt that it is the business of the city itself to extend much more protection to young girls who so thoughtlessly walk upon its streets." Kate Waller Barrett, an authority on the deportation of prostitutes, and a special adviser to the government on matters of immigration, objected also to rash and heartless solutions. In her reports she stressed the social injustice, the

misunderstanding that immigrant women were constantly subjected
to. "Nothing is more in keeping with the wishes of a man when
he has gotten a woman in trouble than to have her deported, and
thus put the ocean between them," she argued on one occasion, as
only a woman of determined militancy could. A holder of doctoral
degrees in medicine and science, President of the National Council
of Women, Mrs. Barrett was appointed as Special Agent of the
United States Immigration Service in 1914. Her task was to join
with European officials in discussions concerning the relationship of
the growing European immigration to the United States and the
white slave traffic. Her final report of this experience, insisting that
the roots of prostitution must be sought in the trans-Atlantic voyage,
stressed the necessity for preventive and precautionary measures on
board the immigrant steamers. Steamship companies should provide
free transportation to woman supervisors, she felt, and urged the
separation of sexes in both living and recreation and the prohibition
of crew members from visiting the steerage quarters "except as their
duties require." Focusing specially upon the case of the deportee, she
urged that an international committee be formed to grapple with the
problem. "The question of the unattached immigrant woman is comparatively new," she pointed out, quite different from that of the
male immigrant with whom America has had years of experience. A
woman accused of prostitution must not be flung out of the country
upon flimsy evidence, without due process of law.

To remove the conditions responsible for the "fall" of alien woman
was a task pre-World War I reformers undertook, and they began
the moment the unaccompanied female arrived. Chicago's Immigrants'
Protective League was founded in part for that reason. Its first Annual
Report in 1910 talked ominously of immigrant girls who failed to
arrive at their expected destination, whose "ultimate fate . . . could
never be discovered." Its agents kept in constant communication with
Ellis Island authorities, in part to request lists of names of alien
women traveling alone to Chicago and other interior cities. Officials
of the League awaited their arrival, and ordered an immediate search
for those who did not appear at the time expected. Each year the
League published its list of "Girls We Have Been Unable to Locate,"
and the names of the missing continued to multiply. According to

Grace Abbott, Director of the League, a 10 per cent annual rate of disappearance was not unusual during the years of the great migration. Worried kin turned frequently to the League for information, which occasionally confirmed their worst fears. "We learned that she had been called for by a notoriously disreputable man and taken to a rooming house on Washington near Halsted," reported League officials after an investigation of the whereabouts of a young Lithuanian girl in 1913. "Everything pointed to the conclusion that the girl either voluntarily or by deception was leading an immoral life, but neither we nor the agencies to which the case was reported could locate the girl."

Immigrant lodging houses and hotels were for this reason frequently attacked by reformers and scrutinized periodically by government and private agents. The insufficient care exercised by such institutions "in discharging young immigrant women and girls who have been placed in their charge by immigration authorities" was a frequent cause of complaint. That a number of such homes served as recruiting centers for houses of prostitution was established by a number of investigations. The founding of the Clara de Hirsch Home for Immigrant Girls in March 1904 was motivated by such discoveries. Its aim, as expressed by its founders, was "to protect the girl at her very entrance to this country, to afford her temporary shelter, to see to it that she reaches her prospective destination in safety." Immediate priority was extended to those without friends or relatives "or such who are called for by single men or married men without their wives." Once housed, declared a spokesman for the Home in 1912, "we do not permit any girls to leave our premises without making a thorough personal investigation of the prospective living quarters . . . surroundings, the number of lodges, and rooming facilities," and "are constantly studying new measures and means for the safeguarding of our girls."

For similar reasons private employment agencies, especially those serving newcomers, were eyed suspiciously. That a number were supplying personnel to houses of ill repute was established by Frances Kellor's investigation of employment agencies early in the century. The link between the alien and commercialized vice, explained Kellor, was the "runner," a "suave, attractive young man who can win the con-

fidence of the immigrant girls." He was expected to have an acquaintance with alien tongues and customs, for "his business is to bring
them to the office by any means." His character "defies description.
There seems to be no meanness to which he will not stoop. . . . If a
girl refuses to enter a questionable place it is part of the work of the
runner to ruin her and make her more amenable to suggestions." Other
investigations during the following years confirmed such findings. One
conducted by the Immigrants' Protective League in 1908 revealed considerable collusion, but the "commonest offense," according to Grace
Abbott, was ignorance of the character of the places to which the
immigrant girl was sent "rather than an active connivance in her
ruin." Two years later New York City's Lillian Wald made a respectable audience squirm in their pews by informing them that numerous
metropolitan employment agencies "were used as markets for selling
girls for prices varying from $3.00 to $50.00 or as procuring places
where immoral women and men came and selected their victims."
New Jersey's Commission of Immigration reported also at this time
that 65 per cent of the agencies investigated "were willing to procure
girls to work as servants in alleged disorderly houses and for immoral
purposes." The United States Immigration Commission confirmed
these findings in 1910 and stamped upon them national concurrence
based upon its own investigations. The link between employment
agencies and immigrant prostitution helps explain why progressives
urged their total abolition and the creation of free publicly-supported
institutions in their stead.

In large part the assault on commercialized vice was led by women
themselves, either speaking through their organizations or as isolated
individuals. The work of the International Institute for Young
Women, launched by the National Young Women's Christian Association in 1910, is an example of a moderate but concerted attack.
To guard "those who have sailed their immigrating journey alone"
and who have gone "through the hazards of arrival with no protection" was its avowed objective. The majority of newcomers, observed
one of its officials, were young, "below thirty years of age and the
largest group of all between sixteen and twenty-one!" The International Institute was impressed with the importance of getting "a girl
started right!" and keeping "her from doing all sorts of things she

wouldn't think of doing back home." The work of Chicago's Immigrants' Protective League and numerous settlement houses pursued the same objectives with considerably less condescension. Especially effective, however, was the program launched by the National Council of Jewish Women. Founded by ninety-five women during the Chicago World's Fair in 1893, the organization dedicated itself "to the service of faith and humanity through education and philanthropy," and elected a scion of a pioneer settler in Chicago, a philanthropist and educator in her own right, Hannah Greenbaum Solomon, as its first president. Within a few years, at the request of the United States Government, the Council became active in immigration affairs and the prevention of the exploitation of alien women became its major concern. Its delegates participated in international white slavery conferences and its workers, whose preventive work at the docks set an example that other organizations would later follow, became permanent fixtures at Ellis Island and other immigration centers. Easily identifiable by their conspicuous badges, able to speak a number of languages, these workers were on a constant lookout for girls traveling alone. Their leaflets and placards, distributed and posted, were also conspicuous at the various ports of entry. "Beware of those who give you addresses, offer you easy, well-paid work, or even marriage," warned one such broadside in three languages. "There are many evil men and women who have in this way led girls to destruction. Always inquire in regard to these persons of the Council of Jewish Women, which will find out the truth for you and advise you." "Bitter experience" had made such warnings necessary, Marion L. Misch, President of the Council, explained in 1912, especially for the benefit of "decent people" who were unable "to comprehend the moral bias of the white slaver," the fiend in human guise who finds "the steamship piers a prolific hunting-ground." Once admitted, young immigrant girls were not easily released from the anxious, watchful eye of the Council. For weeks their movements were observed, the nature of their adjustment studied. If prostitution proved a trap, as it did on rare occasions, legal machinery was put in gear to defend the hapless female from the deportation horror. To the National Council of Jewish Women immigration and prostitution were not causal in their relationship. It "is not a question of immigration," explained the

Council "if an immigrant girl is so unfortunate as to become the victim of some evil man who has traded on her credulity to put her to shame" but "a purely local and American and social question, and we must be careful not to confuse the two."

In the double task of impressing Americans with the need for public protection for the young newcomer, on the one hand, and dispelling the notion that there was a connection between the rise of prostitution and the increase of immigration, on the other, social workers such as Frances A. Kellor, Jane Addams, Grace Abbott and Lillian Wald stand out prominently. Kellor was one of the first to demand that government protection be offered to the female traveler from the moment she commenced her journey to America. "Has our government any matrons or inspectors who make it impossible for the procurer, who wishes to travel steerage or second cabin for the purpose of meeting her, to accomplish his purpose?" she queried. "Is she safeguarded so carefully that members of the ship's crew cannot mislead her?" Jane Addams cautioned immigrant girls against offers of a quick marriage by pleasant-looking strangers, who might well be agents of disreputable houses. Reasons that led to the involvement of immigrant women with vice were many, declared her co-worker, Grace Abbott. Their ignorance of English was in part responsible for their vulnerability. "The more dangerous environment in which they live" was an additional factor. "For it is near an immigrant or colored neighborhood that disreputable dance halls and hotels are usually tolerated." The alien woman also suffers from a hunger for recreation little understood or appreciated by the native-born. In New York City, Lillian Wald, founder of America's first nurses' (Henry Street) settlement in the mid-1890s, met the ugliness head-on. Growing up in a comfortable middle-class environment in Rochester, New York, Miss Wald, like so many other women of her generation, chose a lifetime of service in surroundings of poverty and the struggle of immigrant life. A nurse by training, she preferred to apply her knowledge to the problems of lower Manhattan. "From the very start its poor became her people. She took them to her heart and they gave her quickly their unstinted confidence and trust," Jacob A. Riis, who knew her and the East Side well, wrote in 1913. Like other social and settlement-house workers, she too displayed puritanic zealousness in her desire to protect the alien woman against sexual pitfalls as well as against unsubstantiated charges of prostitution. The vast influx of single women from Eastern Europe did not alarm her, as it did so many others of her generation, for Lillian Wald was certain that the positive value of the European inrush would surely outweigh all sinister nativist forebodings. Nevertheless, she too espoused as necessary a special program of protection and guidance. "The alien is in more danger of moral contamination than the rest of the community," she explained to a convention of social workers in 1908. And, "in the case of the alien girl . . . the danger is increased," especially where she must immediately assume the role of breadwinner. Like Addams, Abbott and Kellor, Lillian Wald sensed the potential danger that grew out of the limited social outlets offered by the American urban environment. The lack of available publicly-supported facilities for amusement and recreation, she cautioned, invariably led to a "pitiful dependence . . . upon the casual pick-up." "A definite and inclusive program is demanded by all ethical standards of a moral society. Existing provisions for meeting such needs," she felt, were "too casual and too haphazard."

In part, the conspicuous evidence of women involved in the attack on vice was due to their relative absence from most movements of social reconstruction in the decades before. America had, after all, never before seen a group of women so well educated, so enlightened, yet with nothing to do. The college-bred women of the late nineteenth century were possessed with an overwhelming desire to act, not just aimlessly, but to participate in some meaningful social and moral venture. They believed, as a perceptive student of the career of Jane Addams wrote, that they had "a special position in history and a special duty to posterity." That they were willing to crash head-on with the most sordid aspects of modern America was also in perfect accord with the utilitarian and activist notions of a blustering, masculine society which credited activity above thought, visible accomplishments above ideas. That the preoccupation of long-sleeved spinsters with the reform of sexual perversions did not totally stun the Victorian mentality was in part due to notions which grew out of the same mythology, a mythology that lifted the native-born American woman above the baser animal passions of her male counterpart, attributing to her the custodianship of sexual purity. In another sense, an attack on prostitution was also a means of warning modern industrial and urban America to make way for the New Woman. It was a sharp exhortation that the exploitation exercised by men in factory, lodgings and on the city streets must cease. Surely if modern urban America could be made safe and comfortable for a defenseless immigrant girl, all women and, for that matter, all men too could dwell there in greater comfort and security.

Here Come the Wobblies!

BERNARD A. WEISBERGER

• Throughout the nineteenth century organized labor in the United States never embraced a majority of the industrial working people. In 1901, only one out of every fourteen non-agricultural workers belonged to any union, about half the proportion in Great Britain. The pattern of organizing only specialized craftsmen resulted partly from the exclusionary policy of the American Federation of Labor and partly from public antipathy for the aspirations and organizations of the unskilled working class. The Knights of Labor championed industrial unionism in the 1870's and attempted to unite the nation into one big co-operative enterprise. But it dwindled in effectiveness after the public's false association of it with the Haymarket Riot and anarchism in 1886.

An even more spectacular effort to broaden the base of organized labor was the formation in Chicago, in 1905, of the International Workers of the World. Led by "Big Bill" Haywood of the Western Federation of Miners, the "Wobblies" wanted to abolish the wage system. They hoped to gain their objectives by violent abolition of the state and the formation of a nation-wide industrial syndicate governed by the workers themselves. The "Wobblies" were strongest among unskilled migratory workers in the West, but they had a hand in a number of strikes in the East. During World War I the "Wobblies" suffered from the patriotic fervor of the government and several vigilante groups, and they waned as a force in the labor movement. Bernard A. Weisberger's essay catches the tragedy and the persecution of the International Workers of the World as they sought to protect the welfare of the American worker.

From *American Heritage*, June 1967. Copyright © 1967 by American Heritage Publishing Co., Inc. Reprinted by permission.

On a hot June day in 1905 William D. Haywood, a thirty-six-year-old miner, homesteader, horsebreaker, surveyor, union organizer, and Socialist, out of Salt Lake City, stood up before a large crowd in a Chicago auditorium. He gazed down at the audience with his one good eye and, taking up a loose board from the platform, impatiently banged for silence.

"Fellow workers," he shouted, "this is the continental congress of the working class. We are here to confederate the workers of this country into a working-class movement that shall have for its purpose the emancipation of the working class from the slave bondage of capitalism."

Thus, in manifesto, the working-class crusade known as Industrial Workers of the World came to birth. It grew amid storms of dissent, lived always in the blast furnace of conflict, and was battered into helplessness over forty years ago. It is still alive, but as a "church of old men" in one author's words, old men still muttering "No" to the status quo. The *Industrial Worker*, the official newspaper of the "One Big Union," still appears, still carries as its masthead motto "An injury to one is an injury to all," still valiantly runs on its editorial page the uncompromising preamble to the constitution adopted at that Chicago convention in 1905:

> The working class and the employing class have nothing in common. There can be no peace so long as hunger and want are found among millions of working people and the few, who make up the employing class, have all the good things of life. . . .
> It is the historic mission of the working class to do away with capitalism. The army of production must be organized, not only for the everyday struggle with capitalists, but also to carry on production when capitalism shall have been overthrown. By organizing industrially we are forming the structure of the new society within the shell of the old.

But the old society is still here, thriving more vigorously than ever; the workers have late-model cars, and the struggle of the I.W.W.'s young radicals to burst its bonds is history now—good history, full of poets and tramps, bloodshed and cruelty, and roads not taken by American labor. The history not merely of an organization but of an impulse that stirred men from the lower depths of the economy—vagrants, lumberjacks, harvest hands, immigrant millworkers—and set them to marching in step with Greenwich Village literary radicals to the tune of gospel hymns and innocent ballads fitted with new, class-conscious verses.

But it was not all ballads and broadsides. The I.W.W. was radical in the word's truest sense. When it denied that the working and employing classes had anything in common, it meant precisely what it said. The I.W.W. put no faith in the promises of bourgeois politicians or in the fairness of bourgeois courts. It made no contracts with employers, and it spurned other unions—like those enrolled in the American Federation of Labor—that did. It was composed of hard, hard-working men, little known to respectability. As a result, it badly frightened millions of middle-class Americans, and it meant to.

Yet it must be understood that the I.W.W. did not grow in a vacuum. It arose out of an industrial situation for which the adjective "grim" is pallid. In the America that moved to productive maturity between 1880 and 1920, there was little room or time to care about the worker at the base of it all. It was an America in which children of ten to fourteen could and did work sixty-hour weeks in mine and factory; in which safety and sanitation regulations for those in dangerous trades were virtually unknown—and in which industrial accidents took a horrible toll each year; in which wages were set by "the market place" and some grown men with families worked ten to twelve hours for a dollar and stayed alive only by cramming their families into sickening tenements or company-town shacks; in which such things as pensions or paid holidays were unknown; lastly, it was an America in which those who did protest were often locked out, replaced by scabs, and prevented from picketing by injunction and by naked force. At Homestead, Pullman, Coeur d'Alene, Cripple Creek, Ludlow, and other places where strikers clashed with troops or police between 1892 and 1914, the record of labor's frustrations was marked with bloody palm prints. And at the bottom of the scale was the vast army of migrant workers who beat their way by rail from job to job—not only unskilled, unprotected, and underpaid but unnoticed and unremembered.

Out of such a situation grew the I.W.W. It gained much not only from the horror of its surroundings, but from the spirit of an infant century when the emancipation of almost everyone—women, workers, artists, children—from the dragons of the past seemed to be a live possibility, and "new" was a catchword on every tongue.

The opening years of the organization's life were not promising. Its

founding fathers were numerous and diverse—discontented trade
unionists, Socialists like Eugene V. Debs and the whiskered, professorial
Daniel De Leon, and veterans of almost every other left-wing crusade
of the preceding twenty years. There was among them all, a recent
I.W.W. historian has written, "such a warfare as can be found only
between competing radicals." They were, however, united in objecting
to the craft-union principles of A.F.L. chieftain Samuel Gompers,
whom Haywood described as "a squat specimen of humanity" with
"small snapping eyes, a hard cruel mouth," and "a personality vain,
conceited, petulant and vindictive."

Gompers' plan of organizing only skilled craftsmen and negotiating
contracts aimed only at securing a better life from day to day struck
the I.W.W.'s founders not only as a damper upon whatever militancy
the labor movement might generate to challenge capitalism, but also
as a betrayal of the unskilled laborers, who would be left to shift for
themselves. The new leaders therefore created a "single industrial
union," as far removed from craft divisions as possible.

All industrial labor was to be divided into thirteen great, centrally
administered divisions—building, manufacturing, mining, transportation, public service, etc. Within each of these would be subgroups. But
each such group would take in all employees contributing to that industry's product or service. On the steam railroads, as an instance,
clerks, telegraphers, and trackwalkers would share power and glory with
engineers, brakemen, and conductors. A grievance of one lowly set of
workers in a single shop could bring on a strike that would paralyze a
whole industry. And some day, on signal from the One Big Union, all
workers in all industries would throw the "Off" switch, and the wage
system would come tumbling down.

Much of the scheme came from the brain and pen of a priest, Father
Thomas Hagerty, who while serving mining parishes in the Rockies
had come to believe in Marx as well as Christ. He had the scheme of
industrial unionism all worked out in a wheel-shaped chart, with the
rim divided into the major industries and the hub labelled "General
Administration." Gompers looked at a copy of it in a magazine and
snarled: "Father Hagerty's Wheel of Fortune!" He did not expect it
to spin very long.

Nor, during the I.W.W.'s first three years of existence, did it seem
likely to. Factional quarrels wracked national headquarters and the

Western Federation of Miners, the biggest single block in the entire I.W.W. structure, pulled out. By spring of 1908 the organization, whose paper strength was perhaps 5,000 but whose actual roster was probably much thinner, was broke and apparently heading toward the graveyard that seems to await all clique-ridden American radical bodies.

But the death notices were premature. The headquarters brawls were among and between trade unionists and Socialists, and the I.W.W.'s future was, as it turned out, linked to neither group. It belonged to a rank-and-file membership that was already formulating surprise tactics and showing plenty of vigor. In Schenectady, New York, for example, I.W.W.-led strikers in a General Electric plant protested the firing of three draftsmen by staying at their machines for sixty-five hours, a use of the sit-down strike thirty years before it was introduced by the auto workers as a radical measure during the Great Depression. In Goldfield, Nevada, the I.W.W. under thirty-one-year-old Vincent St. John organized the town's hotel and restaurant workers into a unit with the local silver and gold miners. This unlikely combination of hash-slingers and miners, an extreme example of industrial unionism, forced the town's employers to boost wage scales, temporarily at least, to levels of five dollars per eight-hour day for skilled underground workers, down to three dollars and board for eight hours of dishwashing by the lowly "pearl divers." It seemed to be clear proof that "revolutionary industrial unionism" could work. The fiery St. John was even able to close down the mines one January day in 1907 for a protest parade—on behalf of Haywood, Charles Moyer, and George Pettibone, three officers of the miners' union who had been arrested (they were later acquitted) in the bomb-killing of former Governor Frank Steunenberg of Idaho. St. John's parade brought three thousand unionists into the small-town streets "all wearing tiny red flags."

The real turning point came at the organization's fourth convention, in 1908. The believers in "direct action at the point of production" forced a change in the I.W.W.'s holy writ, the preamble. It had originally contained the sentence: "A struggle must go on until all the toilers come together *on the political, as well as the industrial field,* and take and hold that which they produce" (italics added). Now this "political clause" was scuttled, over the violent protests of Socialist De Leon, who helplessly denounced the change as an exaltation of "physical force." The shock troops of the direct-action group were twenty

lumber workers known as the Overalls Brigade. Gathered in Portland
by an organizer named Jack Walsh, they had bummed their way to
Chicago in boxcars, raising grubstakes along the way at street meetings
in which they sang, harangued, peddled pamphlets, and passed the hat.
One of their favorite tunes, with which they regaled the convention,
was "Hallelujah, I'm A Bum," set to the old hymn tune "Revive Us
Again":

> O, why don't you work
> Like other men do?
> How in hell can I work
> When there's no work to do?
>
> Hallelujah, I'm a bum,
> Hallelujah, bum again,
> Hallelujah, give us a handout—
> To revive us again.

Sourly, De Leon dubbed Walsh's men The Bummery, but the day was
theirs. The veteran Socialist leader retreated and organized a splinter
I.W.W., which dwindled away in seven years.

It was the I.W.W.'s second split in a short history, but its most important. It gave the organization over to soapbox singers and bums,
brothers in idealism who were poor in all things save "long experience
in the struggle with the employer." They were to break from past labor
practices and give the I.W.W. its true inwardness and dynamism; to
fit it with its unique costume and role in history.

They gave it, first, a musical voice. Walsh's crusaders sang because
when they sought the workers' attention on street corners they were
challenged by those competing sidewalk hot-gospellers, the Salvation
Army. By 1909, the press of the organization's newspaper, the *Industrial Worker*, was able to put out the first edition of *Songs of the
Workers to Fan the Flames of Discontent*. More succinctly known as
the "Little Red Songbook," it has gone through over thirty subsequent
editions—all scarlet-covered and fitted to the size of an overalls pocket.
The songbook and the preamble were to the I.W.W. membership
what the hymnbook and the *Discipline of the Methodist Church* had
been to frontier preachers—the sum and touchstone of faith, the pearl
of revelation, the coal of fire touching their lips with eloquence. Most

of the songs were the work of men like Richard Brazier, an English-born construction worker who joined up in Spokane in 1908; or Ralph Chaplin, a struggling young Chicago commercial artist who wanted to chant "hymns of hope and hatred" at the shrine of rebellion; or Joe Hill, born Joel Haaglund in Sweden, who wrote not parodies alone but also original compositions, which Chaplin described as "coarse as home-spun and as fine as silk"; or bards known simply as T-Bone Slim or Dublin Dan. The I.W.W. members soared on those songs, enjoying them as much for their mockery as anything.

To the patriotic cadences of "The Battle Hymn of the Republic" they sang "Solidarity forever, for the Union makes us strong" (a version which Ralph Chaplin had given them and which the entire labor movement took over without credit). To the sentimental notes that enfolded Darling Nelly Gray they sang of "the Commonwealth of Toil that is to be," and to the strains that had taken pretty Red Wing through ribald adventures in every barroom in the country, they roared that "the earth of right belongs to toilers, and not to spoilers of liberty." They raided the hymnbook of Moody-and-Sankey revivalism for "Hold the fort for we are coming, union men be strong," and for "There is power, there is power, in a working band" (instead of "in the blood of the Lamb"). They laughed in sharps and flats at Casey Jones, of the craft-proud Brotherhood of Railway Engineers, as a union scab who "kept his junk pile running" and "got a wooden medal for being good and faithful on the S.P. line." They sang in the hobo jungles, on the picket line, and in the jailhouse, and it was their singing especially that separated them from the A.F.L. by an abyss of spirit.

The "new" I.W.W. soon had a nickname, as derisive and defiant as its songs: the Wobblies. It is not certain how the name was born, though a popular legend declares that a Chinese restaurant owner in the Northwest was persuaded to grubstake I.W.W. members drifting through his town. His identification test was a simple question, "Are you I.W.W.?" but it emerged in Cantonese-flavored English as "Ah loo eye wobble wobble?" Whatever its origin, the name was a badge of pride.

The I.W.W.'s new leadership provided halls in the towns where a wandering Wobbly could find a warm stove, a pot of coffee, a corner in which to spread a blanket for the night, and literature: the *Industrial Worker* and *Solidarity*, leaflets by St. John or Haywood, and books like Jack London's *The Iron Heel,* Edward Bellamy's *Looking Back-ward,* Laurence Gronlund's *Co-operative Commonwealth.* All of them furnished material for arguments with the unorganized, and also such stuff as dreams were made on.

In 1909 the I.W.W. attracted national attention through the first of its spectacular clashes with civic authority. In Spokane a campaign was launched urging loggers to boycott the "job sharks," employment agents who hired men for work in lumber and construction camps deep in the woods, charging them a fee for the "service." Many a lumberjack who "bought a job" in this way was swindled—sent to a nonexistent camp or quickly fired by a foreman in cahoots with the shark to provide fast turnover and larger shared profits. At street meet-ings, the Wobblies preached direct hiring by the lumber companies. Spokane's thirty-one agencies retaliated by getting the city council to ban such meetings. The *Industrial Worker* promptly declared Novem-ber 2, 1909, Free Speech Day and urged every man in the vicinity to "fill the jails of Spokane."

From hundreds of miles around, Wobblies poured in by boxcar, mounted soapboxes, and were immediately wrestled into patrol wagons. In a matter of weeks, the jail and a quickly converted schoolhouse were overflowing with five or six hundred prisoners. They came into court bloody from beatings; they were put to hard labor on bread and water, jammed into cells like sardines, and in the name of sanitation hosed with ice water and returned to unheated confinement. Three died of pneumonia. Among the prisoners was a dark-haired Irish girl from New York, Elizabeth Gurley Flynn. Eighteen years old and pregnant, she complicated her arrest by chaining herself to a lamp post. "Gurley," a proletarian Joan of Arc, was lodged with a woman cellmate who kept receiving mysterious calls to the front office. It turned out that she was a prostitute, serving customers provided by the sheriff "for good and valuable consideration." This fact was trumpeted by the I.W.W. as soon as Gurley figured it out.

Fresh trainloads of Wobblies poured relentlessly into town, while those already in jail kept the night alive with selections from the Little Red Songbook roared at full volume, staged hunger strikes, refused to touch their hammers on the rock pile, and generally discomfited their captors. In March of 1910 the taxpayers of Spokane threw in the towel,

released the prisoners, and restored the right of free speech to the
I.W.W. Other free-speech fights in the next few years carried the
Wobbly message throughout the Far West and helped in organizing
new locals among the militant.

Two years after the end of the Spokane campaign, the I.W.W. made
headlines in the East. In the textile-manufacturing town of Lawrence,
Massachusetts, on January 11, 1912, more than 20,000 workers struck
against a wage cut that took thirty cents—the price of three loaves of
bread—out of pay envelopes averaging only six to eight dollars for a
fifty-four-hour week. It was an unskilled work force that hit the bitter-
cold streets, and a polyglot one, too. Some twenty-five nationalities,
speaking forty-five languages or dialects, were represented, including
French Canadians, Belgians, Poles, Italians, Syrians, Lithuanians,
Greeks, Russians, and Turks.

There was only a small I.W.W. local in Lawrence, but the tactics
of One Big Union under the slogan "An injury to one is an injury to
all" had never been more appropriate. I.W.W. pamphlets and newspapers in several languages had already appeared. Now the leadership
deployed its best veterans in the field—Haywood, William Trautmann,
Elizabeth Gurley Flynn—and in addition a big, jovial-looking Italian
organizer of steelworkers, Joe Ettor, whose usual costume was a black
shirt and a red tie.

For over two months, something akin to social revolution went on
in Lawrence. A strike committee of fifty-six members, representing all
nationalities, filled days and nights with meetings and parades. Haywood stood out like a giant. He hurdled the linguistic barrier by
speeches partly in sign language (waving fingers to show the weakness
of separate craft unions; balled-up fist to demonstrate solidarity), visited workers' homes, and won the women's hearts by joshing the children or smacking his lips over shashlik or spaghetti. He also shrewdly
exploited the publicity that bathed Lawrence, which was near the nation's journalistic capitals. Demonstrations were called with an eye
not only to working-class morale but to public opinion. It was an education for many Americans to read about "ignorant, foreign" mill girls
carrying signs that said: "We Want Bread And Roses, Too."

The employers played into Haywood's hands. National Guardsmen
were called out. Police arrested more than three hundred workers and,

in a climax of stupidity, clubbed a group of mothers and children preparing to leave town by railroad for foster homes. In defiance of the evidence, Ettor and Arturo Giovannitti, another Italian organizer, were arrested as accessories in the shooting of a woman striker. Authorities held them for seven months before a trial. When it came, it not only let the two men go free but gave Giovannitti a chance to spellbind jury and reporters with an oration on behalf of "this mighty army of the working class of the world, which . . . is striving towards the destined goal, which is the emancipation of human kind, which is the establishment of love and brotherhood and justice for every man and every woman in this earth."

Long before that speech, in March of 1912, the bosses had given up and agreed to the strikers' terms. It was the I.W.W.'s finest hour up to then. Flushed with success, the One Big Union next answered the call of silk workers at Paterson, New Jersey, to lead them in a strike that began in February, 1913. The pattern of Lawrence seemed at first to be repeating. There were nearly fifteen hundred arrests, and in addition police and private detectives killed two workers by random gunfire. One of these, Valentino Modesto, was given a funeral at which twenty thousand workers filed by to drop red carnations on the coffin. But after five months even relief funds and singing rallies could not prevail over hunger. The strike was broken.

Not, however, before it produced a unique project and a strange alliance. One of the reporters who came to Paterson on an April day was John Reed—talented, charming, Harvard '10—who was enjoying life to the hilt in the Bohemian surroundings of Greenwich Village, then in its heyday. When Reed stopped to talk to a striker, a Paterson policeman on the lookout for "agitators" hustled him off to jail. There he stayed for four days, sharing smokes and food with the strikers and amiably teaching them college fight songs and French ballads in return for instruction in the arts of survival in prison. On his release he became an enthusiastic supporter of the embattled workers and brought such friends as Mabel Dodge, Hutchins Hapgood, Walter Lippmann, Lincoln Steffens, and others to hear Haywood and other Wobbly leaders speak.

Between the individualistic rebelliousness of the young artists and writers escaping their bourgeois backgrounds and the hard-shelled but dream-drenched radicalism of the I.W.W. leaders, there was instinctive connection. Reed conceived the idea of a giant fund-raising pageant to present the strikers' case. On June 7, thousands of silk workers came into New York by special train and ferry and marched to Madison Square Garden. There they watched hundreds of fellow strikers reenact the walkout, the shooting of Modesto, his funeral, and the mass meetings that followed. Staged by Reed's Harvard friend Robert Edmund Jones against a backdrop created by the artist John Sloan, the pageant was described by *Outlook* as having "a directness, an intensity, and a power seldom seen on the professional stage." Since it ran for only one night, it failed to earn any money beyond expenses, despite a full house. Yet as a moment of convergence in the currents of radicalism vitalizing American life and letters in the last days of prewar innocence, it has a historic place of its own.

The Lawrence and Paterson affairs were only forays, however. The I.W.W. ran strikes and kept footholds in the East—the dockworkers of Philadelphia were firmly organized in the I.W.W.-affiliated Marine Transport Workers Union, for example—but it lacked staying power in the settled industrial areas. As it moved into its peak years, the future of the One Big Union was in the West, where its message and tactics were suited to the style of migrant workers, and to the violent tempo of what Elizabeth Flynn recalled as "a wild and rugged country where both nature and greed snuffed out human life."

Here, in the mountains and forests, were men who needed protection even more than the unskilled rubber, textile, steel, and clothing workers receiving I.W.W. attention—men like the "timber beasts," who worked in the freezing woods from dawn to dusk and then "retired" to vermin-ridden bunkhouses, without washing facilities, where they were stacked in double tiers like their own logs. The companies did not even furnish bedding, and a lumberjack between jobs was recognizable by his roll of blankets—his "bundle," "bindle," or "balloon" —slung on his back. The bindle stiff who "played the woods," however, was only one member of an army of migrant workers, as many as a half million strong, who as the cycle of each year turned followed the harvests, the construction jobs, the logging operations, and the opening of new mines. Sometimes they got a spell of sea life in the forecastle of a merchant ship; often they wintered in the flophouses of

Chicago or San Francisco; and not infrequently they spent the out-of-season months in jail on charges of vagrancy. The public mind blurred them together, and made no distinction among hoboes, bums, and tramps, assuming them all to be thieves, drunkards, and pan-handlers. But the true migrant was none of these. He was a "working stiff," emphasis on the first word, and thus ripe for the tidings of class war.

The I.W.W. reached him where he lived: in the hobo "jungles" out-side the rail junction points, where he boiled stew in empty tin cans, slept on the ground come wind, come weather, and waited to hop a freight bound in any direction where jobs were rumored to be. The Wobblies sent in full-time organizers, dressed in the same caps and windbreakers, but with pockets full of red membership cards, dues books and stamps, subscription blanks, song sheets, pamphlets. These job delegates signed up their men around the campfires or in the box-cars ("side-door Pullmans" the migrants called them), mailed the money to headquarters, and then followed their recruits to the woods, or to the tents in the open fields where the harvest stiffs unrolled *their* bindles after twelve hours of work in hundred-degree heat without water, shade, or toilets. But there were some whom the organizers could not reach, and the I.W.W. sent them messages in the form of "stickerettes." These "silent agitators" were illustrated slogans on label-sized pieces of gummed paper, many of them drawn by Ralph Chaplin. They sold for as little as a dollar a thousand, and Chaplin believed that in a few weeks a good "Wob" on the road could plaster them on "every son-of-a-bitch of a boxcar, watertank, pick handle and pitchfork" within a radius of hundreds of miles.

The stickers were simple and caught the eye. "What Time Is It? Time to Organize!" shouted a clock. "Solidarity Takes the Whole Works" explained a Bunyan-sized workingman with an armload of trains and factories. The three stars of the One Big Union (Organiza-tion, Education, Emancipation) winked bright red over a black and yellow earth. A "scissorbill"—a workingman without class loyalty—knelt on bony knees and snuffled to the sky, "Now I get me up to work, I pray the Lord I may not shirk." But the most fateful stickers to appear between 1915 and 1917, as the nation moved toward war, were those that urged: "SLOW DOWN. The hours are long, the pay is small, so take your time and buck 'em all"; and those on which appeared two portentous symbols: the wooden shoe of sabotage, and the black cat, which, as everybody knew, meant trouble.

A tough problem for the I.W.W. was how to achieve "direct action" in the migrant workers' spread-eagle world. A factory or a mine could be struck. But how could the I.W.W.'s farmhands' union, the Agricultural Workers' Organization, "strike" a thousand square miles of wheatfield divided among hundreds of farmer-employers? How could the Forest and Lumber Workers' Industrial Union tie up a logging operation spread among dozens of camps separated by lonely miles?

The answer was, as the Wobblies put it, "to bring the strike to the job," or, more bluntly, sabotage. To the average American, sabotage conjured up nightmares of violence to property: barns blazing in the night, crowbars twisting the steel and wire guts out of a machine. The word itself suggested a European tradition of radical workers' dropping their *sabots*, or wooden shoes, into the works. But the I.W.W. leaders insisted that they had something less destructive in mind—merely the slowdown, the "conscientious withdrawal of efficiency," or, in working-stiff terms, "poor pay, poor work." To "put on the wooden shoe," or to "turn loose the black kitty" or "sab-cat," meant only to misplace and misfile order slips, to "forget" to oil motors, to "accidentally" let furnaces go out. Or simply to dawdle on the job and let fruit rot on the ground or let threshing or logging machinery with steam up stand idle while farmers and foremen fumed.

I.W.W. headquarters was vague about where the limits to direct action lay. Nor did it help matters when it printed dim, oracular pronouncements like Bill Haywood's "Sabotage means to push back, pull out or break off the fangs of Capitalism." Such phrases were enough to frighten not only the capitalists, but the Socialists, who in their 1912 convention denied the red sacraments to any who advocated "crime, sabotage or other methods of violence as a weapon of the working class to aid in its emancipation." (The next year, the Socialists fired Haywood from the party's executive board, completing the divorce between the Wobblies and politics.) Still the I.W.W. leaders in the field pushed ahead with their tactics. The Agricultural Workers, to strengthen the threat of mass quittings by harvest hands, organized a "thousand-mile picket line" of tough Wobblies who worked their way through freight trains in the farm belt, signing up new members and unceremoniously dumping off any "scissorbills" or "wicks" who refused a red card. The Lumber Workers forced the camp owners to furnish clean bedding by encouraging thousands of lumberjacks to celebrate May Day, 1918, by soaking their bindles with kerosene and making huge bonfires of them.

Potentially such tactics were loaded with danger, but from 1913 to 1919 they worked. Ralph Chaplin estimated that in early spring of 1917, when the A.W.O. was signing up members at the rate of 5,000 a month, the going wage in the grain belt had jumped from two dollars for a twelve-to-sixteen-hour day to five dollars for a ten-hour day. Two years later northwestern loggers were averaging twenty-five to fifty dollars a month plus board. These facts meant more to the average reader of *Solidarity* and the *Industrial Worker* than I.W.W. theories about the overthrow of capitalism. If he thought about the shape of society after the final general strike, it was only in the vague way of a church deacon who knew there was a celestial crown reserved for him, but did not trouble his mind about it from day to day. Yet the very success of the organization anywhere stirred not only the anger of its enemies but the fears of unsophisticated Americans who were ready to believe that the Wobblies were already putting the torch to the foundations of government and justice. With war hysteria actively feeding the fires of public hostility, the I.W.W. became the victim of new and spectacular persecutions.

Perhaps it was inevitable that the blood of martyrs would splash the pages of the I.W.W.'s book of chronicles. The mine owners, lumber-camp operators, and ranchers whom the Wobblies fought were themselves hard, resourceful men who had mastered a demanding environment. They knew a challenge when they saw one, and the West, in 1915, was not too far past Indian, stagecoach, and vigilante days. Sheriffs and their deputies were ready to use any method to rid their communities of "agitators"—especially those described in the press as "America's cancer sore." The Los Angeles *Times*, for example, said that

> A vast number of I.W.W.'s are non-producers. I.W.W. stands for I won't work, and I want whisky. . . . The average Wobbly, it must be remembered, is a sort of half wild animal. He lives on the road, cooks his food in rusty tin cans . . . and sleeps in

"jungles," barns, outhouses, freight cars . . . They are all in all a lot of homeless men wandering about the country without fixed destination or purpose, other than destruction.

"When a Wobbly comes to town," one sheriff told a visitor, "I just knock him over the head with a night stick and throw him in the river. When he comes up he beats it out of town." Lawmen furnished similar treatment to any hobo or "undesirable" stranger, particularly if he showed a tendency to complain about local working conditions or if, after April 6, 1917, he did not glow with the proper enthusiasm for the war to end wars. Hundreds of suspected and genuine Wobblies were jailed, beaten, shot, and tortured between 1914 and 1919, but some names and episodes earned, by excess of horror or myth-creating power, a special framing among dark memories.

There was the case of Joe Hill. He was the most prolific of the Wobbly bards; the dozens of numbers he composed while drifting from job to job after his emigration from Sweden to America (where his name transformed itself from Haaglund into Hillstrom and then into plain Hill) had done much to make the I.W.W. a singing movement. His songs had, a recent Wobbly folklorist has written, "tough, humorous, skeptical words which raked American morality over the coals." They were known and sung wherever Wobblies fought cops and bosses.

In January, 1914, Salt Lake City police arrested Hill on the charge of murdering a grocer and his son in a holdup. Circumstantial evidence was strongly against him, but Hill went through trial and conviction stoutly insisting that he had been framed. Though a popular ballad written many years afterward intones, "The copper bosses killed you, Joe," Hill was not definitely linked to any strike activity in Utah, and had been in the I.W.W. for only four years. But his songs had made him a hero to the entire radical labor movement, and he had a sure sense of drama. Through months of appeals and protest demonstrations he played—or lived—the role of Pilate's victim magnificently. On November 18, 1915, the day before a five-man firing squad shot him dead, he sent to Bill Haywood, in Chicago, a classic telegram: "Goodbye, Bill. I die like a true blue rebel. Don't waste any time mourning. Organize!" Thirty thousand people wept at his funeral. At his own request, his ashes were put in small envelopes and distributed to be scattered, the following May Day, in every state of the Union.

And there was the "Everett massacre." On October 30, 1916, forty-one Wobblies had travelled from Seattle to Everett, Washington, some forty miles away, to speak on behalf of striking sawmill workers. Vigilantes under Sheriff Donald McRae arrested them, took them to the edge of town, and forced them to run the gantlet between rows of deputies armed with clubs, pick handles, and bats. Next morning the grass was stiff with dried blood. Five days later, two steamer loads of I.W.W. members sailed up Puget Sound from Seattle for a meeting of protest. As they approached the Everett docks singing "Hold the Fort for We Are Coming," the sheriff and his men were waiting. They opened up with a hail of gunfire, and five Wobblies were killed, thirty-one wounded; in the confused firing, two vigilantes were also killed. Seventy-four Wobblies were arrested and tried for these two deaths but were acquitted. No one was tried for killing the I.W.W. men.

The following summer Frank Little, a member of the I.W.W. executive board, died violently in Butte, Montana. Little was a dark-haired man, with only one good eye and a crooked grin. He was part Indian, and liked to josh friends like Elizabeth Gurley Flynn and Bill Haywood by saying: "I am a real Red. The rest of you are immigrants." In June, with his leg in a cast from a recent auto accident, he left Chicago headquarters for Butte to take command of the copper miners' strike, denounced by the mine owners as a pro-German uprising. On the night of August 1, 1917, six armed and masked men broke into his hotel room and dragged him at a rope's end behind an automobile to a railroad trestle, from which he was hanged, cast and all. No arrests were made by Butte police.

As a final gruesome example, there was what happened in Centralia, Washington, on Armistice Day, 1919. An American Legion parade halted before the town's I.W.W. hall, long denounced as a center of seditious efforts to stir lumberjacks to wartime strikes and already once raided and wrecked by townsmen. Now, again, a group of men broke from the line of march and swarmed toward the building. The Wobblies inside were waiting. Simultaneous shots from several directions shattered the air; three legionnaires fell dead. The marchers broke in, seized five men, and pursued a sixth. He was Wesley Everest, a young logger and war veteran. He killed another legionnaire before they captured him and dragged him, with his teeth knocked out, to jail. That night a mob broke in and took Everest to a bridge over the Chehalis River. There he allegedly was castrated with a razor and then hanged from the bridge in the glare of automobile headlights.

The hand of history struck the I.W.W. its hardest blow, however, in September of 1917. The United States government moved to cripple the One Big Union, not because it was a threat to capitalism (the government insisted, without convincing the Wobblies) but because it was impeding the prosecution of the war. Whereas Samuel Gompers had moved skillfully to entrench the A.F.L. deeper in the hearts of the middle class by pledging it fully to Wilson's crusade, the I.W.W. remained hostile. In its eyes, the only war that meant anything to a working stiff was that foretold in the preamble, between the millions who toiled and the few who had the good things of life. Wobblies had seen too many strikes broken by troops to warm to the sight of uniforms. "Don't be a soldier," said one popular stickerette, "be a man."

The General Executive Board knew the dangers of that position once war was declared. The members hedged on expressing any formal attitude toward America's entry, and when the draft was enacted, the board advised them to register as "I.W.W. opposed to war" and thereafter to consult their own consciences. (Wesley Everest had been one of many Wobblies who chose uniformed service.) But the militant I.W.W. campaigns were frank challenges to the official drive for production. Five months after the declaration of war, federal agents, under emergency legislation, suddenly descended on I.W.W. offices all over the country. They confiscated tons of books, newspapers, letters, and pamphlets—as well as wall decorations, mimeograph machines, and spittoons—as evidence, then returned to remove Wobbly officials handcuffed in pairs.

The biggest trial of Wobblies on various counts of obstructing the war effort took place in federal district court in Chicago in the summer of 1918. Relentlessly the prosecutors drew around one hundred defendants a net of rumors and accusations charging them with conspiring to burn crops, drive spikes in logs, derail trains, dynamite factories. Judge Kenesaw Mountain Landis (later to be famous as professional baseball's "czar") presided in shirt-sleeved informality over the hot courtroom as, day after day, government attorneys read into the record every savory piece of I.W.W. prose or verse from which such phrases as "direct action" and "class war" could be speared and held up for horrified scrutiny. The jury took less than an hour to consider thousands of pages of evidence and hundreds of separate alleged offenses, and returned against all but a handful of the defendants a predictable wartime verdict of "guilty" on all counts. The white-thatched Judge Landis handed out sentences running as high as twenty years, as if he were in magistrate's court consigning the morning quota of drunks to thirty days each.

The 1918 federal trials (which were followed by similar episodes in a number of states that hastily enacted laws against "criminal syndicalism") were a downward turning point for the I.W.W. In theory, the One Big Union was wholly responsive to its rank and file, and invulnerable to the destruction of its bureaucracy.* But democratic enthusiasm could not override the fact that the veteran officers and keenest minds of the I.W.W. were behind bars, and their replacements were almost totally absorbed in legal maneuvers to get them out. A pathetic Wobbly fund-raising poster compressed the truth into a single line under a picture of a face behind bars: "We are in here for you; you are out there for us." In 1920 there might still have been fifty thousand on the I.W.W. rolls, but they were riding a rudderless craft.

Other troubles beset the One Big Union. The Communist party rose on the scene and sucked into its orbit some respected veterans, including Elizabeth Gurley Flynn (though she had left the I.W.W. in 1916) and William D. Haywood himself. Released from Leavenworth while his case was on appeal, Big Bill jumped bail and early in 1921 fled to the Soviet Union. Forgivably and understandably, perhaps, his courage had at last been shaken. He was fifty-one years old, seriously ill, and certain that he would die—with profit to no cause—if he had to spend any more time in jail. He was briefly publicized in Russia as a refugee from capitalism. He married a Russian woman, and for a time held a job as one of the managers of an industrial colony in the

---

* The fact was that it made valorous efforts to keep its officialdom humble. As general secretary-treasurer, Bill Haywood received thirty-five dollars a week—just twice what a field organizer took home.

Kuznetsk Basin. But soon there was silence, and rumors of disillusionment. In May of 1928 he died. Half his ashes were sent to Chicago for burial. The other half lie under the Kremlin wall—like those of his old friend of Paterson days, John Reed (see "The Harvard Man in the Kremlin Wall" in the February, 1960, AMERICAN HERITAGE). By and large, however, Bolshevik politicians had as little appeal for old-time Wobblies as any other kind. (Yet in 1948 the leadership of what was left of the organization refused to sign Taft-Hartley non-Communist affidavits. No contract, and no deals with bourgeois governments. Principle was principle still.)

More cracks crisscrossed the surface of solidarity. Some of the more successful I.W.W. unions experienced a yearning for larger initiation fees, and for just a taste of the financial stability of the A.F.L. internationals—the stability which had never been a Wobbly strong point. They quarrelled with the General Executive Board. A few locals chafed under what they thought was too much centralization. And finally, in 1924, there was an open split and a secession of part of the organization, taking precious funds and property with it. The last great schism, in 1908, had freed the I.W.W. for vigorous growth. Now it was sixteen years later, and time and chance were playing cruel games.

Middle age was overtaking the young lions, dulling their teeth—especially those who, one by one, accepted individual offers of clemency and emerged from prison, blinking, to find a changed world. The harvest stiff no longer took the side-door Pullman. He was a "gas tramp" now, or a "flivver hobo," riding his battered Model T to the job, and beyond the reach of the thousand-mile picket line. The logger, too, was apt to be a "home-guard," living with his family and driving through the dawn hours to where the saws whined and the big ones toppled. The children of the sweated immigrants of Paterson and Lawrence were clutching their high school diplomas, forgetting their working-class background, becoming salesmen and stenographers. Even the worker who stayed in the mill or the mine was sometimes lulled into passivity by the squealing crystal set or the weekly dream-feast of the picture-show. The ferment in the unskilled labor pool was hissing out. A new society *was* being built; but Ford and the installment plan had more to do with it than the visionaries who had hotly conceived and lustily adopted the I.W.W. preamble of 1905.

There was some fight left in the old outfit. It could run a free-speech fight in San Pedro in 1923, a coal strike in Colorado in 1927–28. But it was dwindling and aging. When the Depression came, labor's dynamism was reawakened by hardship. The C.I.O. was created, and fought its battles under the pennons of "industrial unionism," the heart of the Wobbly plan for organizing the army of production. The C.I.O. used singing picket lines, too, and sit-down strikes—techniques pioneered by such men as Haywood and Vincent St. John when labor's new leaders were in knickers. The old-timers who had known Big Bill and The Saint could only look on from the sidelines as the younger generation took over. Moreover, the success of organizing drives in the thirties, and the programs of the New Deal, vastly improved the lot of millions of working people. The agony that had nourished the I.W.W.'s revolutionary temper was now abating. Ironically, the very success of labor in uplifting itself through collective bargaining and politics drove one more nail into the I.W.W.'s coffin.

But "coffin" is perhaps the wrong word. Like Joe Hill, the I.W.W. never died. In its offices scattered across the country, old-timers still sit and smoke under pictures of Frank Little and Wesley Everest, or leaf through copies of the *Industrial Worker* like the great readers they always were. They do not give up; they expect that history will knock some sense into the workers soon, and that then the cry of "One Union, One Label, One Enemy" will rise again from thousands of throats. But meanwhile, their offices are, in the words of a recent observer, haunted halls, "full of memories and empty of men."

By contrast, the steel and glass office buildings of the bigtime A.F.L.-C.I.O. unions are alive with the ring of telephones, the hum of presses, the clatter of typewriters, and the clicking of secretaries' heels hurrying through the doors behind which sit organized labor's well-dressed statisticians, economists, lawyers, accountants, editors, co-ordinators, and educators. They have given much to their workers, these unions—good wages, decent hours, vacations, benefits, pensions, insurance. But they may be incapable of duplicating two gifts that the I.W.W. gave its apostles, its knights, its lovers—gifts that shine through a pair of stories. One is of the sheriff who shouted to a group of Wobblies, "Who's yer leader?" and got back a bellowed answer, "We don't got no leader, we're all leaders." The other is a recollection by an unidentified witness at the Chicago trial:

Well, they grabbed us. And the deputy says, "Are you a member of the I.W.W.?" I says, "Yes," so he asked me for my card, and I gave it to him, and he tore it up. He tore up the other cards that the fellow members along with me had. So this fellow member says, "There is no use tearing that card up. We can get duplicates." "Well," the deputy says, "We can tear the duplicates too." And this fellow worker says, he says, "Yes, but you can't tear it out of my heart."

II MATURE NATION
1920–1970

Alcohol and Al Capone

FREDERICK LEWIS ALLEN

• Long before the Civil War temperance enthusiasts had
sought to make the country safe from demon rum. In 1880,
Neil Dow labeled the liquor traffic "the most important political question facing the nation," and thereafter two generations of religious fundamentalists, Anti-Saloon Leaguers,
and Women's Christian Temperance Union members carried on the fight. Enthusiasm for prohibition swept across
the United States in the early years of the twentieth century,
and it became law finally in 1919 by riding the patriotic fervor of World War I. As Frederick Lewis Allen wrote: "If a
sober soldier was a good soldier and a sober factory hand was
a productive factory hand, then the argument for prohibition
was for the moment unanswerable."

At best, the moral amendment to the Constitution was a
mixed blessing. In part it represented the attempt of the middle class to impose its values upon inner-city residents who
found that drinking eased the drabness of their daily lives.
The strong desire for spirits felt by many people was not
quenched by legislation. Some legitimate businesses folded
and alcoholism may have declined, but much of the liquor
trade simply went underground. Speakeasies replaced saloons,
and in booming Chicago Al Capone built a sixty-million-
dollar empire out of the liquor trade. As Allen indicates in
the following essay, it is extremely difficult to alter standards
of personal morality and individual habits by constitutional
dictums.

From *Only Yesterday* by Frederick Lewis Allen. Copyright 1931 by
Frederick Lewis Allen; copyright renewed 1959 by Agnes Rogers Allen.
Reprinted by permission of Harper & Row, Publishers.

If in the year 1919—when the Peace Treaty still hung in the balance, and Woodrow Wilson was chanting the praises of the League, and the Bolshevist bogey stalked across the land, and fathers and mothers were only beginning to worry about the Younger Generation—you had informed the average American citizen that prohibition was destined to furnish the most violently explosive public issue of the nineteen-twenties, he would probably have told you that you were crazy. If you had been able to sketch for him a picture of conditions as they were actually to be—rum-ships rolling in the sea outside the twelve-mile limit and transferring their cargoes of whisky by night to fast cabin cruisers, beer-running trucks being hijacked on the interurban boulevards by bandits with Thompson sub-machine guns, illicit stills turning out alcohol by the carload, the fashionable dinner party beginning with contraband cocktails as a matter of course, ladies and gentlemen undergoing scrutiny from behind the curtained grill of the speakeasy, and Alphonse Capone, multi-millionaire master of the Chicago bootleggers, driving through the streets in an armor-plated car with bullet-proof windows—the innocent citizen's jaw would have dropped. The Eighteenth Amendment had been ratified, to go into effect on January 16, 1920; and the Eighteenth Amendment, he had been assured and he firmly believed, had settled the prohibition issue. You might like it or not, but the country was going dry.

Nothing in recent American history is more extraordinary, as one looks back from the nineteen-thirties, than the ease with which—after generations of uphill fighting by the drys—prohibition was finally written upon the statute-books. The country accepted it not only willingly, but almost absent-mindedly. When the Eighteenth Amendment came before the Senate in 1917, it was passed by a one-sided vote after only thirteen hours of debate, part of which was conducted under the ten-minute rule. When the House of Representatives accepted it a few months later, the debate upon the Amendment as a whole occupied only a single day. The state legislatures ratified it in short order; by January, 1919, some two months after the Armistice, the necessary three-quarters of the states had fallen into line and the Amendment was a part of the Constitution. (All the rest of the states but two subsequently added their ratifications—only Connecticut and Rhode Island remained outside the pale.) The Volstead Act for the enforcement of the Amendment, drafted after a pattern laid down by the Anti-

Saloon League, slipped through with even greater ease and dispatch. Woodrow Wilson momentarily surprised the country by vetoing it, but it was promptly repassed over his veto. There were scattered protests—a mass-meeting in New York, a parade in Baltimore, a resolution passed by the American Federation of Labor demanding modification in order that the workman might not be deprived of his beer, a noisy demonstration before the Capitol in Washington—but so half-hearted and ineffective were the forces of the opposition and so completely did the country as a whole take for granted the inevitability of a dry régime, that few of the arguments in the press or about the dinner table raised the question whether the law would or would not prove enforceable; the burning question was what a really dry country would be like, what effect enforced national sobriety would have upon industry, the social order, and the next generation.

How did it happen? Why this overwhelming, this almost casual acceptance of a measure of such huge importance?

As Charles Merz has clearly shown in his excellent history of the first ten years of the prohibition experiment, the forces behind the Amendment were closely organized; the forces opposed to the Amendment were hardly organized at all. Until the United States entered the war, the prospect of national prohibition had seemed remote, and it is always hard to mobilize an unimaginative public against a vague threat. Furthermore, the wet leadership was discredited; for it was furnished by the dispensers of liquor, whose reputation had been unsavory and who had obstinately refused to clean house even in the face of a growing agitation for temperance.

The entrance of the United States into the war gave the dry leaders their great opportunity. The war diverted the attention of those who might have objected to the bone-dry program: with the very existence of the nation at stake, the future status of alcohol seemed a trifling matter. The war accustomed the country to drastic legislation conferring new and wide powers upon the Federal Government. It necessitated the saving of food and thus condemned prohibition to the patriotic as a grain-saving measure. It turned public opinion against everything German—and many of the big brewers and distillers were of German origin. The war also brought with it a mood of Spartan idealism of which the Eighteenth Amendment was a natural expression. Everything was sacrificed to efficiency, production, and health. If a sober soldier was a good soldier and a sober factory hand was a productive factory hand, the argument for prohibition was for the moment unanswerable. Meanwhile the American people were seeing Utopian visions; if it seemed possible to them that the war should end all wars and that victory should bring a new and shining world order, how much easier to imagine that America might enter an endless era of efficient sobriety! And finally, the war made them impatient for immediate results. In 1917 and 1918, whatever was worth doing at all was worth doing at once, regardless of red tape, counter-arguments, comfort, or convenience. The combination of these various forces was irresistible. Fervently and with headlong haste the nation took the short cut to a dry Utopia.

Almost nobody, even after the war had ended, seemed to have any idea that the Amendment would be really difficult to enforce. Certainly the first Prohibition Commissioner, John F. Kramer, displayed no doubts. "This law," he declared in a burst of somewhat Scriptural rhetoric, "will be obeyed in cities, large and small, and in villages, and where it is not obeyed it will be enforced. . . . The law says that liquor to be used as a beverage must not be manufactured. We shall see that it is not manufactured. Nor sold, nor given away, nor hauled in anything on the surface of the earth or under the earth or in the air." The Anti-Saloon League estimated that an appropriation by Congress of five million dollars a year would be ample to secure compliance with the law (including, presumably, the prevention of liquor-hauling "under the earth"). Congress voted not much more than that, heaved a long sigh of relief at having finally disposed of an inconvenient and vexatious issue, and turned to other matters of more pressing importance. The morning of January 16, 1920, arrived and the era of promised aridity began. Only gradually did the dry leaders, or Congress, or the public at large begin to perceive that the problem with which they had so light-heartedly grappled was a problem of gigantic proportions.

II

Obviously the surest method of enforcement was to shut off the supply of liquor at its source. But consider what this meant.

The coast lines and land borders of the United States offered an 18,700-mile invitation to smugglers. Thousands of druggists were permitted to sell alcohol on doctors' prescriptions, and this sale could not be controlled without close and constant inspection. Near-beer was still within the law, and the only way to manufacture near-beer was to brew real beer and then remove the alcohol from it—and it was excessively easy to fail to remove it from the entire product. The manufacture of industrial alcohol opened up inviting opportunities for diversion which could be prevented only by watchful and intelligent inspection—and after the alcohol left the plant where it was produced, there was no possible way of following it down the line from purchaser to purchaser and making sure that the ingredients which had been thoughtfully added at the behest of the Government to make it undrinkable were not extracted by ingenious chemists. Illicit distilling could be undertaken almost anywhere, even in the householder's own cellar; a commercial still could be set up for five hundred dollars which would produce fifty or a hundred highly remunerative gallons a day, and a one-gallon portable still could be bought for only six or seven dollars.

To meet all these potential threats against the Volstead Act, the Government appropriations provided a force of prohibition agents which in 1920 numbered only 1,520 men and as late as 1930 numbered only 2,836; even with the sometimes unenthusiastic aid of the Coast Guard and the Customs Service and the Immigration Service, the force was meager. Mr. Merz puts it graphically: if the whole army of agents in 1920 had been mustered along the coasts and borders—paying no attention for the moment to medicinal alcohol, breweries, industrial alcohol, or illicit stills—there would have been one man to patrol every twelve miles of beach, harbor, headland, forest, and river-front. The agents' salaries in 1920 mostly ranged between $1,200 and $2,000; by 1930 they had been munificently raised to range between $2,300 and $2,800. Anybody who believed that men employable at thirty-five or forty or fifty dollars a week would surely have the expert technical knowledge and the diligence to supervise successfully the complicated chemical operations of industrial-alcohol plants or to outwit the craftiest devices of smugglers and bootleggers, and that they would surely have the force of character to resist corruption by men whose pockets were bulging with money, would be ready to believe also in Santa Claus, perpetual motion, and pixies.

Yet even this body of prohibition agents, small and underpaid as it

was in view of the size and complexity of its task and the terrific pressure of temptation, might conceivably have choked off the supply of
alcohol if it had had the concerted backing of public opinion. But
public opinion was changing. The war was over; by 1920 normalcy was
on the way. The dry cause confronted the same emotional let-down
which defeated Woodrow Wilson and hastened the Revolution in
Manners and Morals. Spartan idealism was collapsing. People were
tired of girding up their loins to serve noble causes. They were tired of
making the United States a land fit for heroes to live in. They wanted
to relax and be themselves. The change of feeling toward prohibition
was bewilderingly rapid. Within a few short months it was apparent
that the Volstead Act was being smashed right and left and that the
formerly inconsiderable body of wet opinion was growing to sizable
proportions. The law was on the statute-books, the Prohibition Bureau
was busily plying its broom against the tide of alcohol, and the corner
saloon had become a memory; but the liquorless millennium had nevertheless been indefinitely postponed.

III

The events of the next few years present one of those paradoxes which
fascinate the observer of democratic government. Obviously there were
large sections of the country in which prohibition was not prohibiting.
A rational observer would have supposed that the obvious way out of
this situation would be either to double or treble or quadruple the enforcement squad or to change the law. But nothing of the sort was done.
The dry leaders, being unwilling to admit that the task of mopping up
the United States was bigger than they had expected, did not storm
the Capitol to recommend huge increases in the appropriations for enforcement; it was easier to denounce the opponents of the law as Bol-
shevists and destroyers of civilization and to hope that the tide of
opinion would turn again. Congress was equally unwilling to face the
music; there was a comfortable dry majority in both Houses, but it
was one thing to be a dry and quite another to insist on enforcement
at whatever cost and whatever inconvenience to some of one's influential constituents. The Executive was as wary of the prohibition issue
as of a large stick of dynamite; the contribution of Presidents Harding
and Coolidge to the problem—aside from negotiating treaties which

increased the three-mile limit to twelve miles, and trying to improve
the efficiency of enforcement without calling for too much money from
Congress—consisted chiefly of uttering resounding platitudes on the
virtues of law observance. The state governments were supposed to help
the Prohibition Bureau, but by 1927 their financial contribution to the
cause was about one-eighth of the sum they spent enforcing their own
fish and game laws. Some legislatures withdrew their aid entirely, and
even the driest states were inclined to let Uncle Sam bear the brunt
of the Volstead job. Local governments were supposed to war against
the speakeasy, but did it with scant relish except where local opinion
was insistent. Nor could the wets, for their part, agree upon any practical program. It seemed almost hopeless to try to repeal or modify the
Amendment, and for the time being they contented themselves chiefly
with loud and indignant lamentation. The law was not working as it
had been intended to, but nobody seemed willing or able to do anything positive about it one way or the other.

Rum-ships plied from Bimini or Belize or St. Pierre, entering American ports under innocent disguises or transferring their cargoes to fast
motor-boats which could land in any protected cove. Launches sped
across the river at Detroit with good Canadian whisky aboard. Freighters
brought in cases of contraband gin mixed among cases of other perfectly legal and properly labeled commodities. Liquor was hidden in
freight-cars crossing the Canadian border; whole carfuls of whisky were
sometimes smuggled in by judicious manipulation of seals. These diverse forms of smuggling were conducted with such success that in
1925 General Lincoln C. Andrews, Assistant Secretary of the Treasury
in charge of enforcement, hazarded the statement that his agents succeeded in intercepting only about 5 per cent of the liquor smuggled
into the country; and the value of the liquor which filtered in during
the single year 1924 was estimated by the Department of Commerce
at $40,000,000! Beer leaked profusely from the breweries; alley brew-
eries unknown to the dry agents flourished and coined money. The
amount of industrial alcohol illegally diverted was variously estimated
in the middle years of the decade at from thirteen to fifteen million
gallons a year; and even in 1930, after the Government had improved
its technic of dealing with this particular source of supply (by careful
control of the permit system and otherwise), the Director of Prohibition admitted that the annual diversion still amounted to nine million

gallons, and other estimates ran as high as fifteen. (Bear in mind that one gallon of diverted alcohol, watered down and flavored, was enough to furnish three gallons of bogus liquor, bottled with lovely Scotch labels and described by the bootlegger at the leading citizen's door as "just off the boat.")

As for illicit distilling, as time went on this proved the most copious of all sources of supply. At the end of the decade it furnished, on the testimony of Doctor Doran of the prohibition staff, perhaps seven or eight times as much alcohol as even the process of diversion. If anything was needed to suggest how ubiquitous was the illicit still in America, the figures for the production of corn sugar provided it. Between 1919 and 1929 the output of this commodity increased *sixfold*, despite the fact that, as the Wickersham Report put it, the legitimate uses of corn sugar "are few and not easy to ascertain." Undoubtedly corn whisky was chiefly responsible for the vast increase.

This overwhelming flood of outlaw liquor introduced into the American scene a series of picturesque if unedifying phenomena: hip flasks uptilted above faces both masculine and feminine at the big football games; the speakeasy, equipped with a regular old-fashioned bar, serving cocktails made of gin turned out, perhaps, by a gang of Sicilian alky-cookers (seventy-five cents for patrons, free to the police); well-born damsels with one foot on the brass rail, tossing off Martinis; the keg of grape juice simmering hopefully in the young couple's bedroom closet, subject to periodical inspection by a young man sent from a "service station"; the business executive departing for the trade convention with two bottles of gin in his bag; the sales manager serving lavish drinks to the visiting buyer as in former days he had handed out lavish boxes of cigars; the hotel bellhop running to Room 417 with another order of ginger ale and cracked ice, provided by the management on the ironical understanding that they were "not to be mixed with spirituous liquors"; federal attorneys padlocking nightclubs and speakeasies, only to find them opening shortly at another address under a different name; Izzy Einstein and Moe Smith, prohibition agents extraordinary, putting on a series of comic-opera disguises to effect miraculous captures of bootleggers; General Smedley Butler of the Marines advancing in military formation upon the rum-sellers of Philadelphia, and retiring in disorder after a few strenuous months with the admission that politics made it impossible to dry up the city; the Government putting wood alcohol and other poisons into industrial alcohol to prevent its diversion, and the wets thereupon charging the Government with murder; Government agents, infuriated by their failure to prevent liquor-running by polite methods, finally shooting to kill— and sometimes picking off an innocent bystander; the good ship *I'm Alone*, of Canadian registry, being pursued by a revenue boat for two and a half days and sunk at a distance of 215 miles from the American coast, to the official dismay of the Canadian Government; the federal courts jammed with prohibition cases, jurymen in wet districts refusing to pronounce bootleggers guilty, and the coin of corruption sifting through the hands of all manner of public servants.

Whatever the contribution of the prohibition régime to temperance, at least it produced intemperate propaganda and counter-propaganda. Almost any dry could tell you that prohibition was the basis of American prosperity, as attested by the mounting volume of saving-banks deposits and by what some big manufacturer had said about the men returning to work on Monday morning with clear eyes and steady hands. Or that prohibition had reduced the deaths from alcoholism, emptied the jails, and diverted the workman's dollar to the purchase of automobiles, radios, and homes. Almost any wet could tell you that prohibition had nothing to do with prosperity but had caused the crime wave, the increase of immorality and of the divorce rate, and a disrespect for all law which imperiled the very foundations of free government. The wets said the drys fostered Bolshevism by their fanatical zeal for laws which were inevitably flouted; the drys said the wets fostered Bolshevism by their cynical lawbreaking. Even in matters of supposed fact you could find, if you only read and listened, any sort of ammunition that you wanted. One never saw drunkards on the streets any more; one saw more drunkards than ever. Drinking in the colleges was hardly a problem now; drinking in the colleges was at its worst. There was a still in every other home in the mining districts of Pennsylvania; drinking in the mining districts of Pennsylvania was a thing of the past. Cases of poverty as a result of drunkenness were only a fraction of what they used to be; the menace of drink in the slums was three times as great as in pre-Volstead days. Bishop A and Doctor B and Governor C were much encouraged by the situation; Bishop X and Doctor Y and Governor Z were appalled by it. And so the battle raged, endlessly and loudly, back and forth.

The mass of statistics dragged to light by professional drys and professional wets and hurled at the public need not detain us here. Many of them were grossly unreliable, and the use of most of them would have furnished an instructor in logic with perfect specimens of the *post hoc* fallacy. It is perhaps enough to point out a single anomaly—that with the Eighteenth Amendment and the Volstead Act in force, there should actually have been constant and vociferous argument throughout the nineteen-twenties over the question whether there was more drinking or less in the United States than before the war. Presumably there was a good deal less except among the prosperous; but the fact that it was not transparently obvious that there was less, showed how signal was the failure of the law to accomplish what almost everyone in 1919 had supposed it would accomplish.

IV

By 1928 the argument over prohibition had reached such intensity that it could no longer be kept out of presidential politics. Governor Smith of New York was accepted as the Democratic nominee despite his unterrified wetness, and campaigned lustily for two modifications: first, an amendment to the Volstead law giving a "scientific definition of the alcoholic content of an intoxicating beverage" (a rather large order for science), each state being allowed to fix its own standard if this did not exceed the standard fixed by Congress; and second, "an amendment in the Eighteenth Amendment which would give to each individual state itself, only after approval by a referendum popular vote of its people, the right wholly within its borders to import, manufacture, or cause to be manufactured and sell alcoholic beverages, the sale to be made only by the state itself and not for consumption in any public place." The Republican candidate, in reply, stepped somewhat definitely off the fence on the dry side. Herbert Hoover's dry declaration, to be sure, left much unsaid; he called prohibition "a great social and economic experiment, noble in motive and far-reaching in purpose," but he did not claim nobility for its results. The omission, however, was hardly noticed by an electorate which regarded indorsement of motives as virtually equivalent to indorsement of performance. Hoover was considered a dry.

The Republican candidate was elected in a landslide, and the drys took cheer. Despite the somewhat equivocal results of various state referenda and straw ballots, they had always claimed that they had a substantial majority in the country as well as in Congress; now they were sure of it. Still the result of the election left room for haunting doubts. Who could tell whether the happy warrior from the East Side had been defeated because he was a wet, or because he was a Roman Catholic, or because he was considered a threat to the indefinite continuance of the delights of Coolidge Prosperity, or because he was a Democrat?

But Herbert Hoover had done more than endorse the motives of the prohibitionists. He had promised a study of the enforcement problem by a governmental commission. Two and a half months after his arrival at the White House, the commission, consisting of eleven members under the chairmanship of George W. Wickersham of New York, was appointed and immersed itself in its prodigious task.

By the time the Wickersham Commission emerged from the sea of fact and theory and contention in which it had been delving, and handed its report to the President, the Post-War Decade was dead and done with. Not until January, 1931, nineteen months after his appointment, did Mr. Wickersham lay the bulky findings of the eleven investigators upon the presidential desk. Yet the report calls for mention here, if only because it represented the findings of a group of intelligent and presumably impartial people with regard to one of the critical problems of the nineteen-twenties.

It was a paradoxical document. In the first place, the complete text revealed very clearly the sorry inability of the enforcement staff to dry up the country. In the second place, each of the eleven commissioners submitted a personal report giving his individual views, and only five of the eleven—a minority—favored further trial for the prohibition experiment without substantial change; four of them favored modification of the Amendment, and two were for outright repeal. But the commission *as a whole* cast its vote for further trial, contenting itself with suggesting a method of modification if time proved that the experiment was a failure. The confusing effect of the report was neatly satirized in Flaccus's summary of it in F. P. A.'s column in the *New York World:*

> Prohibition is an awful flop.
>   We like it.
> It can't stop what it's meant to stop.
>   We like it.
> It's left a trail of graft and slime,
> It's filled our land with vice and crime,
> It don't prohibit worth a dime,
>   Nevertheless we're for it.

Yet if the Wickersham report was confusing, this was highly appropriate; for so also was the situation with which it dealt. Although it seemed reasonably clear to an impartial observer that the country had chosen the wrong road in 1917–20, legislating with a sublime disregard for elementary chemistry—which might have taught it how easily alcohol may be manufactured—and for elementary psychology—which might have suggested that common human impulses are not easily suppressed by fiat—it was nevertheless very far from clear how the country could best extricate itself from the morass into which it had so blithely plunged. How could people who had become gin-drinkers be expected to content themselves with light wines and beers, as some of the modificationists suggested? How could any less drastic system of governmental regulation or governmental sale of liquor operate without continued transgression and corruption, now that a large element had learned how to live with impunity on the fruits of lawbreaking? To what sinister occupations might not the bootlegging gentry turn if outright repeal took their accustomed means of livelihood away from them? How could any new national policy toward alcohol be successfully put into effect when there was still violent disagreement, even among those who wanted the law changed, as to whether alcohol should be regarded as a curse, as a blessing to be used in moderation, or as a matter of personal rather than public concern? Even if a clear majority of the American people were able to decide to their own satisfaction what was the best way out of the morass, what chance was there of putting through their program when thirteen dry states could block any change in the Amendment? No problem which had ever faced the United States had seemed more nearly insoluble.

V

In 1920, when prohibition was very young, Johnny Torrio of Chicago had an inspiration. Torrio was a formidable figure in the Chicago underworld. He had discovered that there was big money in the newly outlawed liquor business. He was fired with the hope of getting control of the dispensation of booze to the whole city of Chicago. At the moment there was a great deal too much competition; but possibly a well-disciplined gang of men handy with their fists and their guns could take care of that, by intimidating rival bootleggers and persuading speakeasy proprietors that life might not be wholly comfortable for them unless they bought Torrio liquor. What Torrio needed was a lieutenant who could mobilize and lead his shock troops.

Being a graduate of the notorious Five Points gang in New York and a disciple of such genial fellows as Lefty Louie and Gyp the Blood (he himself had been questioned about the murder of Herman Rosenthal in the famous Becker case in 1912), he naturally turned to his *alma mater* for his man. He picked for the job a bullet-headed twenty-three-year-old Neapolitan roughneck of the Five Points gang, and offered him a generous income and half the profits of the bootleg trade if he would come to Chicago and take care of the competition. The young hoodlum came, established himself at Torrio's gambling-place, the Four Deuces, opened by way of plausible stage setting an innocent-looking office which contained among its properties a family Bible, and had a set of business cards printed:

ALPHONSE CAPONE

Second Hand Furniture Dealer   2220 South Wabash Avenue

Torrio had guessed right—in fact, he had guessed right three times. The profits of bootlegging in Chicago proved to be prodigious, allowing an ample margin for the mollification of the forces of the law. The competition proved to be exacting: every now and then Torrio would discover that his rivals had approached a speakeasy proprietor with the suggestion that he buy their beer instead of the Torrio-Capone brand, and on receipt of an unfavorable answer had beaten the proprietor senseless and smashed up his place of business. But Al Capone had been an excellent choice as leader of the Torrio offensives; Capone was learning how to deal with such emergencies.

Within three years it was said that the boy from the Five Points had seven hundred men at his disposal, many of them adept in the use of the sawed-off shotgun and the Thompson sub-machine gun. As the profits from beer and "alky-cooking" (illicit distilling) rolled in, young Capone acquired more finesse—particularly finesse in the management of politics and politicians. By the middle of the decade he had gained complete control of the suburb of Cicero, had installed his own mayor in office, had posted his agents in the wide-open gambling-resorts and in each of the 161 bars, and had established his personal headquarters in the Hawthorne Hotel. He was taking in millions now. Torrio was fading into the background; Capone was becoming the Big Shot. But his conquest of power did not come without bloodshed. As the rival gangs—the O'Banions, the Gennas, the Aiellos—disputed his growing domination, Chicago was afflicted with such an epidemic of killings as no civilized modern city had ever before seen, and a new technic of wholesale murder was developed.

One of the standard methods of disposing of a rival in this warfare of the gangs was to pursue his car with a stolen automobile full of men armed with sawed-off shotguns and sub-machine guns; to draw up beside it, forcing it to the curb, open fire upon it—and then disappear into the traffic, later abandoning the stolen car at a safe distance. Another favorite method was to take the victim "for a ride": in other words, to lure him into a supposedly friendly car, shoot him at leisure, drive to some distant and deserted part of the city, and quietly throw his body overboard. Still another was to lease an apartment or a room overlooking his front door, station a couple of hired assassins at the window, and as the victim emerged from the house some sunny afternoon, to spray him with a few dozen machine-gun bullets from behind drawn curtains. But there were also more ingenious and refined methods of slaughter.

Take, for example, the killing of Dion O'Banion, leader of the gang which for a time most seriously menaced Capone's reign in Chicago. The preparation of this particular murder was reminiscent of the kiss of Judas. O'Banion was a bootlegger and a gangster by night, but a florist by day: a strange and complex character, a connoisseur of orchids and of manslaughter. One morning a sedan drew up outside his flower shop and three men got out, leaving the fourth at the wheel. The three men had apparently taken good care to win O'Banion's trust, for although he always carried three guns, now for the moment he was off his guard as he advanced among the flowers to meet his visitors. The middle man of the three cordially shook hands with O'Banion—*and then held on* while his two companions put six bullets into the gangster-florist. The three conspirators walked out, climbed into the sedan, and departed. They were never brought to justice, and it is not recorded that any of them hung themselves to trees in remorse. O'Banion had a first class funeral, gangster style: a ten-thousand dollar casket, twenty-six truckloads of flowers, and among them a basket of flowers which bore the touching inscription, "From Al."

In 1926 the O'Banions, still unrepentant despite the loss of their leader, introduced another novelty in gang warfare. In broad daylight, while the streets of Cicero were alive with traffic, they raked Al Capone's headquarters with machine-gun fire from eight touring cars. The cars proceeded down the crowded street outside the Hawthorne Hotel in solemn line, the first one firing blank cartridges to disperse the innocent citizenry and to draw the Capone forces to the doors and windows, while from the succeeding cars, which followed a block behind, flowed a steady rattle of bullets, spraying the hotel and the adjoining buildings up and down. One gunman even got out of his car, knelt carefully upon the sidewalk at the door of the Hawthorne, and played one hundred bullets into the lobby—back and forth, as one might play the hose upon one's garden. The casualties were miraculously light, and Scarface Al himself remained in safety, flat on the floor of the Hotel Hawthorne restaurant; nevertheless, the bombardment quite naturally attracted public attention. Even in a day when bullion was transported in armored cars, the transformation of a suburban street into a shooting-gallery seemed a little unorthodox.

The war continued, one gangster after another crumpling under a rain of bullets; not until St. Valentine's Day of 1929 did it reach its climax in a massacre which outdid all that had preceded it in ingenuity and brutality. At half-past ten on the morning of February 14, 1929, seven of the O'Banions were sitting in the garage which went by the name of the S. M. C. Cartage Company, on North Clark Street, waiting for a promised consignment of hijacked liquor. A Cadillac touring-car slid to the curb, and three men dressed as policemen got out, followed by two others in civilian dress. The three supposed policemen entered the garage alone, disarmed the seven O'Banions, and told them to stand in a row against the wall. The victims readily submitted; they were used to police raids and thought nothing of them; they would get off easily enough, they expected. But thereupon the two men in civilian clothes emerged from the corridor and calmly mowed all seven O'Banions with sub-machine gun fire as they stood with hands upraised against the wall. The little drama was completed when the three supposed policemen solemnly marched the two plainclothes killers across the sidewalk to the waiting car, and all five got in and drove off—having given to those in the wintry street a perfect tableau of an arrest satisfactorily made by the forces of the law!

These killings—together with that of "Jake" Lingle, who led a double life as reporter for the *Chicago Tribune* and as associate of gangsters, and who was shot to death in a crowded subway leading to the Illinois Central suburban railway station in 1930—were perhaps the most spectacular of the decade in Chicago. But there were over five hundred gang murders in all. Few of the murderers were apprehended; careful planning, money, influence, the intimidation of witnesses, and the refusal of any gangster to testify against any other, no matter how treacherous the murder, met that danger. The city of Chicago was giving the whole country, and indeed the whole world, an astonishing object lesson in violent and unpunished crime. How and why could such a thing happen?

To say that prohibition—or, if you prefer, the refusal of the public to abide by prohibition—caused the rise of the gangs to lawless power would be altogether too easy an explanation. There were other causes: the automobile, which made escape easy, as the officers of robbed banks had discovered; the adaptation to peace-time use of a new arsenal of handy and deadly weapons; the murderous traditions of the Mafia, imported by Sicilian gangsters; the inclination of a wet community to wink at the by-products of a trade which provided them with beer and gin; the sheer size and unwieldiness of the modern metropolitan community, which prevented the focusing of public opinion upon any depredation which did not immediately concern the average individual citizen; and, of course, the easy-going political apathy of the times. But the immediate occasion of the rise of gangs was undoubtedly prohibition—or, to be more precise, beer-running. (Beer rather than whisky on account of its bulk; to carry on a profitable trade in beer one must transport it in trucks, and trucks are so difficult to disguise that the traffic must be protected by bribery of the prohibition staff and the police and by gunfire against bandits.) There was vast profit in the manufacture, transportation, and sale of beer. In 1927, according to Fred D. Pasley, Al Capone's biographer, federal agents estimated that the Capone gang controlled the sources of a revenue from booze of something like sixty million dollars a year, and much of this—perhaps most of it—came from beer. Fill a man's pockets with money, give him a chance at a huge profit, put him into an illegal business and thus deny him recourse to the law if he is attacked, and you have made it easy for him to bribe and shoot. There have always been gangs and gangsters in American life and doubtless always will be; there has always been corruption of city officials and doubtless always will be; yet it is ironically true, none the less, that the outburst of corruption and crime in Chicago in the nineteen-twenties was immediately occasioned by the attempt to banish the temptations of liquor from the American home.

The young thug from the Five Points, New York, had traveled fast and far since 1920. By the end of the decade he had become as widely renowned as Charles Evans Hughes or Gene Tunney. He had become an American portent. Not only did he largely control the sale of liquor to Chicago's ten thousand speakeasies; he controlled the sources of supply, it was said, as far as Canada and the Florida coast. He had amassed, and concealed, a fortune the extent of which nobody knew; it was said by federal agents to amount to twenty millions. He was arrested and imprisoned once in Philadelphia for carrying a gun, but otherwise he seemed above the law. He rode about Chicago in an armored car, a traveling fortress, with another car to patrol the way ahead and a third car full of his armed henchmen following behind; he went to the theater attended by a body-guard of eighteen young men in dinner coats, with guns doubtless slung under their left armpits in approved gangster fashion; when his sister was married, thousands milled about the church in the snow, and he presented the bride with a nine-foot wedding cake and a special honeymoon car; he had a fine estate at Miami where he sometimes entertained seventy-five guests at a time; and high politicians—and even, it has been said, judges—took orders from him over the telephone from his headquarters in a downtown Chicago hotel. And still he was only thirty-two years old. What was Napoleon doing at thirty-two?

Meanwhile gang rule and gang violence were quickly penetrating other American cities. Toledo had felt them, and Detroit, and New York, and many another. Chicago was not alone. Chicago had merely led the way.

VI

By the middle of the decade it was apparent that the gangs were expanding their enterprises. In Mr. Pasley's analysis of the gross income of the Capone crew in 1927, as estimated by federal agents, the item of $60,000,000 from beer and liquor, including alky-cooking, and the items of $25,000,000 from gambling-establishments and dog-tracks, and of $10,000,000 from vice, dance-halls, roadhouses, and other resorts, were followed by this entry: Rackets, $10,000,000. The bootlegging underworld was venturing into fresh woods and pastures new.

The word "racket," in the general sense of an occupation which produces easy money, is of venerable age: it was employed over fifty years ago in Tammany circles in New York. But it was not widely used in its present meaning until the middle nineteen-twenties, and the derived term "racketeering" did not enter the American vocabulary until the year when Sacco and Vanzetti were executed and Lindbergh flew the Atlantic and Calvin Coolidge did not choose to run—the year 1927. The name was a product of the Post-war Decade; and so was the activity to which it was attached.

Like the murderous activities of the bootlegging gangs, racketeering grew out of a complex of causes. One of these was violent labor unionism. Since the days of the Molly Maguires, organized labor had now and again fought for its rights with brass knuckles and bombs. During the Big Red Scare the labor unions had lost the backing of public opinion, and Coolidge Prosperity was making things still more difficult for them by persuading thousands of their members that a union card was not the only ticket to good fortune. More than one fighting labor leader thereupon turned once more to dynamite in the effort to maintain his job and his power. Gone was the ardent radicalism of 1919, the hope of a new industrial order; the labor leader now found himself simply a man who hoped to get his when others were getting theirs, a man tempted to smash the scab's face or to blow the roof off the anti-union factory to show that he meant business and could deliver the goods. In many cases he turned for aid to the hired thug, the killer; he protected himself from the law by bribery or at least by political influence; he connived with business men who were ready to play his game for their own protection or for profit. These unholy alliances were now the more easily achieved because the illicit liquor trade was making the underworld rich and confident and quick on the trigger and was accustoming many politicians and business men to large-scale graft and conspiracy. Gangsters and other crafty fellows learned of the labor leader's tricks and went out to organize rackets on their own account. Thus by 1927 the city which had nourished Al Capone was nourishing also a remarkable assortment of these curious enterprises.

Some of them were labor unions perverted to criminal ends; some were merely conspiracies for extortion masquerading as labor unions; others were conspiracies masquerading as trade associations, or were combinations of these different forms. But the basic principle was fairly uniform: the racket was a scheme for collecting cash from business men to protect them from damage, and it prospered because the victim soon learned that if he did not pay, his shop would be bombed, or his trucks wrecked, or he himself might be shot in cold blood—and never a chance to appeal to the authorities for aid, because the authorities were frightened or fixed.

There was the cleaners' and dyers' racket, which collected heavy dues from the proprietors of retail cleaning shops and from master cleaners, and for a time so completely controlled the industry in Chicago that it could raise the price which the ordinary citizen paid for having his suit cleaned from $1.25 to $1.75. A cleaner and dyer who defied this racket might have his place of business bombed, or his delivery truck drenched with gasoline and set on fire, or he might be disciplined in a more devilish way: explosive chemicals might be sewn into the seams of trousers sent to him to be cleaned. There was the garage racket, product of the master mind of David Ablin, alias "Cockeye" Mulligan: if a garage owner chose not to join in the Mid-West Garage Association, as this enterprise was formally entitled, his garage would be bombed, or his mechanics would be slugged, or thugs would enter at night and smash windshields or lay about among the sedans with sledge-hammers, or tires would be flattened by the expert use of an ice-pick. There was the window-washing racket; when Max Wilner, who had been a window-washing contractor in Cleveland, moved to Chicago and tried to do business there, and was told that he could not unless he bought out some contractor already established, and refused to do so, he was not merely slugged or cajoled with explosives—he was shot dead. The list of rackets and of crimes could be extended for pages; in 1929, according to the State Attorney's office, there were ninety-one rackets in Chicago, seventy-five of them in active operation, and the Employers' Association figured the total cost to the citizenry at $136,000,000 a year.

As the favorite weapon of the bootlegging gangster was the machine gun, so the favorite weapon of the racketeer was the bomb. He could hire a bomber to do an ordinary routine job with a black-powder bomb for $100, but a risky job with a dynamite bomb might cost him all of $1,000. In the course of a little over fifteen months—from October 11, 1927, to Jaunary 15, 1929—no less than 157 bombs were set or exploded in the Chicago district, and according to Gordon L. Hostetter and Thomas Quinn Beesley, who made a careful compilation of these outrages in *It's a Racket*, there was no evidence that the perpetrators of *any of them* were brought to book.

A merry industry, and reasonably safe, it seemed—for the racketeers. Indeed, before the end of the decade racketeering had made such strides in Chicago that business men were turning in desperation to Al Capone for protection; Capone's henchmen were quietly attending union meetings to make sure that all proceeded according to the Big Shot's desires, and it was said that there were few more powerful figures in the councils of organized labor than the lord of the bootleggers had come to be. Racketeering, like gang warfare, had invaded other American cities, too. New York had laughed at Chicago's lawlessness, had it? New York was acquiring a handsome crop of rackets of its own —a laundry racket, a slot-machine racket, a fish racket, a flour racket, an artichoke racket, and others too numerous to mention. In every large urban community the racketeer was now at least a potential menace. In the course of a few short years he had become a national institution.

VII

The prohibition problem, the gangster problem, the racket problem: as the Post-war Decade bowed itself out, all of them remained unsolved, to challenge the statesmanship of the nineteen-thirties. Still the rum-running launch slipped across the river, the alky-cooker's hidden apparatus poured forth alcohol, *entrepreneurs* of the contraband liquor industry put one another "on the spot," "typewriters" rattled in the Chicago streets, automobiles laden with roses followed the gangster to his grave, professional sluggers swung on non-union workmen, bull-necked gentlemen with shifty eyes called on the tradesman to suggest that he do business with them or they could not be responsible for what might happen, bombs reduced little shops to splintered wreckage; and tabloid-readers, poring over the stories of gangster killings, found in them adventure and splendor and romance.

A Reasonable Doubt *

DAN T. CARTER

• The Scottsboro Case—an infamous series of litigations which was to inflame both the North and the South for many years—began inconspicuously on March 25, 1931, as white and Negro hobos brawled aboard a freight train moving across northeastern Alabama. One of the white youths thrown from the train reported the fight to the nearest stationmaster, and a Jackson County posse stopped the train at the rural village of Paint Rock. When deputies removed the nine Negro teenagers on board they also discovered two young white girls, aged seventeen and twenty-one, who were hitching a ride from Chattanooga, Tennessee, back to their home in Huntsville, Alabama. In the first confusing minutes after the arrests, Ruby Bates whispered to officials that she and her friend, Victoria Price, had been raped by the nine Negroes, who ranged in age from twelve to nineteen. A hasty medical examination revealed evidence of sexual intercourse.

That night, sheriff's deputies, strengthened by the Alabama National Guard, averted a mass lynching after a sullen mob gathered outside the Jackson County jailhouse in the little town of Scottsboro. Two weeks later, while a crowd of eight to ten thousand filled Scottsboro's streets, two court-appointed attorneys half-heartedly defended the frightened boys. Four juries convicted and sentenced eight to death; the trial of Leroy Wright, aged twelve, for whom the state had asked a life sentence, ended in a hung jury.

Cases similar to the Scottsboro one had been largely unnoticed outside the South. But the number of defendants, their extreme youth, the stunning rapidity of the trials, and the harsh sentences the boys received attracted the attention of national newspapers. In April, the International Labor De-

* With headnote exactly as it appeared in American Heritage.

From American Heritage. Copyright © 1969 by Dan T. Carter. Reprinted by permission.

fense, a close affiliate of the Communist party, launched a propaganda campaign to expose what it called "the Alabama frame-up." Although the N.A.A.C.P. belatedly offered legal support to the convicted youths, the I.L.D. swiftly gained the backing of the boys and their parents. In late December of 1931, N.A.A.C.P. attorneys withdrew from the case.

The United States Supreme Court accepted the I.L.D.'s contention that the youths had had inadequate legal counsel at Scottsboro and overturned the convictions in 1932. But the rallies, pamphlets, and flamboyant accusations of the International Labor Defense and the Communist party only stiffened the resolve of Alabamians to repel the accusations of "outsiders" and see the Scottsboro defendants put to death. As the new trials approached in the spring of 1933, the International Labor Defense reluctantly turned to one of the nation's most brilliant criminal attorneys, Samuel S. Leibowitz of Brooklyn, New York. Leibowitz did not subscribe to the I.L.D. ideology, but he felt that the boys' basic civil rights had been violated, and when the I.L.D.'s executive secretary promised to shelve temporarily his organization's revolutionary rhetoric, Leibowitz agreed to defend the youths without fee.

He began the case with a plea for a change of venue, and the presiding judge agreed to transfer the trials fifty miles west of Scottsboro to Decatur, the seat of Morgan County. There, with a National Guard unit on duty to keep order, the second series of trials began in late March. The first defendant to be tried was Haywood Patterson, nineteen.

March 27, the opening day, was warm and clear in Decatur. Before 7 A.M. a large and cheerful crowd had gathered outside the two-story yellow brick courthouse. Even the announcement that there would be a half-day's delay in the proceedings did not seem to dispel the spectators' good nature. Throughout the morning they sunned lazily on the wide lawn or gossiped around the two courthouse statues, one honoring justice and the other paying tribute to those Confederate soldiers "who gave their lives for a just cause—State's Rights." There was some talk about the trial, but mostly the relaxed crowd discussed the Depression. Three and a half years after the crash of 1929, these Alabamians—like most Americans—were optimistically looking to Mr. Roosevelt and his New Deal for relief. For as the cotton mills and railroad shops had closed or curtailed their operations, hard times had come to Decatur. The spring foliage and flowers camouflaged, but they could not conceal, the empty, dilapidated stores downtown and the peeling paint on the outlying houses.

Samuel Leibowitz had been apprehensive when he first arrived in Decatur. He was keenly aware that he and his fellow defense attorney, Joseph Brodsky, were outsiders. Worse, they were New York Jews. To his relief, however, the townspeople greeted him with unaffected hospitality. "[They] . . . impress me as being honest, God-fearing people who want to see justice done," he told reporters.

After lunch, as officials announced that the court would soon convene, an irregular line formed, stretching through the courthouse corridors and past the brass spittoons resting on their tobacco-stained rubber pads. Within minutes, the 425 seats were filled—whites in three sections, Negroes in the fourth. At 2 P.M., Judge James Edwin Horton, Jr., settled into the raised judge's chair, adjusted his tortoise-shell spectacles, and nodded to the prosecutor to begin reading the indictment.

Lank, raw-boned and more than six feet tall, Horton strongly resembled photographs of the young and beardless Lincoln. His family had served prominently in the political life of the ante-bellum South, and the fifty-five-year-old judge spoke without self-consciousness of his obligation to uphold the integrity of the family name. His views on the Negro, like those of the traditionally conservative southerner, were kindly and well-meaning, with a trace of *noblesse oblige*, yet when one of the two Negro reporters present introduced himself on the first day of the trial, Horton, in the presence of disapproving townspeople, unhesitatingly offered a firm handshake. In the Decatur courtroom he was easygoing and lenient, unbothered by the clatter of reporters' noisy typewriters. During the two-week trial he had to rule upon many questions of law that he had accepted without question throughout his legal career; generally he remained calm and unruffled, his voice at an even, conversational level.

To the disappointment of the spectators, the sensational testimony that they expected to hear did not begin right away. In fact, the whole first week of the trial was taken up with a complex constitutional duel between defense and state attorneys over the question of Negro jurors, and the crowd quickly lost interest. Leibowitz argued that Alabama officials had defied the Fourteenth Amendment by excluding Negroes from the Jackson County juries which had originally convicted the nine youths, and from the Morgan County venire from which a new jury would now be chosen to retry the first defendant, Haywood Patterson. The absence of Negro jurors was incontestable; a courtroom official said he could not recall seeing black men in the jury box since before the turn of the century. But a Scottsboro civic leader explained on the witness stand that the absence of Negro jurors was not a matter of racial prejudice. It was simply that Negroes had not been "trained for jury duty in our county . . . and I don't think their judgment—you could depend on it altogether." Besides, he added as the spectators chuckled, "they will nearly all steal." One jury commissioner told Leibowitz that Negroes were not excluded for any particular reason; "Negroes was never discussed."

Thomas Knight, Jr., Alabama's thirty-four-year-old attorney general, was present to handle the prosecution. Affable and charming, he ordinarily conveyed the image of well-bred southern gentility. In the courtroom, however, he was a fierce antagonist. Nervously pacing across the courtroom, he alternately cajoled and threatened the apprehensive Negro leaders from Scottsboro and Decatur who testified on the jury question. The nineteen witnesses included a Pullman porter, the owner of a dry-cleaning shop, a dentist, a seminary-trained minister, and a doctor educated at Phillips Exeter Academy in New Hampshire and the University of Illinois. Knight succeeded in showing that some of them were unaware of the intricate details of the jury selection system and that others did not know all the legal requirements for jury duty. He was not able to conceal, however, what Leibowitz wanted to prove: that the Negro witnesses were completely qualified to serve as jurors yet that, because of their race, none had ever been called.

After four days of testimony and argument, Horton denied Leibowitz's motions to quash the Jackson County indictment and set aside the Morgan County venire. Significantly, however, he also ruled that the jury rolls of both counties contained only the names of whites. A smiling Leibowitz perfunctorily objected to the court's decision; privately he told friends he was confident no conviction could now withstand the scrutiny of the United States Supreme Court.

Despite Leibowitz's pleasure at the progress of the trial, reporters had sensed a shift of local mood from geniality to distrust and then to anger. However well-intentioned Morgan County citizens might be, their ultimate loyalty was to preserving the racial status quo. Still buried in the walls of several of the town's buildings were bullets fired during the Civil War; the entire area had been a center of Ku Klux Klan strength during the Reconstruction era and again in the Klan resurgence of the 1920's. Leibowitz's insistence on referring to Negro witnesses as "Mr." had perplexed the spectators, but when he pressed his demand for Negro jurors, grim hostility appeared on the faces of the overalled farmers. Leibowitz, warned a Black Belt newspaper, had "thrown down the challenge to . . . white supremacy."

Judge Horton's brief remarks to the venire of jurors on Friday afternoon referred obliquely to the rising hostility. "Now, gentlemen," he said, "under our law when it comes to the courts we know neither black nor white. . . . It is our duty to mete out even-handed justice. . . . No other course is open to you"—his voice suddenly became stern and harsh—"and let no one think they can act otherwise." The judge's implicit warning ended the open threats which had been heard on Decatur's streets, but resentment smouldered beneath the surface, a resentment bolstered by the presence of "outside radicals" who had come to observe the proceedings.

The jury was selected in one afternoon. Leibowitz was not altogether satisfied, since the state had used its challenges to exclude younger men who might have had "liberal" ideas, but at least he felt he had managed to keep the most obvious "red-neck" types off the jury.

When the actual taking of testimony began the following Monday, the seats were jammed for the first time since the opening day. Although it was cool in the building when the courtroom doors opened at 8:30 A.M., within an hour the spectators had begun to shed their coats, and by noon courthouse officials were forced to turn on the overhead fans to dispel the oppressive stuffiness caused by constant smoking in the crowded courtroom. Just before 9 A.M. Victoria Price, the older of the two complainants, took the stand. (The other girl, Ruby Bates, was absent; although she had testified at the

trials two years before in Scottsboro, state officials said that she
had recently disappeared.) Mrs. Price wore a blue straw hat and a
black dress with a fichu of white lace at the throat. Her stylish
costume was quite unlike the bedraggled outfit she had worn at
Scottsboro, and in keeping with her new mien, she restrained her
habit of chewing snuff, which at earlier hearings had necessitated
frequent spitting. She seemed nervous in the witness chair, crossing
and uncrossing her legs and fingering her long necklace of glass beads.
When Attorney General Knight began his questioning, however, she
spoke in a clear, firm voice that carried to the back of the courtroom.

Mrs. Price began her story from the time she and her friend Ruby
boarded the train at Chattanooga to return to their home in Huntsville. Just south of Stevenson, Alabama, she said, about a dozen Negro
youths leaped from the top of an adjacent boxcar into the gondola
that she and Ruby were sharing with seven white hobos. After a brief
scuffle, all but one of the outnumbered white boys were thrown from
the train. The only remaining white, Orville Gilley, was forced to
watch the brutal assaults that followed. Thrusting her finger toward
Haywood Patterson, Mrs. Price identified him as one of the rapists.
Knight asked her if Patterson's "private parts penetrated your private
parts." "Yes sir, they did," she replied. Suddenly Knight pulled a torn
cotton undergarment from his briefcase, and asked Victoria Price
to state whether these were the step-ins she was wearing at the time
of the assault. Liebowitz leaped to his feet. "This is the first time in
two years any such step-ins have ever been shown" in connection
with the case, he objected. "They are here now," Knight answered,
grinning, and tossed them into the lap of one of the bewildered
jurors. The courtroom exploded into laughter, and Judge Horton had
to gavel for quiet. In less than twenty minutes the Alabama attorney
general completed his direct examination and, with a gracious smile
toward the defense table, abandoned his star witness to Leibowitz.

The balding lawyer, younger than most spectators had anticipated,
exuded confidence. During his career he had reduced even honest
witnesses to incoherent confusion, and he was convinced that Victoria
Price was lying. Leibowitz had all the skills of a good trial lawyer: an
actor's sense of timing, a flair for the dramatic, and a clear, forceful
voice. But his main strength was an almost infallible memory for
detail and, above all, for contradictions. "I am not a great lawyer,"

he had once said in response to a compliment. "I'm only thorough."
He began his cross-examination gently, almost kindly: "Miss Price
. . . shall I call you Miss Price or Mrs. Price?" "Mrs. Price," answered
the witness sullenly. She looked at her interrogator as though he were
a poisonous snake circling her chair.

For more than three hours Leibowitz put her through a grueling
cross-examination. First, he sought to discredit her testimony by
proving she was a known prostitute and thus unworthy of belief.
Second, by confusing her in cross-examination he hoped to convince
the jury that she was lying. Finally, he planned to reveal what had
really happened during the forty-eight hours preceding the alleged
assault.

It was easy enough to discredit Mrs. Price's claim to be a "southern
lady." In Huntsville, with the nickname of Big Leg Price, she was a
well-known streetwalker. Leibowitz introduced arrest and conviction
records showing she had been found guilty of "adultery and forni-
cation" on January 26, 1931, with a Huntsville married man, L. J.
"Jack" Tiller. But Mrs. Price proved unexpectedly difficult to entangle
in cross-examination. Using a model of the freight train, Leibowitz
tried to illustrate the sequence of events. Mrs. Price adamantly refused
to agree that the model looked like the train she had ridden. What
were the differences? asked Leibowitz. "That is not the train I was on,"
she snapped. "It was bigger, lots bigger, that is a toy." No amount of
cajoling from Leibowitz could force from her an admission that it
was a suitable replica.

During the trials in Scottsboro, Mrs. Price had been colorful
and inventive in her account of the assault. At Decatur she stuck
to a plain, unembroidered story, as lacking in specific details as possible.
She and Leibowitz often shouted back and forth at each other, but
whenever the attorney uncovered contradictions in her testimony, she
would retreat into vagueness: "I can't remember," or "I ain't sure,
that has been two years ago."

"When you got to the doctor's office, were you not crying in any
way?" Leibowitz asked. "I had just hushed crying, the best I remember
I was crying—I won't say, I ain't positive," Victoria said crossly. To
the attentive courtroom, Leibowitz recalled Mrs. Price's story in the
original trials: that she and Ruby had gone to Chattanooga looking
for work and on the night of March 24 had stayed at Mrs. Callie

Brochie's boardinghouse on Seventh Street. The next morning, both girls had testified, they fruitlessly searched for a job in the city's cotton mills before boarding the Huntsville-bound freight at 11 A.M.

Leibowitz pointed out that Mrs. Price had said Mrs. Brochie's house was three or four blocks from the train yards. Wouldn't you rather say it was two miles? asked Leibowitz. "No sir, I wouldn't say two miles," she replied. "Suppose I told you that Seventh Street in Chattanooga, the nearest point . . . to the railroad yards of the Southern Railroad is two miles and show you the map, would that refresh your recollection?" he asked sarcastically. "I don't know," retorted an equally sarcastic Victoria, "I haven't got a good enough education." When he challenged her entire account of the overnight stay in Chattanooga, she broke in, shouting, "That's some of Ruby Bates's dope," and added: "I do know one thing, those Negroes and this Haywood Patterson raped me." Leibowitz stood and stared at her for a moment. She was, he told her, "a little bit of an actress." "You're a pretty good actor yourself," she quickly replied.

After a few questions about her activities on the day before the alleged incident, the tone of Leibowitz's voice suddenly changed. Gravely, he asked Mrs. Price: "Do you know a man by the name of Lester Carter?" She thought he was one of the white boys thrown from the train, she replied. "Mrs. Price, I . . . want to ask you that question again and give you an opportunity to change your answer if you want to," said Leibowitz. "Did you know Lester Carter before that day, Yes or No?" By his intense expression, spectators in the courtroom knew the question was crucial; they leaned forward to hear her answer. Mrs. Price, losing her composure for the first time, mumbled: "Before in Scottsboro—he—was on the train." "I didn't ask you that," said Leibowitz. "Before this day on the train did you know Lester Carter?" "I never did know him," she said firmly.

He continued in the same low voice. Had she asked a companion of hers "to pose as your brother, since you didn't want the authorities to know you were travelling across the state line from Chattanooga . . . [with] somebody with you?" Mrs. Price looked to the table where Knight sat and then back at Leibowitz. "If I said that I must have been out of my mind." "Did you say it?" he asked firmly. Shouting, she clenched the arms of her chair. "If I said it I must have been out of my mind!"

Leibowitz questioned Mrs. Price about Jack Tiller, the married man with whom she had been convicted of adultery. "Did you have intercourse with Tiller a short time before you left Huntsville [for Chattanooga]?" She shook her head emphatically. "In the railroad yards?" he asked, still in the same quiet voice. "I have told you three times, and I am not telling you any more—no, sir, I didn't." Leibowitz returned to Carter. He asked her again if she had arranged with Carter, or "whatever man that was with you, [that] he wasn't supposed to know you on the train because you were afraid to cross the state line and [were afraid of] being locked up for the Mann Act?" She turned angrily to Judge Horton: "I haven't heard no such stuff," she shouted. "That is some of Ruby's dope he has got."

Relentlessly the chief defense attorney continued to probe. He asked Mrs. Price once more where she had spent the night before the alleged assault. Perhaps in a hobo jungle? he asked slyly. Victoria stared at him, her eyes filled with hatred. Columnist Mary Heaton Vorse, one of only two women in the courtroom, found it impossible to describe her "appalling hardness." Only two years before, reporters had described Mrs. Price as "pretty and vivacious." Now, with her hair tightly curled in a new permanent and her face heavily rouged, she seemed more than "tough," Miss Vorse wrote. She was "terrifying in her depravity." Through clenched teeth Mrs. Price repeated again the account of how she had stayed with Mrs. Brochie while she looked for work. Leibowitz asked her if she didn't want to change her story. She shook her head. "By the way, Mrs. Price," said Leibowitz with open disgust, "as a matter of fact, the name of Mrs. Callie [Brochie] you apply to this boardinghouse lady is the name of a boardinghouse lady used by Octavius Roy Cohn in the *Saturday Evening Post* stories—Sis Callie, isn't that where you got the name?" Knight jumped to his feet in protest and Judge Horton sustained his objection. Leibowitz, however, had dramatically made his point; he was pleased with the results of his cross-examination.

The prosecution, concerned about the damaging effects of Leibowitz's questions, re-examined Mrs. Price in order to impress upon the jurors the gravity of the charge. Without the "flutter of an eyelash and in a voice that carried to the furthest corner of the courtroom" (wrote one reporter), she related in the most specific Anglo-Saxon terms the sexual demands made upon her by the defendants. Leibowitz knew the only purpose of the re-examination was to inflame the emotions of the jurors. In a voice shaking with anger he sarcastically asked Mrs. Price: "You are not embarrassed before this huge crowd when you utter these words?" "We object," exclaimed Knight, while Mrs. Price looked at Leibowitz with such venom that one reporter thought she was going to strike him. Suspecting that Victoria's fear of the Mann Act had led her to accuse the Negroes, Leibowitz explained that he had only one more question. "I want to ask you if you have ever heard of any single white woman ever being locked up in jail when she is the complaining witness against Negroes in the history of the State of Alabama?" Without waiting for her answer or Knight's objection, Leibowitz angrily took his seat at the defense table.

The last witness for the state on Monday was Dr. R. R. Bridges, one of the doctors who had examined the girls shortly after the alleged rape. Bridges' testimony and that of his younger colleague, Dr. M. W. Lynch, had been crucial for the state's case at Scottsboro. Under cross-examination, however, Leibowitz brought out facts that made the doctor a stronger witness for the defense than for the state. Bridges admitted that less than two hours after the alleged rape both girls were completely composed and calm, with normal pulse and respiration rates, and no pupil dilation. Even though Mrs. Price claimed she had been brutally raped six times, the doctor testified that there was no vaginal bleeding and that he and Dr. Lynch had had great difficulty finding enough semen to make a smear slide. The semen they did find was completely nonmotile. Bridges readily admitted that this was unusual: spermatozoa normally live from twelve hours to two days in the vagina.

The following morning, Attorney General Knight explained to Judge Horton that the state did not intend to call Dr. Lynch, since his testimony would be repetitious. After Horton's consent, however, a bailiff whispered to the judge that the young doctor urgently wanted to speak to him—in private. The only room available in the crowded building was one of the courthouse restrooms, and there the two men talked. Lynch, visibly unnerved, went straight to the point. Contrary to Knight's explanation, said Lynch, his testimony would not be a repetition of Dr. Bridges', because Lynch did not believe the girls had been raped. From the very beginning, said the Scottsboro physician, he was convinced the girls were lying. Even Dr. Bridges had noted at the examination that the vaginal areas of the two women were "not even red." "My God, Doctor, is this whole thing a horrible mistake?" asked the stunned Horton. "Judge, I looked at both the women and told them they were lying, that they knew they had not been raped," replied the doctor, "and they just laughed at me." *

Horton sent for Knight and confronted him with Lynch's statement. Knight was adamant. It was only the opinion of one doctor, he insisted, and the state was committed to the prosecution of the nine boys.

Judge Horton, now doubting that any rape had occurred, faced a painful dilemma. He could force Dr. Lynch to take the stand or he could himself, by Alabama statute, end the trial. In either case, Lynch—because of his courageous act—would be ruined. In his mind, Horton went over the twelve jurors who sat on his left. He knew more than half of them personally and—in spite of their conventional southern attitude toward Negroes—he believed that the weight of the evidence presented by the defense would convince them of Patterson's innocence. With many misgivings, he decided to allow the trial to continue.

Before the state rested its case on Tuesday afternoon, Knight called to the stand five additional witnesses. Their testimony was inconclusive, and it became clear that the case would stand or fall on the testimony of Victoria Price.

In planning his defense, Leibowitz realized that normal legal assumptions could not be made at this trial. Usually a defense lawyer has only to prove that there is reasonable doubt of his client's guilt. In Decatur, Leibowitz knew he would have to prove beyond a reasonable doubt that Patterson was innocent.

His first witness was Dallas Ramsey, a Negro who lived near the

---

* This account, based upon recent interviews and correspondence with former Judge Horton—and carefully checked by him in manuscript form—has been emphatically denied by Dr. Lynch, who wrote to the author on October 16, 1967, that as "far as I can recall, no such statements were ever made to Judge James E. Horton or anyone else regarding the trial of Haywood Patterson versus Alabama. Of course, it has been 35 years and better since this incident happened; and as far as I can recall, I was never put on the stand as a witness in this case."

hobo jungle in Chattanooga. He testified he had seen and talked with two white girls and two white men on the evening of March 24 and the morning of March 25, 1931. Ramsey picked Mrs. Price from the courtroom as one of the women; from a photograph he identified Ruby Bates. The four had apparently stayed the night in the wooded vagrant's refuge near his home.

George W. Chamlee, a prominent white Chattanooga attorney, took the stand next. He told the jury he had made dozens of personal inquiries and examined city directories in an effort to locate Mrs. Price's "boardinghouse friend," Callie Brochie. He was convinced, he said, that Mrs. Brochie was a figment of Victoria's imagination. No woman by that name had lived in Chattanooga between 1930 and 1933.

Then Leibowitz took a calculated risk. One by one he put six of the Scottsboro boys on the stand. The jury, he knew, would surely discount their insistence that they were innocent; and, if they made an unfavorable impression, Patterson's conviction would be assured. But Leibowitz had to dispel the state's image of the youths as malevolent conspirators acting coldly and methodically to throw the white boys from the train and then rape the two defenseless white girls.

The first two boys who testified were tragic representatives of a society's deprivation and neglect. Homeless, unemployed, illiterate, they had wandered across the South since their early teens. Willie Roberson, short and stocky and with a wild shock of hair, sat quietly in the courtroom with a vacuous stare. Syphilitic since birth, he spoke with a severe speech impediment. At the time of his arrest, he was in great pain from open venereal sores, and walked with a cane. (Four years later a psychiatric examination disclosed a mental age of nine and an intelligence quotient of sixty-four.) Olen Montgomery was blind in his left eye; with his right he could see "good enough not to get hurt, that is all." Yet Victoria Price had identified them "positively" as two of the defendants who had run across the top of a moving boxcar, leaped into the gondola where she sat, fought a pitched battle with the white boys, and then brutally raped her. Montgomery and Roberson told the courtroom they had been riding back toward the rear of the train and had not even known of the disturbance until they were arrested at Paint Rock.

On the witness stand Ozie Powell, Eugene Williams, Andrew Wright, and Haywood Patterson readily admitted participating in the fight. Williams and Patterson, who were travelling with the two Wright brothers (Andy and his twelve-year-old brother, Leroy), explained that somewhere between Chattanooga and Stevenson several whites had begun throwing rocks at them and shouting, "Black son-of-a-bitches." Patterson said that he had rounded up the other Negroes who were hitching on the train to "have it out." Most of the white youths leaped from the gondola before actually being hit. After the fight, the victorious blacks scattered across the train. Unanimously the Scottsboro boys insisted they had not even seen, let alone molested, the two white girls. Patterson in particular, tall, black, and ostentatiously unservile, held his own during Knight's stormy questioning. When the Attorney General made some reference to Patterson's having been tried at Scottsboro, he was bluntly corrected. "I was framed at Scottsboro," declared the young Negro. Knight, flushed with anger demanded, "Who told you to say you were framed?" Patterson retorted: "I told myself to say it."

It is doubtful whether the testimony of the Scottsboro boys had any effect, one way or the other, on the deliberations of the jurors, for it was Leibowitz's scathing cross-examination of Mrs. Price that preoccupied Alabamians. Anyone "possessed of that old Southern chivalry," said the Sylacuga News, could not read of the "'brutal" harassment of Mrs. Price without "reaching for his gun while his blood boils to the nth degree." Within hours after Victoria stepped from the witness stand, reporters overheard angry threats on the streets of Decatur. On Wednesday, Judge Horton learned that a "mass indignation rally" had been held the night before in the local Masonic hall. Several of the two hundred men at the meeting bluntly demanded that the "New York Jew lawyers" be tarred, feathered, and ridden out of Decatur on a rail. For the Scottsboro boys, the prescription was summary justice from the nearest tree.

A grim-faced Judge Horton ordered the jury removed from the courtroom, and then, in a voice betraying deep emotion, he told the spectators that the guilt or innocence of Haywood Patterson and his fellows was for the jury alone to decide. He wanted to make it absolutely clear, he said, that the court intended to protect the prisoners and their attorneys. "I say this much, that the man who would engage in anything that would cause the death of any of these prisoners is a murderer; he is not only a murderer, but a cowardly murderer." For the first time in the trial Horton raised his voice. Anyone who attempted to takes the lives of the prisoners "may expect that his own life be forfeited," he sternly told the silent courtroom. "I believe I am as gentle as any man . . . I don't believe I would harm anyone wrongfully." But he added, emphasizing every word, that there would be no compromise with mob violence. "Now, gentlemen, I have spoken . . . harsh words, but every word I say is true and I hope we will have no more of any such conduct. Let the jury return."

Horton's stern warning ended the open threats of violence. But according to reporters, it also seemed to intensify the community's bitter hostility.

Now under round-the-clock protection by National Guardsmen, Leibowitz continued doggedly to hammer away at the state's case. To intensify the impact for the defense of Dr. Bridges' testimony, he called to the stand Edward A. Reisman, a Chattanooga gynecologist who had spent all his life in Alabama and Tennessee. After reviewing all the medical evidence, Dr. Reisman declared that in his professional opinion it was "inconceivable" that Mrs. Price had been raped six times, as she claimed. But the spectators completely distrusted Dr. Reisman. As one Decatur resident told the New York Times reporter, "When a nigger has expert witnesses, we have a right to ask who is paying for them." On Thursday morning Liebowitz presented his most damaging witness. Lester Carter, a twenty-three-year-old hobo, had been on the train when the fight began; it was his name that had so startled Mrs. Price during Leibowitz's cross-examination. Now, wearing a new gabardine suit and a brightly flowered tie, Carter added graphic details to the story Leibowitz had previously sketched. In January of 1931, Carter testified, a Huntsville police court had convicted him of vagrancy and sentenced him to sixty days in the county workhouse. There he met Victoria Price and her boyfriend, Jack Tiller, who were serving time for adultery. When the three were released in March, Tiller invited Carter to stay around Huntsville for a few days. The hospitable Mrs. Price even offered to arrange a date for Carter with her best girl friend, Ruby Bates. On the night of March 23, approximately forty hours before the alleged rape, Tiller and Carter met the two girls outside the gates of a local mill. Talking and giggling, they walked to the Huntsville hobo jungles.

"What occurred in the jungles that night?" asked Leibowitz. "I hung my hat on a little limb and went to having intercourse with the girl [Ruby]," replied Carter. Less than three feet away, Tiller and Victoria also were "having intercourse." When a light rain began to fall, the four got up from the honeysuckle bushes where they had been lying and crawled into an empty boxcar pulled onto a sidetrack. During the night, in the intervals between love-making, they "talked and started planning this hobo trip," he said. The girls complained that they were sick of Huntsville; perhaps they could go to Chattanooga and "hustle" while the two men got temporary jobs. Tiller explained that he did not want to risk another adultery conviction, but he promised vaguely to meet the other three in Chattanooga if they did not return in a few days. Just before daybreak, the girls went home and collected a change of clothes. They agreed to meet Carter in the freight yards that afternoon.

On the way to Chattanooga, Carter explained, he pretended he did not know the girls; they rejoined each other only after leaving the train. Just beyond the railroad yards, they met Orville Gilley, a slender, self-styled "hobo poet." After Gilley introduced himself, they walked together to Chattanooga's hobo jungle, built a small fire, and shared a meager meal of chili and coffee. During the night, Carter told the court, he once again had sexual relations with Ruby Bates. He could not say for certain about Victoria and their new friend.

The next morning, the four decided they had seen enough of Chattanooga. Tired and hungry, they boarded the 11 A.M. freight for Huntsville. Five white hobos sat in the next car toward the caboose. Just south of Stevenson, Alabama, Carter said, he heard several shouts above the noise of the train. He investigated and saw white and Negro boys fighting in the adjoining car. By the time he and Gilley could get there, however, most of the white youths had jumped or been shoved from the train. Without striking a single blow, Carter "climbed down where the couplings are" and got off. Gilley remained behind. In Scottsboro several hours later, Gilley denied there had been any rape, said Carter.

Although Carter testified persuasively and was unshakable in cross-examination, the jury and spectators listened with open skepticism. His eagerness to testify, his frequent nervous gestures, and his immaculate appearance, one observer said, gave the impression that the defense had "carefully schooled" him. Carter's most damaging mannerism was his insistence on saying "Negro," instead of the typical white southern pronunciation, "Nigra." In cross-examination, Morgan County Solicitor Wade Wright, who was assisting Knight, drew from Carter an admission that the defense had paid his room and board for almost a month and had even bought him the "fancy" new eleven-dollar suit he was wearing.

Shortly after noon on Thursday, the defense rested "with reservations," but Leibowitz had scarcely taken his seat when a messenger brought a note to his table. Walking over to the bench, Leibowitz whispered to Judge Horton, who then announced a brief recess. The courtroom remained quiet but visibly excited. Ten minutes later, National Guardsmen opened the back doors of the room. A heavy-set perspiring woman in her forties came down the aisle; Ruby Bates walked behind, her eyes fixed on the floor. The spectators leaned forward with an audible gasp; at the prosecution table there was open consternation. Miss Bates's chaperone, a social worker from the Church of the Advent in Birmingham, explained that the church rector had asked her to bring the young woman to Decatur. The chaperone knew nothing about the case.

Ruby was dressed in a smart gray coat with matching cloche. In 1931 an investigator for the American Civil Liberties Union had described her as a "large, fresh, good-looking girl" with soft "calflike" eyes. But the freshness now was gone. Unlike the spirited Victoria, Ruby seldom raised her eyes from the floor as she mumbled her testimony. Leibowitz asked few questions in his direct examination. On the night of March 23, 1931, "did you have intercourse with Lester Carter . . . ?" "I certainly did," Ruby replied softly. "Did Victoria Price have intercourse with Jack Tiller . . . in your presence?" he asked. "She certainly did," said Ruby. Judge Horton, who had been sitting behind the bench throughout the trial, got up and moved down to a seat in front of the spectators facing Miss Bates.

Did any rape take place on the Chattanooga-to-Huntsville freight train? continued Leibowitz. Not that she knew of, Ruby replied, and she had been with Victoria Price for the entire trip. While the jury and spectators strained to hear her low voice, she explained why she had decided to testify for the defense. Five weeks before, she said, she had left Huntsville with a boyfriend to avoid any involvement in the new Decatur trials. First she had gone to Montgomery; from there she hitched a ride to New York, where she had worked for a "Jewish lady" for several weeks. But her conscience bothered her, and after reading about a famous New York minister, Dr. Harry Emerson Fosdick ("Dr. Fostick," she called him), she visited him in his study one evening late in March. He arranged for her to go to the Birmingham Church of the Advent and from there to Decatur. Leibowitz completed his questioning in less than fifteen minutes.

For a moment, the Attorney General stared silently at Ruby, who sat with her eyes downcast. "Where did you get that coat?" he finally asked. She hesitated for a moment, and then whispered, "I bought it." "Who gave you the money to buy it?" Knight asked. "Well, I don't know," she replied evasively, her eyes still fixed on the floor. "You don't know?" Knight repeated sarcastically. "Where did you get that hat? Who was the beneficent donor?" There was a long pause as Ruby sat biting nervously at her lower lip. From his seat inside the spectators' rail, Judge Horton leaned forward and gently asked her, "Do you know?" Almost inaudibly she murmured, "Dr. Fostick of New York."

Whenever Knight questioned her about her testimony at Scottsboro, she repeated over and over: "I told it just like Victoria Price told it," or "I said it, but Victoria told me to." The majority of the Attorney General's questions were not, however, about her earlier allegations at Scottsboro. He seemed more intent on proving to the jury that Ruby had been bribed by the defense. Knight suspected that her conscience had been given an assist by representatives of the International Labor Defense. Firing his questions rapidly at the subdued witness, he asked her about her finances. How much money was she making when she left Huntsville? How had she paid for the trip from Montgomery to New York? Who gave her funds for the trip back to Alabama? Although she talked vaguely of loans from her employer in New York, her obvious lack of candor brought smirks and open laughter from the packed courtroom. The Attorney General also drew from Ruby an admission that she was suffering from syphilis and gonorrhea in May of 1931 and had told a Huntsville doctor who treated her that she had contracted it from Negroes who had raped her.

The main testimony in the trial ended when Ruby Bates meekly stepped from the witness stand late Thursday afternoon. Her story caused "an immediate and bitter reaction among the residents of . . . [Morgan] and neighboring counties," said the *New York Times* correspondent. Citizens of the area were convinced she had "sold out" to the defense. Although Attorney General Knight expressed confidence that the "mob spirit" would exhaust itself in harmless talk, reporters noticed that Miss Bates was hustled away from the courtroom and taken to a secret hiding place by a detachment of National Guardsmen. Knight also strengthened the National Guard unit guarding Leibowitz and Brodsky.

On the following afternoon County Solicitor Wright began the state's summation. Renowned among local all-day singers, Wright bellowed his remarks in the singsong chant of a sawdust-trail evangelist. At first he rambled on about the "fancy New York clothes" of the defense's chief witnesses, Lester Carter and Ruby Bates. But soon he was ringing the changes on all the fears and hatreds that had been aroused in the two weeks of the trial. In summarizing the testimony of Carter, he said with mincing sarcasm: "What does Mr. Carter tell you, maybe it is Carterinsky now! If he had a-been with Brodsky another two weeks he would have been down here with a pack on his back a-trying to sell you goods. Are you going to countenance that sort of thing?" From a front-row seat, an excited spectator exclaimed "No!" with the fervor of an "Amen" in church.

As Wright's anti-Semitic tirade poured out, Leibowitz sat at the defense table with a look of stunned disbelief. Attorney General Knight stared fixedly at the floor, his face flushed with embarrassment. The faces of several jurors betrayed their excitement. Horton sharply reprimanded the solicitor, but Wright went tumbling on, almost lost in his own rhetorical fervor. He turned and pointed a finger at the counsel table where Leibowitz and Brodsky sat. "Show them," he paused for effect, "show them that Alabama justice cannot be bought and sold with Jew money from New York." Leibowitz leaped to his feet, slamming his hand on the defense table. "I move for a mistrial," he said. "I submit a conviction in this case won't be worth a pinch of snuff in view of what this man just said." Horton scolded Wright for his "improper statements" but refused to end the trial.

Leibowitz, facing the unenviable task of restoring calm to the feverish courtroom, began his closing remarks late in the afternoon. "Let us assume the prosecution is prejudiced," he began. "Let us assume the defense is also prejudiced. Let us assume both sides are trying to prove their points." He looked squarely into the face of each juror. "It is the sworn duty of each of you," he told them, to convict only upon "hard evidence," not emotion. He summarized the four days of testimony and emphasized what several state officials were admitting privately: that the prosecution's case rested solely on the testimony of Victoria Price. And her story, he said, was the "foul, contemptible, outrageous lie . . . [of] an abandoned, brazen woman."

The defense attorney continued his summation the next morning. By ten o'clock his voice had begun to crack with fatigue. Several times he took a few sips of water, pausing as if to gather his strength. He recalled Wade Wright's tirade, referring to it as a "hangman's speech." "What is it but an appeal to prejudice, to sectionalism, to bigotry?" Wright, he maintained, was simply saying: "Come on, boys! We can lick this Jew from New York!" The jury's verdict, he concluded, would show whether Alabamians would give even this "poor scrap of colored humanity" a "fair, square deal."

When the weary Leibowitz took his seat, Attorney General Knight began the final arguments for the state. In an obvious reference to Wright's tirade, he shouted: "I do not want a verdict based on racial prejudice or a religious creed. I want a verdict on the merits of this case." Knight exhorted the jurors to stand up for Alabama; he expressed his confidence that they were not "cowards." Referring scornfully to the almost forgotten Patterson as "that thing," he told the jury in a tone of unveiled contempt: "If you acquit this Negro, put a garland of roses around his neck, give him a supper, and send him to New York City." There, he said, "Dr. Harry Fosdick [will] dress him up in a high hat and morning coat, gray-striped trousers, and spats." Only one verdict was possible: death in the electric chair.

Horton delivered his charge to the jury before noon. He began with a pointed reference to the state's star witness, Victoria Price. The law was designed to protect all classes of people, he said, but the law also had a "stern duty to perform when women of the underworld come before it." It was the obligation of the jury, in evaluating Mrs. Price's testimony, to weigh her background of promiscuity and prostitution. In an effort to calm the emotionally charged courtroom, the judge concluded with a plea for the jury to put aside extraneous matters. "We are not trying lawyers," he said. "We are not trying state lines. We are not trying whether the defendant is black or white." The only duty of the jury was to ascertain whether there was a reasonable doubt about the guilt of Haywood Patterson. If there was a reasonable doubt, he emphasized, then they should return a verdict of not guilty. Horton, visibly exhausted from the wearing two-week trial, gave the case to the jury just before one o'clock.

The courtroom was soon empty except for lawyers and newspapermen. Patterson and the other Scottsboro boys sat in their cells and played cards or sang gospel songs to pass the time. When the jury still had not reached a decision at 11:30 P.M., Horton ordered them locked up for the night, and told them to resume their deliberations the following morning, Sunday, at 8:30 A.M.

They reached a verdict at 10 A.M. Leibowitz and Brodsky hurried over to the courthouse. There they found Patterson—guarded by two militiamen—sprawled in a chair and smoking a cigarette. Across the room, Knight sat at the prosecution table, the muscles of his face twitching nervously. When Judge Horton arrived at 11 A.M., he called for the jury; the court stenographer opened his notebook to take down the last words of the trial. As the jurors filed in they were still laughing from a joke; they become solemn when they saw the tense courtroom.

"Have you agreed upon a verdict?" Horton asked the foreman. He replied, "We have, your honor," and handed a heavily creased slip of paper to the bailiff, who laid it on the judge's bench. Horton unfolded the slip of paper and read the large pencilled letters: "We find the defendant guilty as charged and fix the punishment at death in the electric chair." There was not a sound in the courtroom as spectators craned to see the defense table. That night a shaking Haywood Patterson would clutch a prison Bible in fear, but he had decided beforehand he would never show his inner terror to the gawking white spectators. His face did not change expression. Leibowitz looked as though he had been struck; he leaned back slackly in his chair.

After the jury had been dismissed and a postponement of further trials announced, Leibowitz walked to the bench and grasped Horton's hand. The judge warmly returned the handshake. "I am taking back to New York with me a picture of one of the finest jurists I have ever met," said Leibowitz, his voice shaking with emotion. "I am sorry I cannot say as much for the jury which has decided this case against the evidence."

Later, reporters learned from several jurors that they had not even discussed, much less considered, the testimony of Ruby Bates. The twelve men had taken their first ballot five minutes after the judge gave them the case. The vote was: guilty 12, not guilty 0. The rest of their deliberation time had been taken up with the question of the sentence. Eleven jurors had voted immediately to send Patterson to the electric chair. One, the foreman, had held out until Sunday morning for life imprisonment.

•

On June 22, 1933, ignoring a warning that he was jeopardizing his own chances for re-election, Judge Horton granted a defense motion and overturned Haywood Patterson's conviction. In a devastating indictment of the state's case, he concluded that Victoria Price's testimony was not only uncorroborated, but also improbable and contradicted by evidence which "greatly preponderates in favor of the defendant." To reporters, Horton implied he would also reverse any future convictions based upon her testimony.

Defense attorneys hoped that Horton's meticulous and persuasively written decision would cause a shift in public opinion in the state. It did not. At the instigation of Attorney General Knight, Horton was removed from the case and another jurist more amenable to the state's position was appointed. (The warning to Judge Horton was not just a threat: in the 1934 Democratic primary he lost his seat on the bench, despite a vigorous campaign. That same year, Attorney General Knight was elected lieutenant governor.) When Patterson and Clarence Norris, another of the Scottsboro boys, were tried again in December of 1933, both received the death sentence. In 1934, the United States Supreme Court accepted the defense contention that Negroes were systematically excluded from Alabama's juries and gave Patterson and Norris another trial. But in 1936, Patterson was convicted for the fourth time and received a sentence of seventy-five years.

The following year, the state began prosecution of the remaining eight defendants, and in rapid succession juries convicted Clarence Norris, Charley Weems, Andrew Wright, and Ozie Powell. But Lieutenant Governor Knight was dead by this time, and the state was in a mood to compromise. Instead of death, the assistant attorney general had asked only for life imprisonment. In the midst of the trials, it was suddenly announced that the state would dismiss the charges against the remaining four defendants. Although Willie Roberson and Olen Montgomery had already spent six years in jail, it was admitted that they were "unquestionably innocent." Since Leroy Wright and Eugene Williams had been only twelve and thirteen years of age in 1931, "the State thinks that the ends of justice would be met . . . by releasing these two juveniles on condition that they leave the State never to return." On this grotesque note, the public story of Scottsboro came to an end.

Of the five who remained in jail, Patterson successfully escaped to Detroit years later, and eventually died of cancer in a Michigan jail. The other four were finally paroled. Andrew Wright, the last of the parolees, left prison nineteen years after he had been taken from the freight train in Paint Rock.

In 1939, Victoria Price offered to recant—for a substantial fee. No one cared to pay it. She and Ruby Bates both died in the same year, 1961, in towns thirty miles apart.

Franklin D. Roosevelt: A Profile

WILLIAM E. LEUCHTENBURG

> . . . I never saw him—
> But I *knew* him. Can you have forgotten
> How, with his voice, he came into our house,
> The President of the United States,
> Calling us friends. . . .

• Through his fireside chats over the radio, Franklin Delano Roosevelt became a father-image to millions of Americans. His warm smile, his oratorical artistry, and his magnetic personality contrasted markedly with the grave, serious, and prudent manner of Herbert Hoover. President Roosevelt injected fresh hope into the sagging American spirit in the Great Depression. His programs to help the people—WPA, CCC, AAA, the Social Security Act—provided jobs and a measure of pride to people who had neither. But the New Deal has also been dubbed a "pill to cure an earthquake." Roosevelt's limited understanding of economics, his commitment to a relatively laissez-faire capitalism, and his traditional approach to politics have been mentioned as shortcomings of his administration. The New Deal extended the boss principle of paternal government to the national level and thereby revitalized a nation afflicted by economic disaster, but it did not serve as a permanent cure-all for the ills of American society.

Franklin D. Roosevelt has been judged as both idealist and Machiavellian, and the many facets of his character and his administration have engaged historians for more than thirty years. In the following essay, Professor William E. Leuchtenburg of Columbia University summarizes the views of some of those who have analyzed the President during

From *Franklin D. Roosevelt: A Profile*, edited by William E. Leuchtenburg. Copyright © 1967 by William E. Leuchtenburg. Reprinted by permission of Hill & Wang, Inc.

his twelve-year occupancy of the White House. Whatever
their interpretation almost all of the commentators recognize that Franklin D. Roosevelt towered among contemporaries in the United States and the world during the long
years of depression and world war.

Of the making of controversies about Franklin Delano Roosevelt there
is no end. In his lifetime, he was literally worshiped by many Americans. One Congressman compared him to Jesus Christ and in a poll
of New York schoolchildren God ran him a poor second. Yet he was
just as strongly detested by others who, as one historian has noted, depicted him "as a liar, a thief, a madman, a syphilitic, and a communist." Since his death, scholars have kept the coals of disputation live.
Some, like Basil Rauch, have contended that the "study of Roosevelt's
words and of all his actions will confirm the instinct of the younger
generation that another hero-President has lately been added to the
company of George Washington, Thomas Jefferson, Andrew Jackson,
Abraham Lincoln, Theodore Roosevelt, and Woodrow Wilson."
Others, like Edgar Eugene Robinson, have asserted that Roosevelt's
reign resulted "in a weakened Constitutional system, in imperiled national security, in diminished national morale, in deteriorated political
morality, and in an overburdened economy."

Roosevelt's admirers argue that he was a creative leader not only of
the United States but of the Western world at a time when democracy
was in peril. They point out that he inspirited the nation in the dark
weeks of March, 1933, and that by the end of the Hundred Days the
country had regained much of its self-confidence. Roosevelt, they note,
inspired faith in man's ability to master events instead of being victimized by them; he saw the world as an unfinished universe in which men
must act to shape their destiny. At the same time, he offered fatherly
reassurance of his own capacity to make the world more secure. He
combined courage in the face of hardship with openness to ideas, he
raised public issues that had long been submerged, and he showed
skeptics that government could be efficient and still democratic. Elected

for an unprecedented four terms, he led the country through the Great Depression, expanded the responsibility of the national government, took giant strides toward the achievement of social justice, guided the country through a victorious war against the Fascist powers, and laid the groundwork for America's entrance into the United Nations.

Roosevelt's critics, however, raise doubts as to whether he was truly a history-making man. They argue that nothing fundamental was altered in the Age of Roosevelt, that the United States at the end of the era remained pretty much what it had been in the beginning, a capitalist nation that rewarded the acquisitive instinct and tolerated a wide range of social injustice. Moreover, they assert that whatever changes did occur were the result less of Roosevelt than of impersonal forces that the President only dimly understood. His conservative campaign in 1932 has been cited to show that he did not intend to be a change maker, and the contradictory character of New Deal measures has been adduced as evidence that Roosevelt lacked a clear sense of direction.

Writers have differed too about whether Roosevelt was a conservative or a liberal. Although most perceive him as a reformer, some view him as an enlightened Tory who preserved capitalism and who never revealed more than "a-basket-for-the-poor-family-down-the-lane approach to social problems." Radicals have complained that he missed an opportunity to nationalize the banks, that he failed to discipline the nation in collectivism, and that he gave indifferent support to the planners like Rexford Tugwell. They see him, at best, as a broker who mediated among interests and who moved only as far as the pressures exerted on him required. They note that groups like the sharecroppers who could not articulate their demands got short shrift in the broker state, and that Roosevelt agreed to measures like insurance of bank deposits and the Wagner Act only because Congress compelled him to do so.

Yet others are convinced that F.D.R. was the paladin of social reform. "He takes his place," writes Henry Steele Commager, "in the great tradition of American liberalism, along with Jefferson, Jackson, Lincoln, Theodore Roosevelt and Wilson." Roosevelt, it has been pointed out, often showed his concern for unrepresented groups, as in his sponsorship of the Federal Arts Project, and frequently drove liberal legislation through a hostile Congress, as in his persistent fight for the death sentence on holding companies. Richard Rovere has written:

> He led us, I think, magnificently. In the early years, to be sure, he was called upon merely to lead us back to where we had been —to keep the ship of state afloat and head it back to its moorings in the snug harbor of 1929. But that is almost always the way statesmen prove themselves. What more did Lincoln do? No more—and yet, in the doing, a great deal more. For the Union restored was not the status quo ante bellum but something very different. And while there was vastly less misery and danger in the late thirties than in the early thirties, the late thirties were very different from the late twenties. It has taken daring and imagination and high intelligence to hold this society together, and the exercise of these virtues proved in itself creative.

Some writers, indeed, have protested not that the New Deal was too conservative but that Roosevelt was a radical who overturned venerated American institutions and even fostered a Communist conspiracy. When in the 1950's Senator Joseph McCarthy asserted that the recognition of Soviet Russia in 1933 had ushered in "twenty years of treason," he was voicing a common suspicion. "Roosevelt's leadership," Edgar Eugene Robinson has written, "was the façade behind which a less understanding but profoundly convinced revolutionary leadership was provided in Congress, in administrative departments, in the press, on the radio, and in the colleges and schools." Yet many writers have observed that if Roosevelt had the squire's contempt for business, he also had the squire's sense of tradition and his conservative instinct to safeguard property rights. Like Lord Grey, who was also damned as a traitor to his class, F.D.R. sought to avert serious class conflict by timely concessions. As a consequence of New Deal measures, it has been argued, capitalism was resuscitated and the Socialist movement all but destroyed. "What cut the ground out pretty completely from under us," observerd the Socialist leader, Norman Thomas, "was Roosevelt in a word. You don't need anything more."

Roosevelt has often been portrayed as the founder of the Welfare State in America. Sir Isaiah Berlin has even written that he was "the greatest leader of democracy, the greatest champion of social progress, in the twentieth century." For the first time, it has been said, the

United States government recognized that men have inherent social rights and that the government must be responsible for guaranteeing at least a minimal livelihood. Yet F.D.R.'s critics have asserted that the Social Security Act was an appallingly limited piece of legislation which compared unfavorably with that adopted in European countries decades before. Moreover, they deny that the United States has achieved even today the rudiments of a Welfare State.

Political scientists and historians have quarreled about Roosevelt's performance as a party builder. F.D.R.'s champions contend that he put together a new coalition that ended a period of Republican supremacy that dated back to the Civil War and inaugurated a new era of Democratic preponderance. They point out that F.D.R. was the only victorious Democratic Presidential candidate in a century to win more than 50 per cent of the vote. They credit the "Roosevelt coalition" with a successful appeal to the masses in the great cities, and note in particular that in the 1930's the Negro broke his historic tie to the Republican party. Other writers dispute these claims. They state that the real builder of the metropolitan coalition was not Roosevelt but Al Smith. Analysts like James MacGregor Burns argue that the President missed an exceptional opportunity to reshape the party by failing to encourage progressive dissidents in states like Wisconsin. Furthermore, Roosevelt, it has been said, was too concerned with advancing his own political interests. As a consequence, at his death, the Democratic party was left divided and leaderless and the prey of entrenched Southern oligarchs and Northern machine bosses.

An even livelier controversy has centered on Roosevelt's economic policies. Critics have pointed out that recovery in the United States was tardier than in almost any other major country. They note that as late as 1939 ten million Americans were still jobless and they argue that only war pulled the nation out of the Depression. They contend that Roosevelt moved in the wrong direction by adopting restrictionist economics in the National Recovery Administration (N.R.A.) and the Agricultural Adjustment Administration (A.A.A.) and by embarking on the gold-buying fiasco. Conservatives claim that government meddling impaired business confidence and thus slowed recovery, while Keynesians lament the fact that Roosevelt proved unwilling to embrace massive deficit spending. On the other hand, F.D.R.'s partisans allege that he inherited from his predecessor an economy so badly impaired that it would inevitably take some years before recovery could be achieved. They insist that significant gains were made under F.D.R., and some believe that prosperity would have been restored even if war had not come. Roosevelt's willingness to break taboos about budget balancing has seemed more remarkable than his reluctance to subscribe to Keynes's unorthodoxy. Most important, it has been said, the New Deal provided a series of underpinnings for the economy that make another depression unlikely.

Almost all commentators have agreed that F.D.R.'s approach was untheoretical, but they have differed about whether this was a virtue or a defect. Roosevelt's critics have emphasized that he was untutored, especially about economics, and that his intellectual interests were superficial. They deplore his preference for puttering with ship models and stamp collections to reading and reflection. It was Roosevelt himself, they note, who said that he was "the least introspective man in the world." They recall his reply when his wife asked him whether their children should go to church: "I really never thought about it. It is just as well not to think about things like that too much." His shallowness and lack of learning, it has been asserted, meant that, as President, he was required to live beyond his intellectual means and that he was reduced in policy making to "catch-penny opportunism."

Those who have been impressed by Roosevelt's record, however, deny that he was ill-informed. Daniel R. Fusfeld has claimed that Roosevelt got a good grounding in economics at Harvard, and had demonstrated his competence in economic matters long before he entered the White House. Others have been astonished by F.D.R.'s grasp of detail in a wide spectrum of subjects. The publisher J. David Stern recalled an occasion when the President recited the average price of ten commodities in 1933 and ten years before and was correct on 90 per cent of them. In June, 1940, *Time* reported:

> For three weeks he had discussed battlefield contours in military detail with U.S. experts; again and again they have whistled respectfully at his apparent knowledge of Flanders—hills, creeks, towns, bridges. The President's particular forte is islands; he is said to know every one in the world, its peoples, habits, population, geography, economic life. When a ship sank off Scotland

several months ago, experts argued: Had the ship hit a rock or
had it been torpedoed? The President pondered latitude and
longitude, said: "It hit a rock. They ought to have seen that
rock." Naval Aide Daniel J. Callaghan recalled the rock, disagreed. "At high tide, Mr. President, that rock is submerged."
No such thing, said the President, even at high tide that rock is
20 feet out of the water.

Roosevelt's sympathizers claim that his "untheoretical" methods
made possible a "pragmatic" approach that liberated government from
the prison of orthodoxy. Uncommitted to dogma, Roosevelt was free
to break traditions and to encourage experimentation. Disrespectful
of the classic taboos, he showed a hospitality to new ideas that made
the 1930's such a remarkable decade. Yet, they add, for all the improvisation and innovation, New Deal thought was more coherent than has
often been recognized, for his administration, as Roosevelt said, had
"a consistency and continuity of broad purpose."

Historians have also disagreed about whether Roosevelt should be
hailed as a master of the art of compromise or faulted as a vacillator.
Roosevelt, it has been said, alertly recognized the necessity of heeding
the demands of a great many divergent interests and working out arrangements that would reconcile them. His critics, however, see F.D.R.
as too often the fox rather than the lion, too unwilling to impose the
national interest on parochial groups, too much a temporizer rather
than a leader. Such disapprobation has been voiced both by radicals,
who believe the President should have scourged businessmen, and conservatives, who castigate him as a demagogue who truckled to labor.

Judgments about whether Roosevelt was a dynamic leader or a time-
server have frequently hinged on a writer's assessment of the President's character. Some have seen him as a deeply moral man, as a
Christian and a Democrat motivated by idealism and a sense of social
responsibility. Others have viewed him as a Catiline willing to cater to
any demand that would serve his lust for power. H. L. Mencken said
of F.D.R.: "If he became convinced tomorrow that coming out for
cannibalism would get him the votes he so sorely needs, he would begin
fattening a missionary in the White House backyard come Wednesday." To some, Roosevelt's buoyant optimism has seemed admirable;
others have deplored it as "Eagle Scout" superficiality and as the in-
souciance of a man unaware of his own limitations. Not a few of his

admirers would concede that Roosevelt had been a rather superficial, supercilious man in his youth but claim that he underwent a "spiritual transformation" after he was crippled by poliomyelitis; he emerged, in Will Durant's words, "softened and cleansed and illumined with pain." Other writers, however, deny that his paralysis resulted in an emotional *crise*.

Both those who esteem Roosevelt and those who abhor him have found it difficult to penetrate his reserve. Roosevelt rarely revealed himself even to intimates. Not even to his minister would he speak of sorrows or disappointments. He seldom confided even in his own family. "You are a wonderful person but you are one of the most difficult men to work with that I have ever known," Harold Ickes told the President bluntly one day. "Because I get too hard at times?" Roosevelt parried. "No, you never get too hard but you won't talk frankly even with people who are loyal to you and of whose loyalty you are fully convinced. You keep your cards close up against your belly." After years of study, many historians have remained puzzled about what kind of man was hidden behind Roosevelt's mask of amiable gregariousness.

Questions about Roosevelt's character have also influenced the whole current of discussion about the President's foreign policy. Collective-security advocates have stigmatized F.D.R. as weak-willed while nationalists have execrated him as deceitful. Internationalists have charged that Roosevelt bowed to the isolationists in scuttling the London Economic Conference, agreeing to neutrality legislation, blocking aid to Loyalist Spain, and delaying too long in intervening in World War II. On the other hand, isolationists have arraigned Roosevelt as a big-navy man who seized on every opportunity to meddle in foreign affairs and who ultimately led the United States into a needless war to cover up his domestic failures. His supporters, however, respond that the President sought both to preserve peace and to mount resistance to fascist expansion and that war came only when these two goals proved irreconcilable. Once again, disputes over Roosevelt's character are significant. Isolationist critics claim that by deceptive statements such as his "again-and-again-and-again" speech in the 1940 campaign and his misrepresentation of the Battle of the Atlantic Roosevelt attempted to lead the country into war with Germany and that when this failed, he provoked the Japanese assault at Pearl Harbor even though it required sacrificing the men and ships at the base. In meeting these charges,

Roosevelt's supporters are sometimes divided; some argue that the President's conduct was straightforward while others state that Roosevelt did good by stealth, that only by a degree of misrepresentation could he have led a nation deceived by the isolationists into a necessary war against the Axis. All of them agree, however, that the allegations about Pearl Harbor are bizarre.

World War II hatched a new flock of controversies about Roosevelt. Rexford Tugwell has written that in war he was "a very different kind of Roosevelt." Some writers have credited the President with many of the achievements of the war years: the victory over the Axis, the unanticipated social gains, the creation of the United Nations. Others have contended that America's war aims were compromised by the means employed: the internment of Japanese-Americans and the deals with collaborationists in North Africa and Italy. Above all, historians have quarreled about the diplomacy of the war. They have disagreed about whether Roosevelt was a skillful statesman who succeeded, where Wilson had failed, in leading the United States into an international association of nations, or was a blunderer who threw away the sacrifices of the war at Yalta and other conference tables.

Finally, writers have differed about the legacy Roosevelt left. A new generation of radicals, distrustful of centralized power, looks back at the New Deal achievements with suspicion. A new generation of conservatives rehearses the old arguments against the New Deal and claims that the attempts to create a Welfare State has produced a Poorhouse State with a permanent class of reliefers. To these arguments, Roosevelt's admirers make two replies. One is that he reigned at a time of perpetual crisis, that if he could only see six months ahead, he almost always had a six-month answer ready. The other is that Roosevelt was, in John M. Blum's words, "the most daring democrat of his time." He made the American government more responsive to the needs of the people than had any other man who had ever held the office of President.

Less than two years after the President's death, Hamilton Basso wrote: "When the historian of the future gets around to evaluating the character and influence of Franklin Delano Roosevelt, he is going to have a man-sized job on his hands." The student who wishes to develop his own interpretation of Roosevelt faces no easy task. He will quite probably find that just at the point when he feels reasonably certain that he knows how to assess Roosevelt he will come upon a new insight that will jar his conviction of certitude. Yet there are rewards, too, in the attempt to decide F.D.R's place in history, for few men have so dominated their times as he did. To come to terms with the significance of the protagonist of the Age of Roosevelt is to move a long way toward comprehending the meaning of both domestic and foreign affairs in the twentieth century.

Half Slave, Half Free

UNEMPLOYMENT, THE DEPRESSION,
AND AMERICAN YOUNG PEOPLE

GEORGE R. LEIGHTON AND RICHARD HELLMAN

• It was 1928 and there were optimistic visions of the banishment of poverty in America—"a chicken in every pot and two cars in every garage." And then it was 1929. The stock market collapsed and depression descended. Investors lost their savings, businesses went bankrupt, and five thousand banks failed within three years. Factories curtailed production; unemployment reached 13,000,000. Those who did have jobs labored for starvation wages; saw-mill hands worked for five cents an hour.

Farmers were hit hard as mortgages were foreclosed, and prices of farm commodities were driven down. There existed a tragic ambivalence of appalling overproduction and staggering underconsumption. Buzzards fed on livestock while men and women scoured garbage cans and refuse piles for meat. Fruit rotted in orchards and grain choked granaries as children ate weeds. A woman wandering in Arkansas hugged a chicken she had found dead in the road and observed with grim humor, "They promised me a chicken in the pot and now I got mine."

By 1932 millions of hungry, footsore hitchhikers roamed the countryside. Many migrants hopped freight cars by day, and their campfires dotted the railway embankments by night. In the cities "Hoovervilles" were erected, where families huddled together in shacks constructed of orange crates and rusted-out car bodies. Watery soup and bland mush were the reward of those willing to wait long enough in the relief lines. Fathers without jobs became demoralized, without pride, and families broke down. Perhaps no one actually starved to death from lack of food, but it cannot be denied that throughout the country deep physical and psychic scars were inflicted.

What must it have been like for college-trained men and women to look forward to years of perhaps unemployment or underemployment after graduation? In the following article, written in the mid-1930's, George R. Leighton and Richard Hellman describe the sense of frustration and desperation that the "lost generation" experienced during the New Deal era. Do you think that the campus youth of the 'thirties had more to object to than today's dissenting young people?

When a resolution offered in the United States Senate paraphrases Gertrude Stein, that is news. Some fifteen years ago, in talking about the spiritual casualties of the War, Miss Stein said to Ernest Hemingway: "You are all a lost generation." On January 30th last Senator Walsh of Massachusetts presented a resolution to the Senate which began:

> Whereas one of the most tragic results of the depression is the effect it has had upon the lives of young men and women emerging from our educational institutions; and
> Whereas there are several million young people between the ages of eighteen and thirty who have graduated from grammar schools, high schools, preparatory schools, trade and normal schools, domestic-science schools, art schools, music conservatories, colleges, universities, and professional schools who have in large numbers entered into a work-world where no opportunities have been open to them to obtain a start in business or to commence the practice of their profession; and
> Whereas this large group may become demoralized and disheartened, and thus constitute a dangerous addition to the discontented and radical-minded elements and also offer a challenge to the system which permits the minds and ingenuities of its youth to be wasted; and

> Whereas it is the duty of the Federal Government to use every possible means of opening up opportunities in private industry and in the Government service for these young people so that they may be rehabilitated and restored to a decent standard of living and insured proper development for their talents. . . .

The resolution ended by asking the Secretary of Labor and the Civil Service Commission to bring in plans to deal with the question. If anyone during the administration of Calvin Coolidge had suggested that the time was not far off when the United States Senate would be asked to take in hand several million young American people lest they become demoralized and dangerous, the man who made such a suggestion would have been thought insane. Since, however, the Senate has seen fit to consider this question, it seems reasonable for the country to give it some attention.

The general public which has yet to find itself on the relief rolls has become accustomed to the depression. It is disturbed and worried and anxious, but it is conditioned to it. In spite of—perhaps because of—all that has been said, written, printed, and broadcast about the condition of our unemployed, there is a disinclination to think about the problem at all. Depending on the point of view of the citizen, he feels that the government is squandering billions to keep people in idleness; that people could get jobs if they wanted to; that relief satisfies most of the unemployed so why worry; that the whole subject is an unmitigated bore and becomes increasingly tiresome and so give us a rest; that what we need is another war to absorb these people; that they ought to go back to the land where at least they can get enough to eat; that no one really starves; that Huey knows what to do, and so on *ad infinitum*.

It has reached a point where in ordinary conversation about unemployment and its effects the talk is carried on in label words. The army of the unemployed. The Lost Generation. The jobless. Through reiteration of these terms the unemployed are no longer persons; they are just collections of people, and their only important characteristic is that they don't have jobs, and so must be fed. They aren't a part of our society; they are an appendage to the nation and an exhausting responsibility.

This is nonsense. The unemployed are just like other persons—they are illiterate or highly educated, they are brave or idle or dishonest or ambitious or generous or envious, just as other persons are. That the circumstances of unemployment can do terrible things to people is true, but they still remain human beings. And they are anything but an appendage. Society cannot divide itself with partitions; we are Hobbes' *Leviathan,* and what touches one must touch all. Unemployment lives in our midst. In one way or another, however subtle, it touches every living person in the Republic. A state of affairs where the lawyer, the architect, tht lettuce picker, the weaver, the doctor, the tenant farmer, the rubber worker, the stockbroker's clerk and the professor, the miner and the milliner, the chemist and the crooner are in the same fix is evidence of the insecurity of all the rest. A nation is the sum of all those persons in it. The anxious hardware merchant looks under his bed at night, fearful lest Emma Goldman has placed a bomb there. It never occurs to him to consider what is going on in the mind and heart of his own son who cannot get a job.

The purpose of this article is to examine the condition of the young people of America—those persons between nineteen and twenty-nine years old—who in one way or another are caught in the clutches of unemployment. They are our Lost Generation. Some of them are married and on relief, some want to be married and can't be, some had jobs before the crash, some emerged from school and have never worked a day. Some of them have families still moderately secure, some have parents who are destitute. But all of those who are considered in this article are affected in some way by unemployment.

Nobody knows how many unemployed—old and young—there are in the United States, nor is there any agreement about the definition of the word unemployed. Under the heading "unemployed" the last census listed six different categories. Estimates vary widely, under the customary influence of political or economic expediency. How ironical it is, as Abraham Epstein has remarked, that in a country where statistics are worshipped, where we can tell, almost to the decimal, how many mules or refrigerators we possess, we have no idea of the size of our unemployed population. The President has promised that a census will be taken but we haven't got it yet. Nevertheless, for the purposes of this article, a careful statistical analysis was made. The conclusion of this analysis was that, excluding agricultural workers of all types,

there are at present some seventeen million workers who are now unemployed. This figure includes all persons sixteen years of age and over.
It includes all those on home or work relief, in C.C.C. camps and
engaged on public works. In a word, the term "unemployed" is taken
to mean all those who are able to work and who have either a relief
job or no job at all.

In this huge aggregation of persons may be found the Lost Generation. It includes all those who left college, high or grade school in
1929 and afterward, and who have had no jobs or who have found only
temporary employment. It includes those a little older who had jobs
and who were mowed down in the years following 1929.

In the United States to-day there are between 11 and 12 million
young men between the ages of 19 and 29. Of these the number in-
voluntarily unemployed is difficult to calculate. Based on the statistics
for marriage, on the work of the Civilian Conservation Corps, and on
the published reports of unemployment among college graduates, we
may conclude that the percentage of unemployment lies between
45 and 70 per cent; in absolute figures, between 5½ and 8 millions.
These figures include men only. Since there is an equal number of
women who look forward to a life of marriage the total of young Americans drawn directly into the dilemma of the lost generation falls between 11 and 16 millions.

No one can hope to present a comprehensive report on the condition of this generation. The best that one can do, to borrow a phrase of
Lytton Strachey's, is to "row out over that great ocean of material, and
lower down into it, here and there, a little bucket, which will bring up
to the light of day some characteristic specimen, from those far depths,
to be examined with a careful curiosity."

II

In many respects the post-1929 college graduate is the American tragedy. He is all dressed up with no place to go. He finds himself trained,
but without any chance to use his training. One sample here will
suffice. There were 50,000 young men studying engineering in 1920;
75,000 in 1930. "Electrical engineering led the increase," says Dr. E.
B. Roberts of the Westinghouse Electric and Manufacturing Company.

"All this was in response to . . . the loud voice of industry demanding more and more technically trained men. If ever an educational system made an effort to adjust itself to the demands thrown upon it, it was our engineering schools." To what end? At the moment there are more than 50,000 unemployed engineers.

The number of male college graduates for the five years of 1929–1934 was between 1½ and 2 millions. During these years college appointment offices have generally placed the percentage of unemployment between 50 and 85 per cent. The actual figures, however, are appreciably higher. A considerable percentage of the 1929–32 graduates who were employed at graduation have since lost their positions. Moreover, a large part of the graduating classes goes on to the professional and graduate schools and, therefore, is not to be included in the base on which the percentage of unemployed is computed.

Now what happens to these young people? Let us suppose that in 1926, at the age of 22, a young man graduated from college and got a position. This left him until 1929, three years of slow, conservative, and uneventful development toward a permanent place in his occupation. After this brief period, which finds him still in the formative stage of his wage-earning career, he loses his job. For many reasons, he is less favorably situated now than at 22. For at 22 his habits were potentially susceptible to direction along the lines of many different occupations. At 25 the fact that he has already worked at one particular calling would make him undesirable from the point of many employers in other kinds of business.

There follows a period of five years of practically complete unemployment. Occasionally he may secure temporary employment at a salary of fifteen dollars a week or less, in what is often a distasteful job that no one else wants. Of hope for the future there is little. Should economic conditions return to the most prosperous level of 1929, his chances of reëmployment are still very uncertain.

The vicissitudes through which this young man and his fellows may pass are sometimes illuminating to the observer if not to the young man. One such, the son of an executive in a large business, graduated from college three years ago and, despite the efforts of his father, has as yet been unable to get a job. Now observe the father. A few weeks ago the father called an employment agency on the telephone. He needed a stenographer who must be male, must have graduated from high school not earlier than 1934, could not be older than eighteen; he must be white, Protestant, and the "American type"; he must be ambitious, aggressive, and accustomed to dealing with people. The pay was fifteen dollars a week, attendance at evening sessions of a local college would be encouraged, and there were opportunities for promotion.

We need not pause for acid comment on the white, Protestant, and "American type" requirements. But the other demands require some translation. There are thousands of competent girl stenographers looking for jobs. Why is a boy asked for? Because the job of a male stenographer can be expanded by degrees into that of a semi-executive and that is where his ambition, aggressiveness, and skill in dealing with people will come in. But he is hired as a stenographer and such he may, in theory, remain and with a great saving in pay. Why must he have graduated from high school no earlier than 1934? There are thousands of boys who have graduated from high school—and college—since 1929 and whose jobs, if any, have been temporary. Business doesn't want them. They're "rusty," they've got into "idle habits," they're "undependable." It's the youngest who are wanted and wanted cheap. But all this while the son of the executive who is doing this hiring is without a job and is himself in the crowd that his father won't touch. The father begs the employment agency to find his son a job elsewhere —where the same attitude is present!

This paradox is repeated with variations. We have trained young people—including those with a technical high-school education that prepares for apprenticeships and college and professional school graduates who hold degrees in medicine or engineering or a dozen other fields. These young people are trained, but they have no experience. If a job calls for experience, the man who has it will probably be someone who was out of school and employed before 1929. If no experience is necessary, the employer will probably fill the job with the youngest, fresh from school. Those who fall in the years between are lost.

A young man out of medical school in '31 and still looking for an interneship has far less chance of getting it than the man who graduates in '35, and it is going to be very difficult for the '35 man with the best of luck. If perchance the graduate is a Jew or a Negro he might as well declare his medical career at an end right now. He was through—forever—before he had a chance to start. And all this despite the fact that there are nowhere near enough doctors to look after our 127,000,000 odd people.

The report of an investigation of unemployment among young people in England makes an admirable statement of the case there which describes our own quite as accurately:

> . . . in the distributive trades large numbers of children, particularly boys, are willing to take employment, because of the absence of other occupation, in the most menial tasks which cannot fit them in any way for a life of useful work. The community is taking advantage of the plight of juveniles to make them hewers of wood and drawers of water for a time until they can be replaced in the same work by a new flood of children direct from school. . . . Finally the depression has produced the paradox that the children who have had the longest training seem least able to obtain employment.

The position of the C.C.C. camps deserves scrutiny, especially since it is argued insistently that the enterprise become an established part of the national policy. Quite aside from food strikes, camp revolts, the discharge of boys for "communistic and bolshevistic plots," the urging of more military training by the Chief of Staff, and other sour episodes which have spotted the history of the C.C.C., there is the vital question of what these camps are supposed to accomplish. Often they have saved boys from destitution and demoralization and have served as a means of physical rehabilitation. But rehabilitation for what? A return to a world where jobs are just as few as they were before? A permanent establishment implies acknowledgment of a permanent state of unemployment. In what way can the camps be regarded as a "solution"? When their period of enrollment expires the boys must go back to the same vicious half slave, half free environment from which they came. Any advantage which has been gained from forest experience must frequently be vitiated—especially in the case of town and city boys—by a newly created conflict between the old and new ways of living.

"The more military training a boy gets, the better employers like it," the authors were told in one instance. The reader may draw from this what conclusions he wishes. Other employers, bilious over the New Deal and all its works, may hesitate to employ boys who have spent time in camps, believing that the C.C.C. means just more vitiating made work. In either way, it's a case of cold storage, and after cold storage, what? Like eggs, a boy will not keep indefinitely.

Confidence in the educational side of the camps has been cracked by the suppression of Professor Ogburn's camp textbook and by the subsequent resignation of Dr. Marsh, the educational director. "There has been a 33⅓ per cent turnover in camp educational advisers. As late as last February 430 camps were still without an adviser serving full time," says a recent article in the *New Republic*. The reader must remember that educational advisers are in a strictly subordinate position under the military camp commanders. "It is not the fault of the officers," says an article officially released by the Emergency Conservation Corps, ". . . if they tend to confuse a work camp with a private training course for themselves and an opportunity for building up a beautiful efficiency record for future use. The army judges results in a C.C.C. camp as it would judge results in an army or militia camp."

Great claims are made of the value of educational projects in the camps. But educational work is done at night after a day's work. A boy may come in to face a condition like this: "There was one schoolroom of moderate size with three tables that might seat ten students. There were no books; the entire equipment for the department cost $58. The library and ping-pong table were in the same room. The director said that 61 per cent of the men had enrolled and about 50 per cent of them were attending. Outside the nature study and forestry, the courses were not popular and did not seem appropriate." The sharing in the responsibility for the camps between the War Department and Mr. Robert Fechner, the Director of the C.C.C., leaves small room for confidence in the camps as a permanent enterprise. Mr. Fechner is an old-line labor-union organizer, and his conduct in the Ogburn case only deepens the profound doubt felt in the social courage and economic intelligence of our labor union bureaucracy.

"Most people who have had anything to do with the C.C.C. wish it to be made permanent and talk of William James's moral equivalent of war," says the *New Republic* article just referred to. "Nevertheless, democratic institutions are probably best preserved when adolescent males remain within the family system and plan for families of their own. Camps might perhaps be continued by the government for boys who wish to make forestry a career. With this exception, the less this country does to prolong the gang age in its youth, the better." But it's being done, all the same, and the quota has just been doubled.

In the United States the tradition of working is extremely strong. Self-respect requires regular occupation. We have a leisure class, but they have never, like their European fellows, been accepted as a part of things. To make a million dollars has been a national passion; but self-made men have cursed any idleness in their own children, and the idle rich have long been taken as a butt of derision, contempt, and hatred by most Americans. To be sure, what a man worked at was less important than the fact that he worked; an industrious bucket-shop operator was more virtuous than an idle Vanderbilt.

We still call upon independence, initiative, and individual effort as our most sterling virtues. For all the discussion about the new leisure, our spiritual and material lives are still dominated by economic necessity. A job is needed even to enable a person to enjoy leisure. Under our civilization, these virtues cannot be realized except by people who possess the economic means to realize them.

> Divorced from the feudal and theological heritage (of Europe) [says Charles Beard], American life has been in the main hard, economic and realistic—a conquest of material things, and American thought has been essentially empirical, not metaphysical and theological. It is largely for this reason that European visitors, with their feudal and theological hangovers, have been almost unanimous in calling Americans "money grubbers." To have food, clothing, shelter, comforts, and conveniences has been an essential preoccupation of Americans. The outstanding positive characteristic of American civilization, then, is preoccupation with economy in practice and empiricism and humanism in thought. Mass production, engineering and gigantic organization have been the outward manifestations of this primary American interest.

When a young man, born and bred in a country with this tradition, cannot find employment, the energy which he would normally expend through participation in the processes of production finds no outlet. He stagnates. His tissues weaken with forced passivity. His morale sags. And his determination becomes increasingly flaccid. Decadence of morale strikes him at the moment when he is beginning the most essential process of his adult life, earning a living. There is no job! The future, at a stroke, is cut off. There is small virtue in damning a young man who, after a year of hopeless salesman-on-commission jobs, thankfully took an imitation relief job. "I get eighteen a week, and I'm eighteen a week better off than I was before."

Examine the young men who find occupation as investigators or in some other capacity in relief administration. Here their wages are fixed—and low. There is practically no prospect of advancement. (Why don't you go down on your knees and thank God you've got a meal ticket? Why?) Their jobs, such as they are, are at the mercy of political forays and the jealous brawling between professional social workers and the political fraternity. Compassed about with such influences, the relief employee covers up. He does not have the protection which the civil service can occasionally extend. If he and his fellows attempt to organize for protection the red scare is raised. Low pay, insecurity, and espionage are his lot, and it is not surprising that he develops a poker face and a profound distrust of the stranger. For the sake of safety he won't—he can't—open his mouth. Whether on relief or off, the lost generation are hemmed in. A bound has been set that they may not pass over.

III

Much has been said and written about career women who are not interested in marriage. By far the majority of women, however, see marriage as a major business. If the man is not in a position, financially, to marry, both are involved in serious social, physiological, and spiritual maladjustments. Although the woman may be employed, marriage is difficult if the man is not, because such a position is repugnant to the average American.

From 19 to 29 is the marrying age. Marriage in many cases has been made possible by aid from the family: by living off the in-laws, by doubling up with them to save rents; by living on the wife's income as a temporary expedient; and even by going on government relief. Those who take the latter course at once find themselves a target for brickbats. "The government is supporting and allowing these people to breed in idleness." Further, at the moment of writing, the allowance for food for one person is 6.97 cents per meal in New York City where the nation's highest relief allowances prevail.

Nevertheless, the drop in marriages has been precipitous. Expressed in marriages per thousand of population, the fall has been even greater. For the first time since 1911 the number of marriages fell below the million mark in 1932. Yet the population in 1911 was 93 millions; in 1932 it was 125 millions, or over 34 per cent greater.

The story of economic enervation, as told in marriages, is repeated in the success of the C.C.C. in filling its ranks. This result has turned upon one factor: the economic helplessness of the lost generation. Despite the fact that 90 per cent of the enrollment is narrowly confined to the ages of 18 to 25, the full quota has always been assembled quickly and easily. In view of the very strong affinity between the sexes at this age, it must be very dire circumstances indeed which will send the young man off to the backwoods. "Boys do not come into the C.C.C. unless they are jobless, unmarried, and members of families on relief," says Jonathan Mitchell. "They know well enough that the normal course for young men of their age would be to find jobs in their native towns, take girls to the movies and plan on getting married and founding homes." For at least some of the boys, their own predicament and that of their families is the cause of intense worry. In a recent issue of the national C.C.C. newspaper, *Happy Days*, there is a naïve story of a fictional C.C.C. boy who performs prodigies of wit and audacity to win a girl in the neighboring village, only to find she is about to marry a non-C.C.C. boy who has a job. A few weeks ago, in Camp 222 in Middleburg, New York, a debate was held before a tense audience on: "Can a Man Support a Wife on $25 a Week?" It would appear useless to labor the obvious further.

From the time he leaves school the young man of the lost generation finds that his world goes into reverse. First he gets no job. Economically debilitated, he can neither sustain his spirit of independence nor express his initiative. Then the Devil begins to wreak his evil. The young man undergoes a profound spiritual metamorphosis. For underlying the need of a position, of the desire to marry and to establish a home, are powerful and fundamental forces. Their abuse may cause serious disturbances to the physical and mental health of the individual.

Most important of these forces is the need of sexual expression. The-oretically it may remain latent; our habits of life, however, stimulate it to a recurrent state of activity. Closely related is the powerful desire of two persons to live under a common roof. The only socially legiti-mate course of sexual expression is under the protection of marriage. If this course is denied there is a probability of increasing sexual ille-gitimacy, and in the absence of the latter, a serious neurotic unbalance.

There is also the desire to establish a normal family life. For most people the spiritual bases of the family are necessary. The stabilizing effect of family life, the mutual stimulation of personalities, mutual support in moments of stress, and a normal participation in com-munity activity: without marriage these are lost.

IV

Family and livelihood are the two first interests of mankind. "That the first want of every man is his dinner and the second want, his girl," said John Adams, "were truths well known by every democrat and aristocrat long before the great philosopher Malthus arose to think he enlightened the world by his discovery."

There is none so illiterate but that he can beget children and none so dumb but that he feels an interest in the source of his bread. Social consciousness is not universal. Large numbers of our people, from birth to death, have no thought about society or the state. Any society, however, requires a degree of co-operation in order to exist, and this co-operation may be given unconsciously through a whole life. But when the opportunity of earning a livelihood is withdrawn and love and marriage become economically impossible, a change is likely to occur in the individual. He may have no more ideas about the state than he had before, the thought of a rational alteration in the existing order may be completely beyond his grasp, but in his actions he will reflect a change.

A migratory worker who has traveled back and forth across the country for twenty years has described the comparatively recent ap-pearance of firearms among the young bums. "In my day," said he, "gats were almost unheard of. Nobody carried one. What would we have used them for? How many Wobblies ever packed a gun? It's different now. Here and there you find high school kids on the road armed. They can't get work and they're sick of begging the old man for cigarette money and they're out for what they can get, while it lasts. Not all of them, of course, but plenty."

A person can live either by peaceful—social—means, or by violent—anti-social—means. If society does not offer a man or woman the opportunity to pursue a normal life his only alternative is to preserve his existence by violence. When a generation, numbering into the millions, has gone so far in decay that it acts without thought of social responsibility, the name for this condition is not socialism but collective anarchy. Assuming the unmitigated demoralization of these people, American society may find itself in the throes of this pathology within another generation. The lost generation is even now rotting before our eyes.

An increase in crime is almost certain. Automatically, forces which are the best guarantees against crime cease to act, and it follows that from this quarter a rise in crime may be expected. The slum grows, its borders expand in both town and country, and in this slum the delinquent children hasten toward their criminal maturity.

A few weeks ago Dr. Sheldon Glueck, the author of *Five Hundred Criminal Careers*, declared that the most important thing the government could do to combat crime was "to act quickly and intelligently in the direction of economic justice." "The layman does not realize," he said, "how early in life appear many . . . manifestations of maladjustment of the young individual to the various social groups in which he finds himself. Fourteen per cent of juvenile delinquents noted showed such symptoms of maladjustment and misconduct at the age of six years or less; 23 per cent at the age of seven or eight; 26 per cent at nine or ten; 21 per cent at thirteen or over, the average age being nine years and seven months. Yet a few years later we condemn and punish these same acts or others growing naturally out of them as crimes for which the offender is regarded as unquestionably and fully responsible."

In this connection, the following from the January 1, 1935 annual report of the Police Commissioner of New York City will be of interest. The italics are the authors':

"The interrogation of prisoners appearing at the line-up discloses the following facts:

"Of those charged with the crime of burglary about 22 per cent had no criminal record and in the majority of cases the losses reported consisted of currency, jewelry and other items of merchandise, less than one hundred dollars in value. *The majority were youths, first offenders and unemployed. Ten per cent of those arrested for assault and robbery were first offenders.*"

The interdependence of crime and unemployment can with difficulty be shown by statistics, if at all; few data exist from which accurate conclusions can be drawn. Nevertheless, since the majority of criminals come from low economic environments, it seems likely that an increase in the number of the destitute will increase our criminal population. The wrecking of large portions of the middle class removes many powerful restraints of custom and tradition, if not in the present mature generation, then in the next.

V

To judge by the samples there is no uniformity of opinion in the lost generation about social change. Many have never even heard of it. The number who demand a change in the system in which we live is very small. The remainder express a multitude of different opinions or no opinion at all. One boy gets out of college in a turmoil of anxiety. He spends a year in Communism and finds it doesn't satisfy. He throws Communism overboard and joins the National Guard in the hope that "discipline" and "no responsibility" will ease him. That doesn't work either. He is now looking for some other recipe. Another boy is not bothered by this particular sort of malaise, but he becomes more and more soured because he can't get a job in aviation, for which he has been trained. His social curiosity is not awakened, nor does he become interested in the slightest degree in any other vocation. He would vote any ticket or wear any uniform for an airplane.

An agency engaged in assisting young people in search of employment discovered that in their general attitude toward business a large number of young men divided into two sharply opposed categories. One part regarded the whole of business as dishonest, an occupation in which cheating and deception were indispensable. Many who felt this way based their opinions on experience gained in business and said that they "would never go back." The attitude of those in the second category was the reverse. Business, they felt, was a racket, and all they wanted was the quickest way into the racket. If Louis Adamic's apprehension of government by gangsters ever materializes, some of its shining lights may easily come from this crowd.

Some young people try to stay in school as long as they can, in the hope that more training will save them. Others, regarding school as useless, throw up the sponge and leave. Generally, among the young, the most coherent and outspoken dissatisfaction comes from the educated, and the more education—no matter how or where secured—the more dissatisfaction. The dissatisfaction is often colored by ignorance of how the world's work is done. They have no jobs and no acquaintance with the processes of working for a living. Experience is the other half of education and this experience they haven't got and can't get. This fact lends point to a recent article which urged the authorities "to take immediate cognizance of the increasing bond of sympathy between unpaid teachers and unemployed high school and college graduates. This army of young people is potentially very dangerous if such numbers remain unemployed and potentially very helpful in creating social stability if they get jobs."

The reader is not to suppose that this means a wholesale espousal of Communism. The radicals get a few, the remainder divide in a thousand ways, angered or baffled or browbeaten or apathetic. These are the ones who provide the material for a future chaos, a sequence of violent upheavals. The corrosive effects of privation and frustration will then have accomplished their terrible work, and the field will be open to native Cæsars and military demagogues. The pressure presumably will be felt in the lower-most strata of the population; proceeding upward through the higher strata, the reverberations will rock the earth, and it is hard to believe that the mansions built at the very top will not go down in the crash.

A girl with graduate training as a chemist is now earning her food and shelter by looking after two small children. High-spirited and ambitious, she had expected that chemistry would be the work of her life. Education had given her assurance and knowledge, chemists were needed, her livelihood was assured. Now, as an individual, she finds that every hope is blasted. As a citizen and as a member of society, able to make a needed contribution to the demands of a highly complex civilization, she is thrown away. Wasted and discarded, she is still alive and thinking and outraged, adding one more to the generation of the lost. How is she, in her present occupation, going to regard the suggestion made at a conference on Youth Problems called by the United States Department of Education, that more young women enter domestic service! Multiply this girl by the others. Put her beside the girl who, after years of training as a typographer both in this country and abroad, was found down and out, jobless, sleeping in a railroad station. Put her with the young doctors driving taxicabs and the young engineers looking for window-washing jobs. What are these people going to be like when they reach middle age? How are they going to think and act—then?

An organization dealing with young people assembled the records of interviews with several thousand young persons between 16 and 21. From these records the agency drew, among others, the following observations:

"Many clients believe jobs are gotten entirely by 'influence' and that training to meet rising occupational standards is not important."

"Many of them regard the depression as temporary and don't think much more about it."

"There is a surprising distrust of present-day advertising and, to some extent, of the press."

"The young men in general have a distrust of war, based on one of three causes, but in almost every case they say 'my mother says—'

"A. Distrust of wars, based on feeling that 'profiteers start them.'

"B. Desire to avoid military service and get high wages as a civilian.

"C. Personal fear of the dangers of modern war."

Another study made by the same organization turned up this: "There is a decided lack of interest and in many cases a distinct antipathy to anything involving international affairs or 'foreign countries.' This was brought out very frequently in general conversation."

Earning a living rather than choosing some special vocation has been the first thought of most young Americans. To a large extent the schools have turned out graduates who "didn't know what they wanted to do" but who expected to be absorbed somehow into our economic life. Now they can't be absorbed. They want jobs, they want to get in, and they can't. The fact that influence has always been an important factor in getting ahead—this was at last demonstrated with imposing figures in 1932 by F. W. Taussig and C. S. Joslyn in *American Business Leaders*—is magnified so that influence appears necessary to get any job. When you add to this a distrust of advertising and the press, it would appear that Mr. Young and Mr. Swope and the other business exhorters had better watch their audience. As for the opinions about war, it is certainly true that there is a growing distrust and fear of war and the whole machinery of war in this country. Because a promise of clothing and food might sweep shoals of these young men into uniform at a time of crisis is no guarantee that they are soaked in devotion to the country which has all but abandoned them nor that they would have much interest in another attempt to save the world for democracy. What has our democracy done to deserve their allegiance?

We are thus confronted with a generation of young people ranging from the illiterate to the highly trained and educated for whom no honorable place in our society has been found. Every day which these young people live, through the mere lapse of time, makes the prospect of employment more dubious. For those who are younger the prospect is more uncertain; for even the advantages of education are being restricted. In the first place, through physical deterioration, due to malnutrition, a rising percentage of young people absorb instruction with great difficulty. In the second place, school funds are shrinking. There is less school than there was, or, if schools are available, other reasons prevent attendance. A year ago the New York *Times* reported three and a half million children ready for school—with no schools to attend. The same paper in January, 1935, reported that five hundred school children of Mt. Vernon, N. Y., were out of school for lack of clothing. Whatever the reasons, the young people and the schools are being separated. Seldom anywhere is there recognition of the fact that in such a complex civilization as ours education is indispensable.

What freedom remains to the schools is being still further constricted by the efforts of business, the patriots, and the red baiters to shut off any realistic study of our present crisis. If perchance the youth is interested in such study, our schools give him little or no opportunity for

it. If he is not interested, present conditions guarantee that his ignorance shall remain unscratched until the time when he is turned out
of school to join the generation already adrift.

It is impossible to forecast what action this generation may take in
the future. Germany affords one illustration of what may happen to an
unwanted generation in a highly industrialized country. The original
intellectual nucleus of German discontent, which made the Hitler revolution possible, was contained in the abandoned youth of Germany. It
was composed mainly of young men who had slaved and starved their
way through the German universities, only to graduate without the
prospect of even a street-cleaner's job.

To this element of the German population, anything was better than
its present plight. Youthful vitality compelled them to action; war and
death were preferable to their passive, helpless, pauper role. Hence
their support of the first movement which offered them hope of change
(which was, incidentally, Hitlerism). Recently, in *Social Frontier*, the
membership of two typical Storm Troop Battalions in Berlin was analyzed. In a workers district 80 per cent of the troopers were under
thirty years of age. In a middle-class district 78 per cent were under 30.

There is no sure reason to suppose that the fate of Germany will be
duplicated in this country, but the prospect does not promise anything
much better. The present efforts of the government do not apply sub-
stantially to the young people. Such courses of action as the Civilian
Conservation Corps are scarcely palliatives. Recently an allocation of
$96,000,000 was asked for use in various work and educational projects
for young people. This cannot get us very far.

We have bred a population numbering into the millions whose position is now little better than that of serfdom. These people are not an
appendage, an amorphous mass tied to the periphery of the nation.
They are the nation, they are in it and of it, and they have been left to
rot. There is no one who reads this article who is not in some way or
other involved. No longer can anyone be reasonably sure that with education, industry, and effort his children may attain a degree of security.
There is no assurance that they may, in decency, be able to rear families
of their own. Many of them, whether they will or no, are marked to
join this rotting population. Rot spreads.

Twenty years hence this present lost generation, sideswiped, battered, and warped, will have reached middle age. And then what? That famous Promise of American Life is not worth a continental. We may with good reason recall the words uttered by an eminent citizen on the 17th of June, 1858: "'A house divided against itself cannot stand' . . . this government cannot endure half slave and half free." Which it is to be?

A Fateful Friendship

STEPHEN AMBROSE

• On September 1, 1939, when the German Army crossed
the Polish frontier to begin World War II, Dwight David
Eisenhower was an obscure lieutenant colonel in the regular
army. Six years later "Ike" was famous all over the world as
the victorious supreme commander of the Allied Expedi-
tionary Force in Europe. He became a five star general before the war ended, and in subsequent years served as president of Columbia University, supreme commander of the
North Atlantic Treaty Organization and President of the
United States.

In the years when he was responsible for integrating the
air, naval, and land forces of many nations, General Eisenhower won his greatest accolades as a manipulator of men
because he successfully co-ordinated the efforts of strong-
willed and feuding subordinates. One of Eisenhower's most
persistent "problem" officers was General George S. Patton,
whose Third Army led the sweep of United States forces
through Brittany and northern France in 1944. Patton was
an extremely able tank commander whose personal courage
and iron discipline inspired both fear and loyalty among his
men. But Patton's battlefield brilliance was sometimes over-
shadowed by serious lapses in judgment. When General Patton impulsively slapped a soldier suffering from battle fatigue, General Eisenhower was forced to examine critically
Patton's value to the Allied military effort. As Professor
Stephen Ambrose makes clear in the following essay, the
long relationship between the two powerful men was indeed
a "fateful friendship."

From *American Heritage*, April 1969. Reprinted by permission of the
author.

They never had much in common. George Patton was a conceited, spoiled child from an extremely wealthy, snobbish family. He dressed as he pleased, said what he liked, and did as he wished. He cursed like a trooper and told off his inferiors—and sometimes his superiors—with profane eloquence. Although he moved easily in America's highest society, many people, soldiers included, thought Patton vulgar. Dwight Eisenhower came from the wrong side of the tracks in a tiny midwestern town. He had to support himself while in high school by working nights in a creamery; he wanted to be well liked, and he obeyed his superiors. The only thing he did to attract attention was to do his duty quietly and efficiently.

Patton was an erratic genius, given to great outbursts of energy and flashes of brilliant insight. He was capable of sustained action, but not of systematic thought. A superstitious man, he was much taken by his own *déjà vu*, his sensation of having been somewhere before; he devoutly believed that he had fought with Alexander the Great and with Napoleon, among others. Eisenhower had a steady, orderly mind. When he looked at a problem he would take everything into account, weigh possible alternatives, and deliberately decide on a course of action. Patton seldom arrived at a solution through an intellectual process; rather, he *felt* that this or that was what he should do, and he did it.

Patton strutted while Eisenhower walked. Both were trim, athletic, outdoor types; but Eisenhower was usually grinning, Patton frowning. Patton indulged his moods, while Eisenhower kept a grip on his temper.

Despite the differences, the two soldiers shared a friendship that survived two decades and (according to Eisenhower) "heated, sometimes almost screaming arguments. . . ." Their common West Point training—Patton graduated in 1909, Eisenhower in 1915—helped hold them together; other factors were, however, more important. Both had a deep interest in tanks and armored warfare. Patton, five years Eisenhower's senior, had led tanks in battle during World War I; Eisenhower had trained tank crews in Pennsylvania. After 1918, when the War Department almost ignored the new weapon, Patton and Eisenhower, like those junior officers in England, France, and Germany who believed that the tank would dominate the battlefield in the next war, naturally drew together. But beyond this mutual interest, they respected each other. Patton's dash, courage, and recklessness complemented Eisenhower's stubborn, straightforward caution. Each admired the other and benefited from the relationship.

The two young majors met in 1919, and almost immediately they began an argument that would last until Patton's death. Patton thought that the chief ingredient in modern war was inspired leadership on the battlefield. Eisenhower felt that leadership was just one factor. He believed that Patton was inclined to indulge his romantic nature, neglecting such matters as logistics, a proper world-wide strategy, and getting along with allies.

A letter Patton wrote to Eisenhower in July, 1926, illustrated the difference between the two men. "Ike" had just spent a year at the Command and General Staff School at Fort Leavenworth. He had applied himself with almost monastic diligence to his studies, and had graduated first in his class. Patton, fearful that his friend had concentrated too hard on such subjects as transportation, staff functioning, and how to draft a memo, decided to set him straight. After congratulating Eisenhower on his achievement, Patton declared, "We talk a hell of a lot about tactics and stuff and we never get to brass tacks. Namely what is it that makes the Poor S.O.B. who constitutes the casualty list fight." Leadership was Patton's answer. Officers had to get out and inspire the men, keep them moving. One or two superheroes would not do; Patton thought any such notion was "bull." Finally, he concisely summed up the difference between his and Eisenhower's approach to battle. "Victory in the next war will depend on EXECUTION not PLANS." By execution, Patton said, he meant keeping the infantry advancing under fire.

Eisenhower disagreed. Plans, he said, mean that food and ammunition and gasoline would continue to reach the men in the front lines, that pressure would be applied where it hurt the enemy the most, that supreme effort would not be wasted. The most difficult tasks in the next war, Eisenhower believed, would be raising, training, arming, and transporting the men; getting them ashore in the right places; maintaining good liaison with allied forces. Execution would matter, of course, but it was only one part of the total picture.

During the thirties their Army assignments kept the two men apart, but they stayed in touch. It was a bad time for armor advocates: the army had practically no tanks. Patton, disgusted, joined the cavalry, where he could at least play polo, while Eisenhower worked patiently through a series of staff jobs. Patton lived expensively—entertaining, racing around in sports cars, keeping his own string of polo ponies, and travelling by private yacht and private plane. This was in an army that was, for most practical purposes, poverty-stricken. During the Depression, Congress cut officers' salaries and introduced annoying economy measures on army posts. Most career men tightened their belts, entertained frugally, and associated only with their fellows. Patton's ostentatious display of his wealth was offensive to most of his colleagues, especially his superiors; they could not begin to compete with him.

Eisenhower, meanwhile, kept begging for assignments with the troops, but his superiors, most notably General Douglas MacArthur, liked to have the hard-working, efficient major around. He lived according to the accepted pattern and was one of the best-liked officers in the Army. While Patton disported himself outside the system, Eisenhower worked from within. In 1940, for example, Patton—who had finally become a colonel in 1938—took command of a tank brigade of the 2nd Armored Division. He found that most of his tanks were not working because of an absence of spare parts. When a mechanic pointed out that many usuable parts were available from Sears, Roebuck, Patton ordered them and paid out of his own pocket. He kept the bill a secret, but it probably ran into many thousands of dollars. As chief of staff of a division, Eisenhower often faced similar problems. His solution was to write to a friend in the War Department and, with this extra prodding, get the material he needed through proper channels.

When World War II began in Europe, Patton quickly forgot about polo and his active social life. Eisenhower was certain that Patton would go straight to the top when America got into the war, and in September, 1940, he wrote his friend: "I suppose it's too much to hope that I could have a regiment in your division, because I'm still almost three years away from my colonelcy." Still, he thought he could do the job.

Patton may have had his doubts, and in any case he had a better idea about what Eisenhower could do for him. Apply for armor, Patton advised, and join up with me as my chief of staff. "He needs a brake to slow him down," General George C. Marshall once said of Patton, "because he is apt to coast at breakneck speed, propelled by his enthusiasm and exuberance." Patton himself understood this, and he thought Eisenhower would be the perfect brake.

They did not get together, however, until two years later. Eisenhower, by 1941, had become a temporary colonel and was chief of staff for the Third Army. His son, John, was considering whether to go to West Point or to study law, and he asked his father's advice. Eisenhower said that the Army had been good to him, although he expected to retire as a colonel and admitted that his hopes had once been higher. Still, he had to be realistic; he warned John that he would never get rich or famous in the Army. He could get instead the satisfaction of knowing he had made a contribution to his country. John took West Point.

Patton, meanwhile, continued to move ahead in armor. He did so because of his abilities, of course, but more to the point because the Army Chief of Staff, General Marshall, was a remarkable man, able to overlook idiosyncrasy and to judge by performance. A rigid soldier and old-fashioned gentleman himself, Marshall had seen the impetuous Patton in action at Saint-Mihiel in World War I. He had marked him favorably in his famous little black book, a book he used ruthlessly after he became Chief of Staff to weed out the unfit and to jump men like Patton over their superiors. Marshall moved Patton up to temporary brigadier general in 1940 and, in April, 1941, to major general.

When America entered the war in December, 1941, Marshall called Eisenhower to Washington; he did not know Eisenhower, but he had read his efficiency reports and observed his brilliant staff work in maneuvers in Louisiana in 1941. Within three months Eisenhower was head of the Operations Division of the War Department. Marshall was so favorably impressed that three months later he sent Major General Eisenhower to London to take command of the European Theatre of Operations. In July, 1942, Great Britain and America decided that their first joint offensive of the war would be an invasion of French North Africa. Eisenhower had pleased the British as much as he had Marshall, and they agreed that he was the ideal Supreme Commander for the invasion. He could choose his own assault commanders; the first man he picked was Patton. It was an ironic reversal of what Eisenhower had hoped for two years earlier.

Eisenhower gave his old acquaintance the potentially toughest assignment, that of hitting the beach at Casablanca. Shortly after Patton arrived, however, the French quit fighting, as a result of Eisenhower's deal with Admiral Jean Louis Darlan, Vichy's chief of state in French Africa. This brought the North African French into the Allied camp,

and Patton lost his chance for glory. He compensated by competing
with the local sultans in lavish living during three months as head of
United States occupation forces in Morocco, and by hobnobbing with
upper-echelon Vichy Frenchmen so convivially that it struck some
Americans as aid and comfort to the enemy.

In March, 1943, following the Battle of Kasserine Pass, Eisenhower
brought Patton to Tunisia to take command of the II Corps, which
had been badly battered. He told Patton to restore morale, raise the
image of American troops in British eyes by winning a victory or two,
and take care of himself. Patton, Eisenhower said, did not have to
prove to him that he was courageous.

Patton had always been a martinet when it came to morale. He himself indulged in gaudy uniforms, but he insisted that his enlisted men
dress meticulously according to regulations, even in the front lines. He
worked them hard, subjecting them to twice as many drills and training exercises as most generals. His insistence on spit and polish was so
great that he once tried to get Bill Mauldin's famous "Stars and Stripes"
cartoons banned from his area because Mauldin's G.I.'s always looked
like the sloppiest soldiers in the world. (Eisenhower, incidentally, over-
ruled Patton on the issue, after Patton had called Sergeant Mauldin into
his headquarters and raked him over.) It is doubtful that Patton's men
ever loved him—that notion was mainly journalists' copy—but they
did respect him, and they respected themselves as a result. He used his
techniques with the II Corps, and they worked. He made the men
shave regularly and stand straight, and then scored a tactical victory
over the great German tank commander, Erwin Rommel. A grateful
Eisenhower gave Patton the most coveted combat position in the Army
—command of the invasion of Sicily.

Patton did well. His Seventh Army sent the German and Italian opposition reeling across Sicily past Palermo. It was a campaign that left
the British, especially General Bernard Montgomery, awe-struck. Patton had proved himself to be a master of pursuit, a general who could
keep the troops going under all conditions. He was not so good at a
set-piece battle. When he turned his army east for the drive to Messina,
across from the Italian toe, the Germans were waiting. Progress was
exasperatingly slow. The narrow roads, winding through the mountains,
gave the Germans every advantage. Patton was almost beside himself.

On August 3, while he was in this mood, he tried to make himself

feel better in a way that had often worked well before: visiting an evacuation hospital near the front and talking to brave soldiers who had recently been wounded in action. This time it backfired. The General had
gone around the tent and chatted with a number of bandaged men,
asking them how they got hit, where they were from, and so on, when
he came to Private C. H. Kuhl, a young infantryman from Mishawaka,
Indiana. Kuhl was sitting on a box, and had no visible sign of wounds.
To Patton's query, the soldier said simply, "I guess I can't take it."

As Patton admitted later, he "flew off the handle." In his opinion,
most cases of "shell shock" or "battle fatigue" were just plain cowardice,
and he proceeded to say so to Kuhl in a high, excited voice and with an
appropriate selection from his rich lexicon of profanity. Then he slapped
Kuhl across the face with his gloves and turned to the medical officer in
charge, shouting: "Don't admit this son of a bitch. I don't want yellow-
bellied bastards like him hiding their lousy cowardice around here,
stinking up this place of honor!" Patton then stalked out. Kuhl, who
had indeed been admitted to the hospital on a diagnosis of psychoneu-
rotic anxiety, was found upon examination to have chronic diarrhea,
malaria, and a temperature of 102.2°F.

This slapping incident, although it shocked those who witnessed it,
was not widely reported. Patton felt that he had done the right thing;
he dictated a brief account of the episode for inclusion in his diary, and
added in his own hand: "One sometimes slaps a baby to bring it to."
He then issued a memorandum to the officers of his command direct-
ing that any soldiers pretending to be "nervously incapable of combat"
should not be sent to hospitals but, if they refused to fight, should be
"tried by court-martial for cowardice in the face of the enemy."

Having rehearsed his hospital scene with Private Kuhl, Patton repeated it a week later with added flourishes. Early on the hot Monday
afternoon of August 10, while on his way to a military conference with
General Omar Bradley (who was then Patton's subordinate), his command car passed a sign pointing the way to the 93rd Evacuation Hospital. Patton told his driver to turn in. A few minutes later he was
going from litter to litter, talking to the battle casualties and commend-
ing them for doing a good job against the Germans. Then he came to a
man who, like Private Kuhl, was fully dressed, unbandaged, and apparently in good health. "What's the matter with you?" the General asked.

When the soldier said the trouble was "my nerves" and began to sob,

Patton exploded. "Your nerves hell, you are just a goddamn coward, you yellow son of a bitch," he screamed. He then struck the soldier twice, knocking his helmet liner off so hard that it rolled into the next tent; Patton even pulled out one of his famous pearl-handled revolvers and waved it in the man's face. "You ought to be lined up against a wall and shot," one witness reported the General as shouting. "In fact, I ought to shoot you myself right now, goddamn you!"

The commanding officer of the hospital was incensed. Private Paul Bennett, the victim of Patton's outburst, was a regular-army soldier with a good fighting record; he had begun to show signs of unusual nervous tension only after receiving from his young wife a picture of their newborn baby. Moreover, he had gone to the hospital reluctantly, insisting that he did not want to leave his unit. Within a week a detailed report of the incident had worked its way from the hospital through channels to Eisenhower's headquarters in Algiers.

It was 10:30 A.M., August 17, and Patton's men had just triumphantly entered Messina. Eisenhower was feeling friendly toward Patton, and after reading the report he said mildly, "I guess I'll have to give General Patton a jacking up." He then praised Patton for the "swell job" he had done in Sicily. Eisenhower did order Brigadier General Frederick Blessé, his surgeon general, to go to Sicily and conduct a full investigation, but he warned him to keep it quiet. "If this thing ever gets out," Eisenhower told Blessé, "they'll be howling for Patton's scalp, and that will be the end of Georgie's service in this war. I simply cannot let that happen. Patton is *indispensable* to the war effort."

Eisenhower then sat down and wrote a personal letter to Patton. By now he was beginning to feel the seriousness of Patton's offense and to realize that more than a "jacking up" was required. "I clearly understand that firm and drastic measures are at times necessary in order to secure desired objectives," Eisenhower wrote, "but this does not excuse brutality, abuse of the sick, nor exhibition of uncontrollable temper in front of subordinates." Eisenhower said he did not intend to institute any formal investigation, or put anything in Patton's official file; but he did warn that if the reports proved true, he would have to "seriously question your good judgment and your self-discipline." This would "raise serious doubts . . . as to your future usefulness."

In conclusion Eisenhower declared, "No letter that I have been called upon to write in my military career has caused me the mental anguish of this one, not only because of my long and deep personal friendship for you but because of my admiration for your military qualities." But, Eisenhower warned, "I assure you that conduct such as described in the accompanying report will *not* be tolerated in this theater no matter who the offender may be."

But by this time the press corps in Sicily had got hold of the story. The reporters had conducted their own investigation and were prepared to make it public. "If I am correctly informed," one reporter noted, "General Patton has subjected himself to general court-martial by striking an enlisted man under his command." They wanted to know, a committee of correspondents told Eisenhower's chief of staff, what Eisenhower was going to do to punish Patton.

All of Eisenhower's famous abilities as a mediator were needed now. He called the reporters into his office and frankly confessed that he was doing all he could to hold on to Patton. He asked them to keep the story quiet so that Patton could be "saved for the great battles facing us in Europe." The effort worked. The correspondents entered into a gentleman's agreement to sit on the story.

Patton, meanwhile, tried to make amends. He apologized, although somewhat curtly, to Private Bennett and to the nurses and doctors of the 93rd Evacuation Hospital. He wrote Eisenhower, "I am at a loss to find words with which to express my chagrin and grief at having given you, a man to whom I owe everything and for whom I would gladly lay down my life, cause for displeasure with me." The incident was closed, or so Eisenhower hoped.

Three months later Drew Pearson learned of the Patton slapping incident and gave it full treatment in a radio broadcast. Eisenhower's chief of staff made matters worse when, in a press conference, he admitted that Eisenhower had not officially reprimanded Patton. Since there was a shortage of battlefront news at the time, the story received front-page treatment everywhere. Eisenhower, the War Department, and the White House each received hundreds of letters, most of them demanding that any general who would strike a private in a hospital be summarily dismissed from the service. The letter writers were especially upset because Eisenhower apparently had done nothing to censure Patton.

Eisenhower made no public defense of his actions. Nor was he willing to throw Patton to the wolves. He did answer a number of the incoming letters of criticism, carefully pointing out that Patton was too important to lose. In each case he asked that the letter be regarded as strictly personal. He advised Patton to keep quiet, since "it is my judgment that this storm will blow over." In the end, it did.

In the late fall of 1943 Eisenhower received his appointment as Supreme Commander for OVERLORD, the invasion of France. One major factor in his selection was his ability to get British and American officers to work together, something that would be even more important in OVERLORD than it had been in the Mediterranean. For this reason he was tempted to leave Patton behind. "Georgie" was something of an Anglophobe and loved to tweak sensitive English noses, especially Montgomery's; and Montgomery would be one of the chief commanders in OVERLORD. But despite this, and despite the slapping incident, Eisenhower decided to bring Patton along. He told Marshall, who had doubts, that he thought Patton was cured of his temper tantrums, partly because of his "personal loyalty to you and to me," but mainly because "he is so avid for recognition as a great military commander that he will ruthlessly suppress any habit of his own that will tend to jeopardize it." Marshall, remembering his own earlier admiration for Patton, and bending to Eisenhower's insistence, agreed.

Eisenhower's most important responsibility as Supreme Commander was the defeat of the German armies. He felt that whatever trouble Patton caused him in other ways, he would make a tremendous combat contribution to victory. Without accepting Patton's contention that execution was more important than planning, Eisenhower recognized that "the first thing that usually slows up operations is an element of caution, fatigue or doubt on the part of a higher commander." Patton was never affected by these.

So Patton, who had been in the doghouse without a real command since Sicily, went to England to prepare for the great invasion. On April 25, 1944, he went to the opening of a Welcome Club that the people of Knutsford had organized for the growing number of American troops in the town. About sixty people were there, sitting on hard-backed chairs in a cold, damp, depressing room, listening to insipid speeches on Allied unity. Patton was thoroughly bored. When asked to speak, he ad-libbed: he thought Anglo-American unity important "since it is the evident destiny of the British and Americans to rule the world, [and] the better we know each other the better job we will do."

Patton thought the meeting was private; but a reporter was present. The statement went out over the British wire services, and the next morning the British press indignantly featured it. Some editorial writers were angry because Patton had omitted Russia from the list of ruling powers; others cited the implicit insult to the smaller nations. The next day Patton's remarks were widely circulated in the United States, where he was denounced by both liberal and conservative congressmen. All agreed that generals ought to stay out of politics.

Patton, in short, had put his foot in his mouth. Eisenhower was disgusted. In his small office at SHAEF headquarters in Bushey Park, on the Thames River near London, he dictated a letter to Patton. "I have warned you time and again against your impulsiveness in action and speech and have flatly instructed you to say nothing that could possibly be misinterpreted. . . ." Eisenhower said he was forced to "doubt your all-round judgment, so essential in high military position." Then he sent General Marshall a cable expressing his disgust over the incident. He added, "I have grown so weary of the trouble he constantly causes you and the War Department to say nothing of myself, that I am seriously contemplating the most drastic action"—namely, sending Patton home.

Marshall told Eisenhower to do what he thought best, and on April 30 Eisenhower replied: "I will relieve him unless some new and unforeseen information should be developed in the case." Eisenhower felt Lieutenant General Courtney H. Hodges would be satisfactory as Patton's replacement—and Hodges had no record of getting his superiors in trouble. Eisenhower admitted that he had about given up on Patton: "After a year and a half of working with him it appears hopeless to expect that he will ever completely overcome his lifelong habit of posing and of self-dramatization which causes him to break out in these extraordinary ways."

At 11 A.M. on May 1, Eisenhower met with Patton at Bushey Park. An old hand at getting out of a fix, Patton let out all the stops. He told Eisenhower that he felt miserable, but that he would fight for his country if "they" would let him. Alternatively, he dramatically offered to resign his commission to save his old friend from embarrassment. He seemed on the verge of tears. The outpouring of emotion made Eisenhower slightly uncomfortable; he did not really want Patton on his knees begging. He ended the interview by dismissing Patton without having made a decision.

For the next two days Eisenhower mulled it over. He finally decided that Patton was too valuable to lose, and sent a wire informing him that he would stay on. Patton celebrated with a drink, then sent a sentimental letter to Eisenhower expressing eternal loyalty and gratitude. To his diary, however, he confessed that his retention "is not the result of an accident" but rather "the work of God."

Eisenhower's aide, Harry Butcher, noted that Patton "is a master of flattery and succeeds in turning any difference of views with Ike into a deferential acquiescence to the views of the Supreme Commander." But if Butcher saw something that Eisenhower missed, there was a reverse side to the coin. Patton bragged that he was tolerated as an erratic genius because he was considered indispensable, and he was right. The very qualities that made him a great actor also made him a great commander, and Eisenhower knew it. "You owe us some victories," Eisenhower told Patton when the incident was closed. "Pay off and the world will deem me a wise man."

Patton paid off. On July 30, 1944, eight weeks after the invasion of Normandy, his Third Army began to tear across France in a blitzkrieg in reverse. Eisenhower used Patton's talents with the skill of a concert master, giving him leeway, holding him back when necessary, keeping him away from Montgomery's throat (and vice versa), and making sure that Bradley kept a close watch on his movements. It must be added that Patton showed small appreciation of Eisenhower's peculiar responsibilities. To hold the alliance together, Eisenhower had to humor Montgomery on a number of occasions. When he learned that Eisenhower had given more supplies to Montgomery than to the Third Army, Patton is said to have mumbled, "Ike's the best damn general the British have got."

Patton had something of the boy in him. He liked to believe that he was putting something over on his superiors, that he was getting away with mischief. On a number of occasions Patton thought that he was fooling both Bradley and Eisenhower. When he received orders to carry out a reconnaissance in force at the German border, for example, he turned it into a full offensive. He thought neither Bradley nor Eisenhower realized what he was up to; but of course they did, and had counted on it.

Aside from his drive through France, Patton's two great moments
came during the Battle of the Bulge and when he crossed the Rhine
River. On December 19, three days after Hitler's last offensive began,
Eisenhower and his chief subordinates at SHAEF met at Verdun with
Bradley, Patton, and other field commanders. The Germans had caught
the Allies by surprise and were making significant gains. Sitting around
a potbellied stove in a damp, chilly squad room of an old French bar-
racks, Eisenhower opened the meeting by announcing that he wanted
to see only cheerful faces at the table. "The present situation is to be
regarded as one of opportunity for us and not of disaster," he said.
Patton grinned and declared, "Hell, let's have the guts to let the ——
—— —— go all the way to Paris. Then we'll really cut 'em off and chew
'em up." Eisenhower grinned back, but said that the Germans would
never get across the Meuse River.

When the Germans struck, Patton had been preparing an offensive
of his own, headed east. Eisenhower ordered him to switch directions,
attack north, and hit the Germans in the Bulge on their left flank. In
three days Patton got all his divisions turned and was on the road. By
December 26 he had battered his way through to Bastogne and, along
with Montgomery's forces on the German right flank, had stopped the
German thrust.

In March, 1945, Patton's Third Army reached the Rhine. A few
American troops had already made a surprise crossing at Remagen,
where they had found a bridge intact, but the main crossings were yet
to come. The big effort was to be made in the north, near the Ruhr
industrial concentration, by Montgomery's British and Canadian troops.
Ever since Sicily, Patton had been in keen competition with Montgomery, and he was determined to get his men across the historic river
first. The British general's preparations were detailed and meticulous.
On March 24, after a massive artillery barrage, Montgomery started to
cross. To his astonishment, he learned that Patton and his men were
already over. Patton had been carrying bridging equipment and a Navy
detachment with landing craft close up behind his infantry ever since
the liberation of Paris, for just this moment. With less than half Montgomery's strength, he beat the British to the east bank. While he himself was going over one of the Third Army's pontoon bridges, Patton
paused and deliberately undid his fly. "I have been looking forward
to this for a long time," he said.

Six weeks later the war was over. Peace highlighted the contrasting personalities of Eisenhower and Patton. Eisenhower moved smoothly into his new job as head of the occupation. He faithfully and without question carried out his superiors' orders. Patton chafed. He talked about driving the Russians back to the Volga River. He got chummy with German generals. As military governor in Bavaria, he kept former Nazis and even some SS officials in the local administration because, he argued, no one else was available. Actually, there were others available, men of Konrad Adenauer's stamp; but it was easier for Patton to work with the old hands. In any case Patton's policy ran exactly counter to the national policy, and Eisenhower ordered him to get rid of the Nazis. But except for a few prominent officials, Patton did nothing. He was sure that, before long, German and American generals would be fighting side by side against the Russians.

His area soon gained a dubious reputation, and the press waited for a chance to bait Patton into damning the de-Nazification policy. It came on September 22, when he called a press conference and asserted that the military government "would get better results if it employed more former members of the Nazi party in administrative jobs." A reporter, trying to appear casual, asked, "After all, General, didn't most ordinary Nazis join their party in about the same way that Americans become Republicans or Democrats?"

"Yes," Patton agreed. "That's about it."

The headlines the next day screamed that Patton had said the Nazis were just like Republicans and Democrats back home.

Eisenhower phoned Patton and told him to get over to his headquarters in Frankfurt right away. Patton arrived wearing a simple jacket and plain trousers rather than his fancy riding breeches, and he left behind the pearl-handled pistols he usually wore. The generals were together for two hours. When Patton walked out he was pale: Ike had taken the Third Army away from him.

Eisenhower gave Patton a meaningless paper army to command. He stayed in Germany, spending most of his time hunting. In December, on a hunting expedition, his neck was broken in an automobile accident. Eisenhower, who had returned to Washington to become Chief of Staff, wrote him on December 10. "You can imagine what a shock it was to me to hear of your serious accident," the letter began. "At first I heard it on the basis of rumor and simply did not believe it, thinking it only a story . . . I immediately wired Frankfurt and learned to my great distress that it was true."

Eisenhower told Patton he had notified Mrs. Patton and had given orders that everything possible should be arranged, including the fastest transportation available to fly Mrs. Patton to his bedside. "By coincidence, only the day before yesterday," Eisenhower continued, "I had directed that you be contacted to determine whether you wanted a particular job that appeared to be opening up here in the States. The real purpose of this note is simply to assure you that you will always have a job and not to worry about this accident closing out any of them for your selection."

Eisenhower confessed that "it is always difficult for me to express my true sentiments when I am deeply moved," but he wanted Patton to know "that you are never out of my thoughts and that my hopes and prayers are tied up in your speedy recovery. If anything at all occurs to you where I might be of some real help, don't hesitate a second to let an aide forward the message to me."

Mrs. Patton arrived at her husband's bedside the next day, and she read Eisenhower's letter to him. When she reached the end, he asked her to read the part about the job again.

Nine days later, George Patton died.

The Use of American Power in the Post-Colonial World

HERBERT I. SCHILLER

• Since the end of World War II the United States and the
Soviet Union have been engaged in a world-wide struggle for
power, prestige, and influence. In particular, the newly
emerging nations of Asia and Africa have been the scene of
considerable cold-war skirmishing. The United States has
reversed its traditional policy of avoiding permanent alliances,
and through such vehicles as the Truman Doctrine, the
North Atlantic Treaty Organization, and the Southeast Asia
Treaty Organization has pledged its enormous military
strength toward the defense of its allies.

Most Americans are familiar with such foreign aid programs as the Marshall Plan, the Point Four Program, and the
Alliance for Progress, and they believe that the United
States government has been using its resources to promote
what is best for underprivileged people in the world.
Unfortunately, the rhetoric and the realities of American
foreign policy have not always been in agreement. Although
professing the ideals of democracy and national self-determination, the United States has sometimes supported dic-
tators of the most vicious sort. In the words of The New York
Times, the United States and its European allies seem "dangerously indifferent to the crisis that is brewing in the poverty-stricken areas of the world, a crisis that is not unlike
that which has already exploded in the impoverished ghettos
of American cities."

In the following selection, Professor Herbert Schiller discusses United States policies since 1945 and suggests that
this nation has actually hindered the economic development
of emerging nations. Much of his evidence comes from the
United Nations Conference on Trade and Development in

From *The Massachusetts Review*, copyright © 1968 by The Massachusetts Review, Inc.

1964. For instance, he notes that the United States delegation voted against a proposal whereby "a significant portion of resources released in successive stages as a result of the conclusion of an agreement on general and complete disarmament under effective international control should be allocated to the promotion of economic development in developing countries."

As a matter of practical fact, however, an affirmative vote on such a statement would have committed the American taxpayer to an increase of billions of dollars in foreign aid. Is it reasonable, therefore, to attack the United States on the basis of conference votes? Do you find Schiller's thesis convincing or do you find his view overly harsh?

Self-delusion has never been a national monopoly. Our English friends not so long ago colored the world's maps with their own particular hue (curiously it was red) indicating their global paramountcy—all the while exclaiming that their steadily expanding empire was indeed even a surprise to themselves. As one English chronicler of the late 19th century put it, "We seem, as it were, to have conquered and peopled half the world in a fit of absence of mind."

Since then, we have overtaken and surpassed the English in many fields, not least of which is apologetics. American explanations of what has been unfolding on the international scene in recent decades substitute concern and generosity for absent-mindedness as the motivating elements in the nation's overseas economic behavior. Beginning a long line of self-justifications, President Truman in his 1949 inaugural address, for example, affirmed that "The old imperialism—exploitation for foreign profit—has no place in our plans. What we envisage is a program of development based on the concepts of democratic fair-dealing."

Academics likewise have put a good face on American practices overseas since Hiroshima, and they have assured us that we differ greatly from this century's earlier predators. One writes "It is certainly misleading to describe by the same word 'imperialism' both the European statesmen who plan ruthlessly to overrun a country in Asia or Africa and the American company building an automobile assembly plant in Israel." Another asserts that "What was regarded as exploitative imperialism about a half-century ago is now regarded on almost all sides virtually as benevolences extended to economically backward nations starved for development capital. . . ."

These reassuring comments notwithstanding, any serious effort to explain what has been going on internationally since 1945 must take into account some elemental economic relationships, both *inside* the United States and *between* the United States and its world associates. Without invoking a conspiracy conception of American enterprise, if anyone can review the evidence—the positions argued by policy-makers and diplomats over the last twenty years—without discerning a very marked elaboration of economic-political stances conducive to the world-wide expansion of United States private economic power, above and far beyond any reasonable representation of this power in our allegedly pluralistic society, then one is turning a blind eye on proceedings.

Explanations of this country's recent economic behavior, global and domestic, that exclude the analysis of group interests, approximate as such analysis must be, can resort in the end, only to vague and mystical categories—the tiresome and unrevealing conceptions of "honor," "face," "maturity" and "character."

Joseph Schumpeter, though he denied its connection to the capitalist economy and saw imperialism as a carryover from an earlier tribal or national belligerency, asked the proper question when writing about Roman imperialism. He noted: "Here there was neither a warrior nation in our sense, nor, in the beginning, a military despotism or an aristocracy of specifically military orientation. Thus there is but one way to an understanding: *scrutiny of domestic class interests; the question of who stood to gain.*" (Italics added)

More sharply put and more willing to move out of antiquity, but essentially in agreement, Baran and Sweezy in their "Notes on the Theory of Imperialism" assert that ". . . the relevant actors on the imperialist stage are classes and their subdivisions down to and including their individual members. And this means in the first instance the dominant classes in the most advanced capitalist countries to which the less developed and underdeveloped countries stand in various relations of subordination."

The departure point, consequently, in this analysis is the belief that eclectic aggregation obscures more than it reveals of international interaction. We must, with Schumpeter, inquire throughout this appraisal, "Who Stands to Gain?"

This understood, we identify next the environmental setting in which the dynamics of internationalism occur. The international community that has emerged in the last quarter-century presents a vastly different complexion to the order prevailing before World War II. The new age is defined by a massive shift in the global distribution of power points. More than matching the recession of European authority, once exercised internationally, has been the thrusting forward of American strength. Samuel P. Huntington writes about this: "By the year 2000 it should be clear retrospectively that the dominant feature of international politics during the thirty years after World War II was neither the East-West confrontation between the U.S. and the Sino-Soviet bloc nor the North-South conflict between the developed and the underdeveloped countries. Instead, the crucial relationship was that between the United States and Western Europe, and the dominant feature of international politics during this period was the expansion of the power of the United States. A critical feature of this expansion was the extension of American power into the vacuums that were left after the decline of the European influence in Asia, Africa, and even Latin America. . . . Americans devoted much attention to the expansion of Communism (which, in fact, expanded very little after 1949), and in the process they tended to ignore the expansion of the United States influence and presence throughout much of the world."

Alongside this sweeping power transfer have occurred two other significant developments. One is the extension of the state-owned enterprise sector from the isolation of its initial quarantined Soviet base to a position that embraces much of Europe and Asia, though the past summer's Soviet-Czechoslovak developments indicate that this extended socialist area is by no means as stable as it once seemed to be. The other is the transition of a good portion of the rest of the world from a position of formal *total* subordination, colonialism, to a condition of *political* independence and national sovereignty.

The interplay of American power, newly felt, with diminished European strength, an expanded but divided and therefore vulnerable Socialist geographical and material base and the newly-independent but economically feeble "third world" is the setting for the drama now enacted on the world stage.

American power, physically apparent throughout the twentieth century, achieved its global eminence during and since World War II. The full implications of this power only slowly seeped into the general consciousness of the nation, though certain groups were earlier alert to its significance.

The outlines of a national expansionist economic policy, evident in bits and pieces of war-time negotiations, took some time to be formulated into an all-embracing theoretical structure. When it finally was articulated in the immediate postwar years, it reflected the already deep imprint that public relations and salesmanship had made on national life. The country's new doctrine for international relations consolidated all concerns under the rubric of freedom. Freedom of trade, freedom of enterprise and freedom of speech became the catchwords of American foreign policy and have remained the apparent guideposts of national decision-making for an uninterrupted twenty-year span. As early as 1947, President Truman made an explicit declaration of governmental intentions. He stated unequivocally that "There is one thing that Americans value even more than peace. It is freedom: freedom of worship—freedom of speech—and freedom of enterprise."

The association of the objectives of American expansionism with the concept of freedom, in which the former are obscured and the latter is emphasized, has been a brilliant achievement of American policy. Rarely has a word, "freedom," produced so much confusion and obtained so much misdirected endorsement.

The opportunity to benefit from unrestricted freedom in trade or enterprise is a very uncertain advantage for those whose strength is puny or whose capital is limited. Small enterprises in undeveloped economies competing against the industrial giants of the Western world may find freedom of trade something less than an unmixed blessing. Similarly, freedom of speech, viewed as the unrestrained opportunity for the dissemination of the messages of powerful American mass media in the world arena, threatens to swamp the feeble communications systems of the poor nations who comprise the vast majority of the global community.

Information moving between nations on the basis of "economic opportunities" and "competition," unimpeded by other national or cultural considerations, affords American communications media the same advantages American commerce now receives from "free" world trade patterns that are also minimally controlled by national states. Accordingly, the material interests of American commerce and American mass communications find their expression in the continuing official declarations of freedom of speech and freedom of enterprise. Their joint interests are further promoted, when, over time, it becomes apparent that the championing of freedom of communications (speech) most often has, as an indirect benefit, the global extension of American commerce and its value system. More of this later.

The conception of a well-arranged international economic order, though newly-announced as American doctrine twenty years ago, had an earlier counterpart in another world-embracing system. Writing about English national policy in the middle of the nineteenth century, two English economic historians used the felicitous phrase "free trade imperialism." The concept of empire, they noted, cannot be judged by *formal* empire alone. "Refusals to annex are no proof of reluctance to control." The mechanics of informal empire, in the British experience, these writers found, "was the treaty of free trade and friendship made with or imposed upon a weaker state." The policy as they describe it was "trade with informal control if possible, trade with rule when necessary." A brilliant opportunity for the practice of free trade imperialism was offered to the English in Latin America after that area's breakaway from Spain in the early 1800's. Canning, the British minister in 1824, put the issue in terms that are stunningly contemporary. "Spanish America is free," he said, "and if we do not mismanage our affairs sadly, she is English."

A century and a half later, American leaders view the dissolution of the British, French, Dutch and Portuguese empires with equal enthusiasm if less candor. All the same, the opportunities for informal control, both material and ideological, of the newly-independent nations are irresistible to the new American power complex. This is implicit in Landes' bland explanation of American practices ". . . as a multifarious response to a common opportunity that consists simply in disparity of power," and that "whenever and wherever such disparity has existed, people and groups have been ready to take advantage of it."

The United States, ready and willing to exert its will, is at the top of the power pyramid that exists today and scores of recently independent states are at the bottom. Internationally the new order is represented by a visible 55 billion dollars of invested private capital (and untold billions not identified) and another 55 billion dollars of annual U.S. foreign trade, organized by an extremely concentrated group of commercial commanders.

To believe that the commercial and ideological connection-points that join the economically feeble nations to the technologically powerful American economy are beneficial to both sides of the union is to outdo Voltaire's good doctor Pangloss. In the recently-independent states, as Balogh and Fanon have both noted, "the new bureaucracy which was created is to a large extent a faithful reflection of the social failures of the imperial regime." This governing stratum accepts, often uncomplainingly, the socio-economic relationships which represent in Balogh's words "a severe limitation on the possibility of full development of the weaker parties in the 'colonial pact,' even if there is no conscious policy which aims at exploitation for the benefit of the metropolitan areas." Balogh affirms that "neo-imperialism does not depend on open political domination. The economic relations of the U.S. to South America are not essentially different from those of Britain to her African colonies. The International Monetary Fund [the chief instrument of Western International financial assistance] fulfills the role of the colonial administration of enforcing the rules of the game."

Whatever one may think of Kwame Nkrumah, his understanding of the functioning of the international economy eliminates rhetoric and muddle. He makes this point: "The issue is not what return the foreign investor receives on his investments. He may, in fact, do better for himself if he invests in a non-aligned country than if he invests in a neo-colonial one. The question is one of power. A State in the grip of neo-colonialism is not master of its own destiny."

The efforts of the developing states to shake off the network of controls, automatic or otherwise, that straitjacket them into an international system which distributes rewards unequally, reached a climax with the United Nations Conference on Trade and Development, convened in Geneva in March through June, 1964. At this international meeting, 120 nations and over 2000 delegates were assembled. A coalition of 77 developing states proposed at the outset of the conference to begin the reshaping of the international economy to a direction more favorable to the weaker parties. Their chief purpose was to expose and change the economic rules of international trade. It is these, they believe, that, unaltered, assign them to continuing inferiority. Balogh sums it up well: "So long as the rules of international trade and international payments are based on a theory which itself is derived from the fiction of equal partnership between small and large, poor and rich, sluggish and dynamic, any endeavor to overcome the inequality in income distribution will be frustrated. No magic formula or economic gadget or policy trick exists which would deal with the worsening of the relations of the rich and the poor countries without fundamental long-term aid and development planning."

Consider the issues that arose at the conference. In its final act the United Nations Conference on Trade and Development agreed on fifteen general and twelve special principles to govern international trade relations and trade policies in the interest of fostering economic development.

Of the fifteen General Principles adopted, the United States voted against nine and abstained on two, endorsing only four. Of the twelve Special Principles, the United States voted against four, abstained on five and endorsed only three. No other participant in the conference was so frequently in opposition. Only a handful of Western European states came anywhere close to the negativism exhibited by the American delegation. On several important principles, the United States stood alone in the voting. On General Principle One, for instance, "Economic relations between countries, including trade relations, shall be based on respect for the principle of sovereign equality of States, self-determination of peoples, and noninterference in the internal affairs of other countries," the votes tallied 113 to 1 with 2 abstentions. In opposition to this principle was the United States. Abstaining were the United Kingdom and Portugal.

Almost identical line-ups occurred on General Principles Four (pledge "to help to promote in developing countries a rate of growth consistent with the need to bring about substantial and steady increase in average income in order to narrow the gap between the standard of living in developing countries and that in the developed countries"); Six (cooperation in creating international trade conditions "conducive in particular to the achievement of a rapid increase in the export earnings of developing countries and, in general, to the promotion of an expansion and diversification of trade between all countries, whether at similar levels of development, at different levels of development, or having different economic and social systems"); and Twelve ("a significant portion of resources released in successive stages as a result of the conclusion of an agreement on general and complete disarmament under effective international control should be allocated to the promotion of economic development in developing countries"). In each of these instances the United States cast the only negative vote.

The other General Principles against which the United States voted, generally in the company of a handful of industrialized states representing the North Atlantic enclave were Two ("no discrimination on the basis of differences in socio-economic systems"); Three ("Every country has the sovereign right to freely trade with other countries, and freely to dispose of its natural resources in the interest of the economic development and well-being of its own people"); Seven (positive measures to increase exports of developing countries and international cooperation to stabilize commodity export earnings and to maintain "a mutually acceptable relationship between the prices of manufactured goods and those of primary products"); Eight (special preferences on tariffs should be granted to the developing countries by the developed states without seeking reciprocity); and Eleven (obligation of international institutions and developed countries to provide an increasing net flow of international financial, technical and economic assistance; "such assistance, should not be subject to any political or military conditions"; whatever its form and source it "should flow to developing countries on terms fully in keeping with their trade and development needs. International financial and monetary policies should be designed to take full account of the trade and development needs of developing countries").

United States voting on the twelve Special Principles followed the same negative pattern. It cast the only vote against Special Principle Eight on applying internationally agreed criteria of surpluses and stockpiles "for the promotion of economic development of all developing countries whether producers or recipients." It voted against Special Principles One, Seven and Twelve with the same scant support of a few industrialized partners from Western Europe.

Most revealing perhaps, was the United States position on Special Principle Four. This stated simply that "Developing countries have the right to protect their infant industries." This modest attempt to protect the developing industries of the poorer countries was adopted by a roll-call vote of 115 to 0 with 1 abstention, the United States of America, which in doing so turned its back on its own developmental history.

The United States voted against all the measures that were designed to permit developing countries to organize their own affairs in their own interest. It allowed no room for genuine international decision-making. It expressed no willingness to permit the slightest intrusion on its own internal or external right of decision for the benefit of a larger community.

The United States voted unswervingly and often alone for the continuation of a world market organized in its own interest. In the face of the overwhelming opposition of the entire, underdeveloped world as well as all of the Socialist bloc and a good section of the noncommunist industrialized nations, the United States insisted on the workability of an international economy that has been demonstrably ineffective in raising living standards in two-thirds of the world. No other single episode in the last twenty years demonstrates so conclusively and comprehensively the implacable resistance of United States policy to fundamental change in the economic condition of the poor world as does the behavior at Geneva. Even as kind and generous an observer of United States policy as Professor Harry Johnson was compelled to write that ". . . the United States appeared at UNCTAD as the arch-defender of a system of international trade they (the poor world) believe to be strongly biased against their trade and development interests and the chief opponent of changes they believe essential to the foundation of a more equitable international trading order." Johnson concluded, perhaps wishfully, that ". . . the United States cannot persist in maintaining this predominantly negative stance. In purely political terms it has suffered a serious defeat from the less developed group. . . ."

The sole argument that was mustered by the defenders of American economic policy at Geneva is that which Johnson invoked in his account of the meeting. This is the charge that the UNCTAD majorities were proposing economically inefficient policies—that costs all around, in the developed and in the developing societies would be higher if protectionist devices, commodity agreements, unreciprocated tariff preferences, infant industry sponsorship, et al. were adopted.

Actually, the answer to this criticism was given a long time ago. Friedrich List, writing in the first half of the 19th century to promote the development of a still-weak German economy, noted that ". . . the loss which a nation undergoes in consequence of protective tariffs consists in any case only in *values*; whereas, on the other hand, it gains *powers* whereby it is enabled permanently to produce values which are incalculable in their amount. This expenditure of value is, accordingly, to be regarded simply as the price of the industrial development of the nation."

Put differently, economic efficiency is not sufficient excuse against policies or actions that aim to break a prevailing power pattern. The issue is not inefficiency for its own sake, but inefficiency as perhaps an inescapable accompaniment of essential structural change. List had recognized a century and a quarter ago the vital interconnections of economics and politics. In our time, Sartre has described how the Cuban revolution shattered the bones and ripped apart the tissue of the old social order. Can this be done neatly? To balk at change that may be temporarily inefficient is to accept the survival of the way things are.

While totally resisting UNCTAD's 1964 proposals for improving the situation of the hungering many, the United States nevertheless continues to emphasize its selfless concern with these problems. In the President's 1967 *Economic Report*, for example, it was asserted that "The United States will continue to respond constructively to the aspirations of the developing nations."

Meanwhile, at the second UNCTAD Conference, convened in Delhi in the spring of 1968, nothing was changed in the scenario. The United States and the North Atlantic industrialized elite states continued to resist any fundamental restructuring of the world economy that might benefit the less advantaged nations. The *New York Times* editorialized: "Underlying the failure of this conference was the preoccupation of its natural leader, the United States, with the Vietnam War, plus the fiscal and monetary problems precipitated by that war at home and abroad. Because of these and other domestic considerations, the wealthy nations of the West have remained dangerously indifferent to the crisis that is brewing in the poverty-stricken areas of the world, a crisis that is not unlike that which has already exploded in the impoverished ghettos of American cities."

Given the refusal of the world's most powerful nation to accept significant changes in the international trading economy and its insistence on economic structures in other states that correspond to its own parochial notions of freedom and efficiency, the matter of financial assistance, the so-called foreign aid program, assumes a perspective altogether different than that which it is generally given, either by its promoters or detractors. Issues such as waste, corruption, inadequacy and length of the aid commitment that have received much of the attention of the program's critics, are obviously secondary or even irrelevant considerations. They are a piece with those charges of waste against the Armed Forces, not because of their very existence, but because the services throw away too much edible food in their garbage.

If national rather than commercial interest was foremost, the country would be channeling its entire economic assistance through a United Nations agency. This organ, in turn, by standards Washington has often endorsed on paper, would be distributing these resources largely to those countries which have already had their revolutions (or, at least, partial revolutions) and are in a position to utilize the materials constructively. Egypt, Cuba, Guyana (under Jagan), The Dominican Republic after the ill-starred uprising against its generals, Ben-Bella's Algeria, and, the Committee of One Million notwithstanding, Mao's China, would be (or should have been) the foremost recipients of American largesse. In all of these countries the spirit of change is or was manifest and the aspirations of the many for development clearly expressed. That many of these states have received not aid but unremitting hostility is a matter of public record. Their culpability in the eyes of U.S. leadership springs from their lack of hospitality to foreign investment and the absence of freedom of enterprise and free trade, though the bill of particulars drawn up for domestic consumption in the United States is, of course, less candid.

Instead we give our substance to the "free" countries along the frontier of the Sino-Soviet land-mass, Vietnam, Laos, Thailand, Taiwan, India, Pakistan, Turkey. With what is left over, in the words of the President's latest special message on foreign aid, we "seek new breakthroughs in private investment in Africa, particularly the current efforts by private American banks and other financial institutions."

Despite being told for twenty years that bilateral aid-giving is humiliating to both the recipient and the donor, we steadfastly maintain our bilateral habits, and there is a very good reason for this obstinacy. "Bilateralism is appropriate to a world of nations with unlimited sovereignty," writes Senator Fulbright, and, he adds, "multilateralism to a world that is at least groping toward a broader community." Unlimited sovereignty reinforced with arrogant power makes bilateral aid a useful instrument of persuasion, pressure and coercion. This is not the place to document these activities. One of the most blatant examples was the hold-up of grain to famine-threatened India until that unhappy country's government accepted private ownership for the chemical fertilizer industry in which American firms are active.

Of course, bilateralism is not an exclusive American practice. Ohlin estimates that in 1963, "as much as 84 percent of global development assistance was bilateral." The Western Europeans "aid" their ex-colonial territories. The relatively large-scale French effort of which we hear so much is concentrated on former possessions in tropical Africa. The British program, as Ohlin notes, "has its roots in colonial policy" and continues to be directed, albeit modestly, to former empire holdings. The Belgian aid activity is concentrated in the Congo and the West Germans, whose pre-war colonial holdings were inconsequential, unashamedly use their aid program, such as it is, for a policy of export promotion.

Another aspect of foreign aid instrumental in preserving the present character of the international economy is military assistance for the maintenance of "order." When angry people rampage in the streets against pitiful destinies, the investment climate that business considers so essential to its affairs suddenly turns raw and chilly. No better business climate regulator has yet been devised than the military strongman who sweeps the streets clear with his loyal legions. Senator Fulbright ironically notes "that we are sustaining over three million non-fighting men along the borders of Russia and China" and he "wonders whether some of the countries which maintain these forces would not be more stable and secure today if much of the money spent on armaments over the years had been used instead for development and social reform." Furthermore, he adds, "Viewed in the physical and economic context

of a poor country in Central America, United States military assistance
no longer appears small and innocent: it contributes in an important
way to the perpetuation of military oligarchies."

Many other criticisms can be leveled against the foreign aid program. It has served the narrowest market interests of the export community. It has offered a haven for former officers of the National Student Association, who like old generals, do not die but only fade away
into overseas intelligence activity with A.I.D. It has sometimes misused
the counterpart funds at its disposal and often grossly interfered in the
internal affairs of sovereign states. It nourishes corrupt elites in many
places. But its chief limitation, its fatal flaw, is that it serves, before
anything else, the commercial aims of its founders and promoters and
these are antithetical to significant change and development abroad.

Much like domestic social welfare work, foreign aid has its dedicated
individuals and engages in some useful, if limited activity. But also like
social welfare in America, it is basically a sordid, patch-up job which
temporarily prevents the mess from spilling over onto the orderly
avenues of the well-off. It is tragic too, because the generous impulses
of American society have been soured by the sorry record of a program
which is superficially a national contribution but which in practice is
something else. At a time when the world requires an expanding stream
of American resources, the popular attitude grows more resentful and
mistakenly (if understandably) attributes to the concept of assistance
itself the failures of those who manipulate and distort the program
for private goals.

Finally, a discussion of the contemporary methodology of international economic control, however limited, cannot be completed without
at least a few words on the very unlikely subject of ideology. Half a
century ago, Rosa Luxemburg came to the end of her study on *The
Accumulation of Capital* and concluded that ". . . Capitalism is the
first mode of economy with the weapon of propaganda, a mode which
tends to engulf the entire globe and stamp out all other economies,
tolerating no rival at its side." The legitimacy of this statement is more
apparent now than ever. Matching the dazzling advances in communications technology has been the equally remarkable takeover of
communications structures and systems by American electronics superpower. Consider the dilemmas of Britain and France, striving to main-

tain communications conti   er their former empires while the communications instrumentation of the future, satellite communications, leapfrogs their cables and wire systems and develops rapidly under the control and guidance of their relentless ally, the United States.

The organization of INTELSAT, the international communications satellite consortium, is illustrative of the stranglehold that American electronics leadership presently exercises in the world community. Comsat, the American communications satellite corporation, privately owned but carrying some governmentally-appointed directors, controls roughly 53 percent of the voting stock in this purportedly international organization. The terms of the agreement are now so drawn that Comsat's share can never drop below 50.5 percent, an absolute control percentage. As might be expected, Comsat is also the general manager and executive agent of the new, global communications system.

If already-industrialized states are apprehensive over American power, what is the situation of the not-yet-developed societies? Their industrial feebleness is legendary. Less well appreciated is their total vulnerability to economic domination through the cultural mechanism. Their ability to withstand the ideological barrage of modern communications artillery is practically nonexistent. Moreover, the messages and information that emanate from the American electronic culture complex are far more effective instruments of control than the visiting naval flotillas of an earlier age.

Furtado points out that in contemporary development the historical order of interaction between base and superstructure is reversed. Unlike the Western growth experience, the non-material culture in the new societies today changes faster than the technology and the productive relations, creating unique problems for development designers. Balogh, too, has considered what this means for a poor society. Consumer want stimulation in India after the American pattern, he believes, would be disastrous, not only because "the creation of new wants is directly hostile to savings and accumulation," but in addition, it would introduce into India "the social escalation of material desires which has led to such frustration in the highly developed industrial countries of the West."

To be sure, it is no startling discovery to declare that the determination of the character and the direction of the national community slips out of the exclusive control of indigenous leaderships in propor-

tion to the exposure of the society to external contacts. What is
remarkable in this age is the speed and the totality by which the process
operates, permitting little time for insulation and adjustment. In one
swoop, so to speak, the weak society is deprived of its right to decide
for itself the options it will follow on its developmental course. Once
the consciousness of any considerable fraction of a population has
been awakened to the possibilities of consumerism, for instance, woe
be to leaderships not equally beguiled and disinclined to move the
developmental machinery in that direction.

This is the *general* problem that American commercially-dominated
communications presents to any society exposed to its wares. On an
individual basis it goes much deeper and affects the very process of
character formation. It involves relationships and attitudes that oppose
privatism to community, personal acquisition to collective enjoyment
and the self to the group. The ideological problems of socialist development are illustrative. The movement to socialism, one writer observes,
requires ideological development at least as rapid as technological progress, otherwise the transformation of the society may be postponed or
carried forward in distorted fashion. Yet it is further noted that "in
an imperfect situation, communists cannot separate foreign technology
from foreign ideology perfectly."

Our domestic strategy makers are not unaware of this dilemma.
When the Russians contract with the Italians to have Fiats manufactured in the USSR, the United States Government revokes its
decades-old embargo on credits to the Soviet Union to help finance
the importation of American machine tools for automobile assembly
lines. The official explanation of the Defense Department is that "a
loan that would induce the Soviet Union to devote greater resources
to the production of consumer goods at the expense of applying those
resources to military purposes is in our national interest." Of course,
the real motive lies elsewhere. It is the recognition of the Department
of Defense and its allied governmental associates that the ideology
of consumerism in the USSR is enormously strengthened, that personal
acquisitiveness is enhanced, and that the Soviet society has taken
another step away from its socialist goal.

Socialism aside, from the standpoint of a developing nation attempting to preserve its cultural integrity, the present situation is menacing.
The British, the French and the Dutch have had to capitulate in one

way or another to the commercial programming of off-shore pirate radio stations. What then are the chances in economically feeble countries to safeguard cultural and material development from the influence of powerful external financial and communications systems?

It is difficult to determine whether United States global power, built up so rapidly in the last twenty years, will continue its ascendancy or will begin to wane in the years immediately ahead. Huntington hypothesizes that "in the year 2000 the American world system . . . will be in a state of disintegration and decay." Furthermore, he believes that ". . . the decline of American influence will tend to undermine and disrupt American politics. The American political system," he concludes, "could be less likely than that of the French Republic to adjust successfully to the loss of empire."

The domestic strains produced by one Vietnam indicate that Huntington's vision, grim as it is, may not be far off the mark, give or take a decade or two in the timing. Conflict, domestic and international, seems certain to be with us, as America ultimately goes through the painful process of imperial dissolution.

Kennedy in History: An Early Appraisal

WILLIAM G. CARLETON

• The assassination by rifle fire of the President of the United States on November 22, 1963, stunned the world and brought to a tragic and premature end one of the nation's most glamorous idols. John Fitzgerald Kennedy aroused a generation that had lived through depression, hot and cold war, and the threat of nuclear annihilation. As James Reston of The New York Times has written: "What was killed in Dallas was not only the President but the promise. The death of youth and the hope of youth, of the beauty and grace and the touch of magic."

About the charismatic qualities of the nation's first Roman Catholic President there has never been any dispute. In the realm of accomplishment, however, he achieved less than any Democratic President since Grover Cleveland. His administration negotiated a nuclear test ban treaty and won approval of the Trade Expansion Act of 1962, but his other major aims—farm legislation, a civil rights bill, tax reform, medicare, federal aid to schools—bogged down in Congress. His approval of the disastrous Bay of Pigs invasion of Cuba in 1961 and of increased involvement in Vietnam raise searching questions about the wisdom of his foreign policy, although most contemporaries approved of his handling of the Cuban missile crisis in 1962.

In the following essay, William Carleton evaluates the man and the President. He concludes, as have most writers, that despite his limitations, John F. Kennedy gave the nation, and indeed the world, a lift. How would you evaluate Kennedy's place in history? What does constitute evidence of presidential greatness?

From The Antioch Review, volume XXIV, number 3 (1964). Reprinted by permission of the editors.

Although John F. Kennedy has been dead less than a year, it is not too early to assess his place in history. Judgments about historical figures never come finally to rest. Reputations fluctuate through the centuries, for they must constantly do battle with oblivion and compete with the shifting interests and values of subsequent generations. Even so, contemporary estimates are sometimes not markedly changed by later ones.

The career of a public man, the key events of his life, most of his record, the questions he confronted, the problems he tackled, the social forces at work in his time are largely open to scrutiny when he leaves public life. The archives and subsequently revealed letters, memoirs, and diaries will yield important new material, but usually these merely fill out and embellish the already known public record.

What more frequently alters an early historical appraisal than later revealed material is the course of events after the hero has left the stage. For instance, should President Johnson, during the next few years, succeed in breaking the legislative log-jam and driving through Congress a major legislative program, then President Kennedy's failure to do this will be judged harshly. But should the congressional stalemate continue, then the Kennedy difficulties likely will be chalked up not so much against him personally but against the intricacies of the American system of separation of powers and pluralized, divided parties. Even so, it will not be easy to defend the meager Kennedy legislative performance.

If popular passion is running high at the time an historical personage makes his exit, then it is difficult for a contemporary to be relatively objective in his evaluation. (At no time is there absolute objectivity in history.) For instance, Woodrow Wilson left office amidst such violent misunderstanding that few contemporaries could do him justice, and only now, four decades later, is he being appraised with relative fairness. With Kennedy, one collides with adoration. The uncritical bias in favor of Kennedy derives from his winsome personality, his style and elan, the emotional euphoria arising from his tragic death, and the sympathetic spiritual kinship with him felt by historians, political scientists, intellectuals, and writers. There is, to be sure, considerable hate-Kennedy literature, most of it written before his death and reflecting ultra right-wing biases, but few will be fooled into taking diatribes for serious history.

WILLIAM G. CARLETON

II

Although as president he clearly belongs to the liberal tradition of the Democratic party's twentieth-century presidents, Kennedy's pre-presidential career can scarcely be said to have been liberal. During his congressional service he refused to hew to an ideological or even a party line. Kennedy often asked: "Just what is a liberal?" He confessed that his glands did not operate like Hubert Humphrey's.

Reviewing Kennedy's votes in House and Senate from 1947 to 1958, the AFL-CIO's Committee on Political Education gave him a pro-labor score of twenty-five out of twenty-six, which in considerable part may be explained by the large number of low-income wage-earners in his district. Kennedy usually followed the views and interests of his constituents, and this gave his congressional career its greatest measure of consistency. With respect to welfare programs which did not much concern his constituents—farm price supports, flood control, TVA, the Rural Electrification Administration—Kennedy sometimes joined the Byrd economy bloc. On occasion, Kennedy could fly in the face of New England sentiment, as when he supported reciprocal tariff laws and the St. Lawrence Seaway, and again when he publicly stated that he thought President Eisenhower, in an attempt to salvage the Paris summit conference, should apologize to Khrushchev for the U-2 incident. At such times, Kennedy displayed a disarming candor.

In foreign policy, Kennedy's early pronouncements had a right-wing flavor, especially with respect to China, but he soon developed a greater interest in foreign affairs than in domestic ones, and he moved away from right-wing attitudes to favor foreign economic aid, to rebuff the Committee of One Million devoted to keeping Red China out of the United Nations, to speak up for abandoning Quemoy and Matsu, to fight for economic help to Communist Poland, to advocate Algerian independence, and to encourage international arms-control negotiations.

In general, through the years, in both domestic and foreign policy, Kennedy moved from positions right of center or at center to positions left of center.

Since Negro rights played so important and dramatic a part in his

Presidency, historians will always be interested in Kennedy's earlier stand on civil rights. Until the presidential campaign of 1960, Kennedy was not an aggressive fighter for the Negro. During his quest for the vice-presidential nomination in 1956, he wooed the Southern delegations and stressed his moderation. After 1956, he sought to keep alive the South's benevolent feeling for him, and his speeches in that region, sprinkled with unflattering references to carpetbaggers like Mississippi Governor Alcorn and praise for L. Q. C. Lamar and other Bourbon "redeemers," had a faint ring of Claude Bowers' *Tragic Era*. In 1957, during the fight in the Senate over the civil rights bill, Kennedy lined up for the O'Mahoney amendment to give jury trials to those held in criminal contempt of court. Civil rights militants regarded this as emasculating, since those accused of impeding Negro voting would find more leniency in Southern juries than in federal judges.

What will disturb historians most about Kennedy's pre-presidential career was his evasion of the McCarthy challenge. In his early congressional days, Kennedy himself often gave expression to the mood of frustration, especially with reference to the loss of China, out of which McCarthyism came. In a talk at Harvard in 1950, Kennedy said that "McCarthy may have something," and he declared that not enough had been done about Communists in government.

By the time McCarthyism had emerged full blown, Kennedy was caught in a maze of entanglements. His Irish-Catholic constituents were ecstatically for McCarthy, and Kennedy's own family was enmeshed. Westbrook Pegler, McCarthy's foremost journalistic supporter, was close to father Joseph P. Kennedy; the elder Kennedy entertained McCarthy at Hyannis Port and contributed to his political fund; brother Robert Kennedy became a member of McCarthy's investigating staff. John Kennedy himself not only kept mum on the McCarthy issue but actually benefited from it. During Kennedy's senatorial campaign against Lodge, the latter was portrayed as soft on Communism, leading McCarthyite politicians and newspapers in Massachusetts backed Kennedy, and McCarthy was persuaded to stay out of Massachusetts and do nothing for Lodge there.

When McCarthyism finally climaxed in the debate and vote in the Senate over censuring the Great Inquisitor, Kennedy was absent because of an illness which nearly cost him his life. At no time did

Kennedy ever announce how he would have voted on censure. He did not exercise his right to pair his vote with another absent colleague who held an opposite view. It may be that Kennedy was too ill for even that. Kennedy's subsequent private explanations—that to have opposed McCarthy would have been to commit political hara-kiri and that he was caught in a web of family entanglements—were lame and unworthy.

Nevertheless, there can be no doubt that McCarthyism was a searing experience for John Kennedy. During his convalescence, as a sort of personal catharsis, he wrote his book *Profiles in Courage*, which dealt with famous senators of the past who had to choose between personal conscience and violent mass execration and political extinction. Kennedy seems to be saying: "This is the kind of cruel dilemma I would have faced had I been present in the Senate when the vote was taken on the McCarthy censure." *Profiles in Courage* is Kennedy's examination of his own Procrustean anguish. Such soul-searching may have helped him psychologically, but it added not a whit to the fight against McCarthy's monstrous threat to the free and open society.

Some years later, when even then Eleanor Roosevelt sought to prod Kennedy into making an *ex post facto* condemnation of McCarthyism, he wisely refused. He observed, with that candor which was his most engaging hallmark, that since he had not been in opposition during the controversy, to take a decided stand after Senator McCarthy was politically dead would make him (Kennedy) a political prostitute and poltroon.

In the future, historians sympathetic to President Kennedy are likely to seriously underestimate the right-wing influences that played upon him and his brother Robert during their formative years and early life in politics. The influence of Joseph P. Kennedy was strong, and in the pre-Pearl Harbor years the Kennedy household was the center of "America First" leaders, journalists, and ideas, and in the early 1950's of McCarthy leaders, journalists, and ideas. It is not remarkable that John and Robert reflected some right-wing attitudes in their early political careers; what is remarkable is that first John and then Robert, who is less flexible, emancipated themselves from these attitudes.

III

In all likelihood, John Kennedy would never have become president had his brother Joe lived; or had he (John) been nominated for vice-president in 1956; or had the Paris summit of May 1960 not blown up.

All of those who have followed the Kennedy story know well that it was the eldest son of the family, Joe, Jr., and not John, who was slated for politics. If Joe, Jr., had lived, John would not have gone into politics at all. (This is not to say that Joe, Jr., would have "made the grade" in high politics, as believers in the Kennedy magic now assume.) Joe, Jr., was an extrovert; he was obviously the political "type." John's mind was more penetrating and dispassionate, and he did not fit the stereotype of the politician, particularly the Irish politician. What endeared John to the status-seeking minorities was that he appeared more the scion of an old aristocratic Yankee family than the authentic scions themselves. Had Joe, Jr., lived, the Kennedy family in all probability would never have had a president at all.

Had John Kennedy been nominated for vice-president in 1956, he would have gone down to disastrous defeat along with Stevenson. That year Eisenhower carried even more of the South than he had in 1952. Both the elder Kennedy and John are reported to have felt that this poorer showing by the Democratic national ticket in 1956 would have been attributed to the continued vitality of anti-Catholic sentiment, thus rendering Kennedy unavailable for the 1960 nomination. It seems that this is a sound judgment.

Despite the fact that more Americans were registered as Democrats than as Republicans, the chances for Republican success in 1960 looked rosy indeed until after the dramatic U-2 incident and the collapse of the Paris summit conference. Had the summit accomplished anything at all, the result would have been hailed as the crowning achievement of Eisenhower, the man of peace, and Nixon would have been effectively portrayed as Eisenhower's experienced heir, one who could be both resolute and conciliatory. The explosion of the summit paved the way for Republican defeat and gave plausibility to the kind of "view-with-alarm" campaign waged by Kennedy. In any

general climate favoring Republican victory, even Kennedy's ability
to win the Catholic vote would not have elected him.

Will historians be hard on Kennedy for his extravagant charges
during the 1960 campaign that the Eisenhower administration had
been remiss about America's missiles and space programs? (The fact
is that the "gap" in intercontinental missiles was decidedly in favor
of the United States.) No, for presidents are rated in history by the
records they make in office, not by how they wage their campaigns.
In his first campaign for the Presidency, Lincoln assured voters that
the South would not secede; Wilson promised his New Freedom
but in office wound up closer to Theodore Roosevelt's New Nationalism; and Franklin Roosevelt pledged ceonomy and a balanced
budget but became the founder of the New Deal. Kennedy's zeal will
likely be put down as no more than excessive "campaign oratory."
Oddly enough, it may be Eisenhower who will be blamed for failing to
"nail" Kennedy and to tell the nation bluntly the true state of its
defenses, for missing the opportunity to add credibility to America's
nuclear deterrent. Liberal historians, impressed by Kennedy's domestic
promises and, except for Cuba, his more liberal program than Nixon's
in foreign policy—Quemoy and Matsu, emphasis on foreign economic aid, stress on international arms control—will not be prone
to hold Kennedy accountable for the alarmist flavor of his campaign.

Of 1960's "issues," only the religious one will loom large in history. It was the religious implication which gave Kennedy the victory.
Democratic gains in the pivotal Catholic cities in the states with the
largest electoral votes were greater than Democratic losses in the
Protestant rural areas. It was the Democrats, not the Republicans, who
actively exploited the religious aspect. In the Protestant areas, citizens
were made to feel they were bigots if they voted against Kennedy. But
Catholics were appealed to on the grounds of their Catholicism. Any
evidence of Protestant intolerance was widely publicized to stimulate
Catholics and Jews to go to the polls to rebuke the bigots. But
history will treat these Democratic tactics—a kind of bigotry in reverse
—with kindness. The means may have been objectionable, but the
good achieved was enormous. For the first time in American history
a non-Protestant was elected president. The old barriers were downed.
Now that an Irish-Catholic had been elected president, the way was

opened for the election of an Italian Catholic, a Polish Catholic, a Jew, eventually a Negro. A basic American ideal had at last been implemented at the very pinnacle of American society.

The second permanent contribution of the 1960 election lies in its underscoring the large degree to which presidential pre-convention campaigns and election campaigns have been geared to democratic mass behavior. Kennedy and his team wisely recognized that a mere pursuit of the politicians and delegates was not enough, that beginning with 1928, conventions had nominated the outstanding national favorite as indicated by the primaries and the polls. In Kennedy's case, winning the primaries and the polls was especially necessary to convince the doubters that a young man and a Catholic could be elected president. Hence Kennedy organization, money, and high-level experts were directed not merely to bagging delegates but even more to winning mass support, primaries, and high ratings in the polls. In this they succeeded marvelously well. In effect, the Democratic convention merely ratified the choice already made by the primaries, the polls, and the mass media. The revolution in the presidential nominating process had been in the making for over three decades, but it took the Kennedy campaign to make the public and even the pundits aware of it.

During the election campaign itself, Kennedy kept alive his personal organization; brother Bob, his personal manager, was more important than the chairman of the Democratic National Committee; the nominee himself made all the meaningful decisions and virtually monopolized the limelight; other party leaders were dwarfed as never before. The TV debates further spotlighted the nominees. Again, as in the pre-convention campaign, the Kennedy team did not create the trend to a personalized campaign, to glamourous celebrity politics. The trend and the techniques to make it work had been on the way for decades. Basically these emerged from the increasingly mass nature of American society. But Kennedy exploited the trend and the techniques in conspicuously successful fashion; he widened, intensified, and accelerated them; he made the nation aware of them; he did much to institutionalize them.

Thus the Kennedy campaigns will always be remembered for the dramatic way they contributed to the personalized and plebiscitic Presidency.

IV

No administration in history staffed the executive departments and the White House offices with as many competent, dedicated, and brilliant men as did Kennedy's. Kennedy paid little attention to party qualifications at top level; the emphasis was on ability, drive, imagination, creativity. Politicians made way for specialists and technicians; but Kennedy was on the lookout for specialists *plus,* for men who had not only technical competence but intellectual verve. Kennedy himself was a generalist with a critical intelligence, and many of the most prized of his staff were men of like caliber—Sorensen, Goodwin, Bundy. After the brilliance of the Kennedy team, and with the ever-growing complexity of government problems, no administration is ever likely to want to go back to the pedestrian personnel of earlier administrations, although few presidents are apt to have the Kennedy sensitivity and magnetism capable of gathering together so scintillating an administration as his. FDR will be known as the founder of the presidential brain trust, but Kennedy will be known as the president who widened and institutionalized it.

In contrast to his performance in the executive departments, Kennedy's relations with Congress can scarcely be said to have been successful. The dream of enacting a legislative program comparable to that of Wilson and FDR soon vanished. The one outstanding legislative achievement of Kennedy was the Trade Expansion Act of 1962. All of Kennedy's other major goals—farm legislation, tax reform, a civil rights law, medicare, federal aid to schools—bogged down in Congress.

Since 1938, major welfare legislation had repeatedly been smothered in Congress at the hands of a Republican-conservative-Southern Democratic coalition. During the bobtail, post-conventions session of 1960, both Kennedy and Johnson, the Democratic party's new standard bearers, had met humiliating legislative failure when they found themselves unable to budge the Democratic Congress. Kennedy had explained that once the powers of the Presidency were in his hands, things would be different. But when he achieved the Presidency and still failed with a Democratic Congress, Kennedy apologists contended that after Kennedy's re-election in 1964 he would be in a position to press more boldly for legislation. This argument stood experience on its head, for most presidents have secured much more legislation during their honeymoon first years than during their lame-duck second terms.

Kennedy will not escape all blame for his legislative failures, for despite his awareness of the stalemate since 1938, he had promised a "strong" legislative leadership like that of Wilson and the second Roosevelt. Moreover, in various ways Kennedy contributed to the personalized and plebiscitic Presidency: by the manner in which he waged his 1960 campaign, by his assigning to key posts not party leaders but men personally chosen for their expertise and creative intelligence, and by his monopolizing of the limelight. Kennedy and his family naturally made exciting publicity, but the President seemed to go out of his way to get even more—holding televised press conferences, for example, and permitting TV cameras to capture the intimacies of decision-making in the executive offices and of private life in the White House. All of this further exalted the Presidency, further dwarfed politicians, party, and Congress, and added to Congress' growing inferiority complex.

Now, Kennedy was not unaware of the susceptibilities of Congress. He carefully cultivated individual congressmen and senators, frequently called them on the phone, had them up for chats, extended them an unusual number of social courtesies and parties in the White House. His legislative liaison team, headed by Kenneth O'Donnell and Lawrence O'Brien, was diplomatic and astute, pumped and twisted congressional arms, applied both the carrot and the stick. But Kennedy left too many of the congressional chores to his liaison team. He simply did not give this aspect of the Presidency enough attention. Foreign affairs interested him intellectually much more than domestic measures. Despite his years in Congress and his love of politics, Kennedy did not really like or feel at home with small-bore politicians and congressional "types," and he was not skillful in his personal bargaining with them.

Moreover, Kennedy made no attempt to initiate and institutionalize new devices for easing presidential-congressional relations, nor did he even explore this problem intellectually. The breath of life to politicians is publicity, but no effort was made to share the presidential glory, of which there was a superabundance. What could be done to

enhance the publicity and prestige of congressional leaders and committee chairmen who consented to carry the administration ball in
Congress? How give them credit for "creating" and "initiating" the
administration's legislative measures? How let them become spokes-
men before the nation of the administration's legislative goals? True,
other presidents had made no such probings, but in recent years, with
a legislative log-jam piling up, the presidential-congressional deadlock
had reached crisis-like proportions. The President did not give this
question, inherently baffling at best, his full creative effort.

Kennedy's Presidency will be known as the time of the Negro revolution, when Negro aspirations widened to include desegregation in the
private sector and were spectacularly supported by sit-ins and street
demonstrations. As President, Kennedy not only gave full executive
backing to the enforcement of court decisions but personally identified
himself with the goals of the Negro revolution and gave them the
full moral support of the Presidency.

By 1960, Kennedy had become an aggressive fighter for Negro
rights. With the South lined up behind the Lyndon Johnson candi-
dacy, Kennedy's nomination depended on the support of the Northern
liberals and the metropolitan areas outside the South. During the
election campaign, Kennedy's strategy was geared to winning the
Negro vote in the big cities of the states with large electoral votes.
Kennedy's new militancy carried over to his Presidency.

But by 1963, it appeared that what had been a political advantage
might turn into something of a political liability. "The Kennedys"
were denounced in the South, and the President faced the loss of much
of that section in 1964. More serious, there were indications that the
civil rights issue would cost Kennedy many votes in the North, where
considerable opposition to the Negro drive had developed. However,
by this time Kennedy had chosen his course, and while there might
be temporary shifts in tactics, there could be no turning back. Robert
Kennedy has stated that at this point the administration really did
not have any choice and that, besides, the administration's course
was the correct one. He reports the President as saying: "If we're
going to lose, let's lose on principle."

There seems little question that Kennedy would have been re-
elected in 1964, but the civil rights issue would have been his biggest
worry. In sizing up Kennedy as a politician, it is significant that he

appears not to have anticipated the extent to which his position on civil rights might become politically hazardous. Otherwise it is difficult to explain the appointment of his brother as attorney general, upon whom the brunt of enforcing the civil rights court decisions would necessarily fall. Astute rulers take care to divert the political lightning of an offended public from themselves to subordinates. But in appointing his brother attorney general, the President left himself no "out." Those hostile to the Negro revolution could not say: "President Kennedy is all right; it is that attorney general of his." Instead, they blamed "the Kennedys." With another attorney general, President Kennedy might well have escaped some of the venom of the opposition. And incidentally, Robert Kennedy, in some other important job, would have been made better available for high politics in the future.

V

In foreign policy, the first two years of Kennedy were ambiguous. In the third year, there was a clearer sense of direction, one which promised to harmonize American policy with emerging new realities in the world.

At the time of the Kennedy accession, the postwar world was disintegrating. Bipolarization was giving way to depolarization. The Sino-Soviet rift was widening. With the single exception of little Vietminh, all the old European colonies that had recently gained their independence had escaped Communism, although there were Communist guerrilla activities in some of them. The trend was to a new pluralism, a new diversity. The nuclear revolution in war and the American-Soviet nuclear deterrents had rendered an ultimate military showdown unthinkable. The United States was ahead in the nuclear arms race.

In Europe, despite Khrushchev's bluster about West Berlin, the existing arrangements in East and Central Europe were ripening into a more overt *modus vivendi*, by way of tacit understanding rather than formal political agreements. Trade and intercourse between East and West Europe were increasing, the satellites were operating more independently of Moscow, and an all-European economic and cultural co-operation seemed slowly to be replacing the postwar's clear-cut division between the "two Europes." West Europeans were becoming less interested in NATO because they were more and more convinced that there would be no Soviet military aggression in Europe, due to the nuclear deterrent and other reasons. The drive to West European political integration was slackening, owing to the decline of external pressures and to De Gaulle's opposition to the supranational approach. Forces within the Six, composing the Common Market, were honestly divided over whether they wanted an inward-looking European community or an outward-looking Atlantic one.

In short, Kennedy was confronted with a new fluidity, a necessity and an opportunity for a reappraisal of American foreign policy. How much of the old foreign policy was still applicable? What aspects required a new orientation? To what degree was it safe, realistic, and advantageous to strike out in new directions? In some ways this ambiguous situation was more agonizing to decision makers than the obvious crisis situation with which Truman and Acheson had had to deal in the late 1940's and early 1950's. It is no wonder that some aspects of the Kennedy record in foreign affairs seem somewhat confused, even contradictory.

The chief stumbling block to an American-Soviet *détente* continued to be Berlin, the two Germanies, and the territorial arrangements in East and Central Europe. Kennedy rejected explorations of a definitive settlement, and if in the future a genuine American-Soviet *rapprochement* develops, this rejection is likely to be held against him. However, he did move informally in the direction of a more openly tacit recognition of the existing arrangements in East and Central Europe. He deferred less to Adenauer's views than previous administrations had done. In his interview in *Izvestia*, remarkable for its clarity and candor, he agreed that it would not be advisable to let West Germany have its own nuclear weapons. After the Communists built the Berlin Wall, Kennedy resisted all pressures to use force to tear it down.

Nevertheless, during his first two years in office, Kennedy seems needlessly to have fanned the tensions of the dying Cold War. (It may be that "needlessly" is too strong a word; perhaps Kennedy thought he needed to arouse the country to obtain a more balanced military program, more foreign economic aid, the Alliance for Progress; perhaps he thought, too, that a truculent tone was necessary to convince Khrushchev that America would stand firm under duress for its rights in Berlin.) His inaugural address was alarmist, already historically off key, more suited to the Stalinist era than to 1961. His first State of the Union Message was even more alarmist. The nation was told that the world tide was unfavorable, that each day we were drawing near the maximum danger. His backing of the Cuban invasion in April, 1961, further fanned the Cold War. His statement to newspaper publishers and editors gathered at the White House in May— that the United States was in the most critical period of its history— increased the popular anxieties. He over-reacted to Khrushchev's Vienna ultimatum in June, for in recent years Khrushchev's repeated deadlines and backdowns over West Berlin had become a kind of pattern. But for Kennedy, Vienna seems to have been a traumatic experience. On his return home he appealed to Americans to build do-it-yourself bomb shelters, and this produced a war psychology in the country and all manner of frenetic behavior, caused right-wingism to soar (1961 was the year the membership and financial "take" of the right-wing organizations reached their peak), and weakened confidence abroad in Kennedy's judgment.

There are no defenders of the Cuban fiasco of April, 1961. Even had the expedition of the Cuban exiles been given American naval and air support and forced a landing, there is scant evidence that the Cubans, at that time devoted to Castro, would have revolted en masse and welcomed the invaders as deliverers. More likely a nasty civil war would have followed, with the Americans, giving increasing support to the invaders, cast in the role of subjugators. The C.I.A. had already rejected the social-revolutionary leadership of the anti-Castro Manuel Rey for a non-leftist leadership, and this would have made the task of overthrowing Castro even more difficult. The world would have looked on with dismay, and outside the United States the whole affair would have come to be regarded as "another Hungary." It is ironical that Kennedy, the generalist with a critical intelligence, the politician with a feel for popular moods, should on this occasion have been taken in by the bureaucrats and the "experts." Prodded by his own anti-Castro stand during the election campaign, Kennedy must have wanted desperately to believe in the reliability of those dossiers of the intelligence agents.

With respect to Western Europe, the Kennedy administration underestimated those forces within the Common Market that wanted a European community rather than an Atlantic community, at first regarded De Gaulle as a kind of maverick without group support for his position, and framed the Trade Expansion Act of 1962 in such a way that the most decisive tariff cuts between the United States and the Common Market would depend upon Britain's inclusion in the Market. Nevertheless, the Act as written still allowed for much liberalization of trade, even with Britain outside the Market, and the responsibility for failure to take advantage of this opportunity must be borne by parochial-minded groups and interests inside the Market.

The Kennedy administration's contributions to national defense were notable. It emphasized a balanced and diversified establishment—both strategic and tactical nuclear weapons, conventional arms, and guerrilla forces—so the nation would never have to make the choice between the ultimate weapons and no other adequate defense. It was realistic in its shift from bombers to missiles as the chief nuclear carriers of the future, and in its dismantling of the intermediate missiles bases in Britain, Italy, and Turkey as the Polaris submarines and intercontinental missiles became increasingly operational. Its attempt to find a formula for a NATO multilateral nuclear force was a way of countering De Gaulle's blandishments to the West Germans and of balancing the possibility of a détente with Russia with reassurances to Bonn. Its experiments with massive airlifts of ground troops was in part a response to the desires of many of America's NATO allies for less rigidity, less insistence on fixed ground quotas, and more flexibility. However, NATO was plainly in transition, and while the Polaris submarines and intercontinental missiles were making the United States less dependent on European bases, ways were not yet actually implemented to share America's nuclear weapons with European allies on a genuine multilateral basis and satisfy their desires for less centralized direction from the United States.

There was an honest facing up to the terrible responsibilities inherent in the nuclear deterrent. That deterrent was put under tighter control to guard against accident and mistake, and the "hot line" between Washington and Moscow was set up. A much more determined effort was made to get arms-control agreements and a treaty banning nuclear-weapons testing than had ever been made by Kennedy's predecessors. Negotiations with the Soviet Union had been going on for years, but the Americans now so yielded in their former demands for strict international inspection as to put the Russians on the defensive, making world opinion for the first time believe that it was the Russians and not the Americans who were the obstructionists. Kennedy's administration believed that the United States and Russia had an enormous common interest in preventing the spread of nuclear weapons to other countries, that the Sino-Soviet rift gave Khrushchev a new freedom and a new urge to make agreements, and that the increasing accuracy of national detection systems made the possibility of cheating on a test-ban treaty, even one without international inspection, "vanishingly small."

Kennedy's regime also showed its international-mindedness in its firm support of the United Nations. It defended the Secretariat, the executive, from Soviet attacks, and in practice the activities of the Secretariat were widened. The organization was saved from bankruptcy by American financial aid. The operation of the United Nations military force in the Congo, backed by the United States, showed that the American government had no sympathy for "neo-colonialism" as practiced by the Katanga secessions, and it added another successful precedent for international enforcement of international decisions.

With respect to the underdeveloped nations, the Kennedy policies paralleled the trend of history. Anti-colonialism and self-determination were more valiantly espoused than in the preceding administrations. The Dulles doctrine that neutralism is "immoral" was abandoned, and neutralism was cordially accepted for nations which wanted it. Neutralism was positively encouraged in Laos and in the Congo. Help to South Vietnam was so hedged as to prevent the guerrilla war there from escalating into another Indo-China war, another Korea. Foreign economic aid was increased. The Food-for-Peace program was expanded. The Peace Corps was launched. The Alliance for Progress, an ambitious economic-aid program in Latin America coupled with domestic reforms, an experiment in "controlled revolution," was undertaken.

However, Kennedy, like his predecessors, did little to make the average American understand foreign economic aid—that it is not only an attempt to raise living standards, prevent Communism, and contribute to the world's economic well-being and stability, but is also a substitute for those obsolete ways in which the old colonialism supplied capital to the underdeveloped areas. Until an American president takes to television and in a series of fireside chats explains to Americans in simple terms the real meaning of the foreign-aid program, that program will be in jeopardy.

The Cuban crisis of October, 1962, provoked by the discovery of secret Soviet intermediate missiles in Cuba, was the high point, the turning point, in the Kennedy administration. Could this crisis have been avoided? This will be debated by future historians. True, Khrushchev could not have declined giving Castro economic aid, technical assistance, and some military help, even had he desired to do so, for to have refused this would have been tantamount to surrendering Communist leadership to the Chinese. But why did he go to the length of planting intermediate-missile bases in Cuba? As an appeasement to the Stalinist and Chinese opposition? As a countermeasure to American missile bases in Turkey (which were soon to be dismantled)? As a means of blackmailing Americans into making a compromise on Berlin? To extract a promise from the Americans not to invade Cuba? Whatever the causes, some future historians will have nagging questions: Might this terrible gamble in nuclear brinkmanship have been prevented had Kennedy previously shown more disposition to come to a *détente* with the Soviet Union by a somewhat clearer recognition of the two Germanies and other *de facto* boundaries and arrangements in East and Central Europe; and if so, did this Kennedy reluctance, coming in part out of regard for West German opinion, represent a realistic appraisal of the world situation?

Anyway, when the crisis came, even neutralist opinion seemed to feel that Khrushchev's attempt to compensate for his own intercontinental-missiles lag and the open and avowed American intermediate missiles in Turkey did not justify the sneaky Soviet operation in Cuba. America's quiet, deliberate planning of countermeasures, both military and diplomatic, was masterly. America's prudent use of force, enough but not more than enough to achieve its objective, won world-wide acclaim. Khrushchev and Castro lost face. The Chinese denounced the Soviet backdown, and Chinese-Russian relations worsened. Most important, the peak of the crisis, a spectacular nuclear brinkmanship, cleared the atmosphere like a bolt of lightning. The lunacy of an ultimate nuclear showdown was traumatically revealed. Khrushchev's personal correspondence to Kennedy, reputedly revealing a highly emotional state and a genuine horror of nuclear war, the President had the grace, sportsmanship, and wisdom to keep secret.

Thereafter Khrushchev spoke even more insistently about the need to avoid nuclear war and pursue a policy of peaceful but competitive coexistence. From then on Kennedy gave more public recognition to emerging new international realities, the world's escape from monolithic threats, the trend to pluralism and diversity. In his address at American University in June, 1963, Kennedy spoke as if the Cold War scarcely existed and emphasized the common stake both the United States and the Soviet Union had in world peace and stability. This address, one of the noblest and most realistic state papers of our time, will be remembered long after Kennedy's inaugural address is forgotten.

The new spirit in world affairs expressed itself concretely in the consummation of the limited nuclear test-ban treaty in the summer of 1963, the first real break in the American-Soviet deadlock. After this, Kennedy proposed a joint American-Soviet effort to explore the moon, and he agreed to permit the Soviet Union to purchase American wheat.

By 1963, then, Kennedy had come to much awareness that the postwar world was ending and to a determination to attempt more shifts in American foreign policy in harmony with the emerging fluidity. By this time, too, he had developed close personal relations with a large number of premiers and heads of state the world over. It was felt that after his re-election in 1964 he would be in an unusually strong position to give American foreign policy a new direction, that the test-ban treaty was but a foretaste of more significant measures yet to come, measures which might lead to an American-Soviet *détente*, eventually even to a *rapprochement*. Thus the President's life ended in a tragic sense of incompleteness and unfulfillment.

Every twentieth-century American president with a flair for world politics and in power in time of momentous international decision has been felled by sickness or death before his term was over, before his work was completed. First Wilson. Then Roosevelt. Then Kennedy. For sheer bad luck, this is a record unique among nations.

VI

Because of the vividness of his personality and the shortness of his tenure, Kennedy will be known more for the intangibles—a taste-maker, a symbolic embodiment of the values of his time, a romantic folk hero—than for his achievements in statesmanship.

Government requires pageantry, and rulers are expected to put on a show. The Kennedys put on a superb one. Never before, not even under Dolly Madison, was the White House the scene of such a dazzling social life, one which combined beauty and intelligence, radiance and creativity. There were, to be sure, crabbed Mrs. Grundys who derided "peacock opulence" and looked back longingly to the decorous days of Lucy Webb Hayes. But most Americans were fascinated, pleased as punch that even Elizabeth and Philip appeared a bit dowdy in contrast to those two young American thoroughbreds in the White House. They figuratively crowned Jacqueline Queen of Hearts. This aspect of the Kennedy reign has been inimitably described by Katherine Anne Porter, and no historian will ever record it with more grace, insight, and tenderness.

Kennedy's contributions to the cultural life of the nation also belong to the intangible, and they are difficult to measure. Now of course President Kennedy did not engage in as wide-ranging an intellectual life as President Jefferson or President Theodore Roosevelt. He did not carry on a voluminous and polemical correspondence with American and foreign intellectuals as these men had done, even when they were in the White House. And Kennedy himself realized that his "little promotions" did not help young and struggling artists and writers in the direct and material way the New Deal works projects had done.

But never before Kennedy's time had the White House paid so much personal and social attention to the nation's writers, artists, musicians, scientists, and scholars. At first some of the public was inclined to take a snidely skeptical view of all this. Was not this celebrity-hunting, highbrow name-dropping, a further drive to presidential glamour? The recipients of these attentions did not think so. Only William Faulkner, in bad-tempered petulance, rebuffed the President. For the rest, a chat with the President or an invitation to an event in the White House was an occasion of a lifetime, and these felt that Kennedy was not merely honoring them but the creative work they represented. As Richard Rovere has pointed out, Kennedy was tremendously concerned that the American society become a good, even a brilliant, civilization. He thought of himself as a promoter, an impresario, of excellence in every phase of American life, and he hoped that future presidents would emulate him in this.

To latter twentieth-century Americans, Kennedy will be a kind of beau ideal reflecting what they consider admirable in the politician— a shunning of corniness and hokum, an accent on youth and wealth, the glamorous videographic personality favored by Hollywood and TV, a contrived casualness in dress and manner, the sophistication and urbanity of the ivy league, direct and clear speech sprinkled with wit, an avoidance of doctrine and dogma, a pragmatism just emotionally enough involved to be effective, the capacity for using expertise and Madison Avenue techniques, the ability to create and sustain an "image." In these, most of them externals, Kennedy will have many imitators.

The Kennedy clan will not be easy to imitate. Even more difficult of imitation will be the Kennedy mind—rational and balanced thinking, objectivity, the ability to see all around a question, resilience, elusiveness, the capacity for keeping judgment in suspense, a detachment reaching to one's self and one's own image, an avoidance of absolute commitment combined with genuine intellectual involvement, a general critical intelligence brought to bear on the findings of the specialists. The Kennedy magic lies in its combination of the various elements: the externals, the verve with which the externals were carried off, and the cast of mind.

There is still another Kennedy intangible, perhaps the most important, one which belongs to the non-rational. Kennedy is becoming a folk hero, a subject of myth and legend, one of those few in history who capture the poetic imagination and affection of the masses. Solid achievement may have something to do with arriving at such a place in history, but very often it has little or nothing to do with it. Indeed, the titans who have wrought most mightily and in the end been felled by tragedy inspire awe and reverence more frequently than they do folk affection. They are too mature, their lives too devoid of colorful gallantries and foibles, their achievements too overwhelming for the average man to identify himself with such figures. To this class belong

2 WILLIAM G. CARLETON

Caesar, William the Silent, Lincoln. Increasingly Lincoln has become a father image and "the martyred Christ of the democratic passion play."

The folk hero in the affectionate, indulgent sense is one who leaves behind him an over-all impression of elan, style, beauty, grace, gaiety, gallantry, bold and light-hearted adventure, valor—mingled in one way or another with the frail, the fey, the heedless, the mystic, the tragic. This is the romantic tradition, the tradition of Achilles, David, Alcibiades (despite his damaged soul), Arthur, Roland, Abelard, Richard the Lion Hearted, St. Francis, Bayard, Raleigh, Henry of Navarre, Gustavus Adolphus, Byron. Alexander the Great is often put in this tradition, but his exploits were so dazzling, so epoch-making, that he became more a god than a hero.

Kennedy's death has in it the touch of religious epic, of man pitted against fate. Here surely was one favored by the gods, one possessed of power, wealth, youth, the aura of manly war heroism, zest for living, personal charm and beauty, glamour, imagination, keen insight, intelligence, immense popularity, the adoring love of family and friends. Great achievements were to his credit, and even greater ones seemed in store. Then in the fullness of his strength, he was cut down in a flash. History has no more dramatic demonstration of the everlasting insecurity of the human condition.

Was Kennedy himself a romantic? In some ways, mostly in appearance and manner. There are photographs of him, for instance several public ones taken in Tampa five days before his assassination, which reveal him in a kind of narcissistic euphoria. (Those who understand how wondrously flexible human nature can be will see nothing damaging in this.) James Reston once observed that the effect Kennedy had on women voters was "almosty naughty." In his personal relations —and this is a matter not of appearance but of substance—Kennedy had an outgoing freshness and (there is no other term for it) a sweetness of temper. But basically Kennedy was not a romantic. He was a rationalist with a critical intelligence, a realist who knew the hard and subtle uses of power.

However, one need not be a romantic to become a romantic hero of history. Many romantics miss it—sometimes for a variety of reasons just barely miss it: Bolívar, Garibaldi, Gambetta, Jaurès, Michael Collins. In modern times romantic heroes have become rare. Kennedy is the first in this tradition in a long time, and he is the only American in its top echelon. Strange that he should have come out of the America of the machine and mass production. Or is it? People in our prosaic age, particularly young Americans, were yearning for a romantic hero, as the James Dean cult among our youth revealed. Now they have an authentic one.[1]

Violence in the Cities: An Historical View

RICHARD C. WADE

• The United States witnessed both triumph and tragedy in the 1960's. During the decade its citizens enjoyed unparalleled material prosperity, its gross national product approached a trillion dollars per year, and its space program was climaxed by the successful placement of American astronauts on the moon. But the 1960's will also be remembered for the war in Southeast Asia, for the numerous domestic assassinations, and probably for the untoward violence which broke the uneasy racial calm of the 1950's. In the summer of 1965 a six-day race riot in Los Angeles left thirty-four dead and more than 850 injured; in 1967 battles between black militants and police claimed twenty-five lives in Newark and forty-three in Detroit. And disturbances in more than one hundred cities followed the assassination of the Reverend Martin Luther King, Jr., in April of 1968.

President Lyndon Johnson's National Advisory Commission on Civil Disorders (the Kerner Commission) placed the blame for the rioting on "white racism." It reported that the civil rights gains of the previous fifteen years had actually done very little to improve the quality of life in the black ghetto, where millions of youngsters continued to be denied an equal chance in American society. The principal response to the riots had been increased expenditures for police and weaponry rather than serious attempts to alleviate the causes of the distress.

The United States has, of course, always been a violent nation. Even now the murder rate exceeds that of any other "advanced" nation; in a typical recent year there were more homicides in Houston, Texas, than in all of England. But while personal violence continues to increase, the incidence

From *Urban Violence* (The University of Chicago Center for Policy Study, 1969), pp. 7–26.

of large-scale American disorder has actually been reduced
in the twentieth century. As Richard C. Wade points out,
nativist and labor violence is now largely a thing of the past.
What is alarming about racial rioting is that it conflicts with
the larger trend and seems to confirm the Kerner Commission's judgment that we are moving toward two societies,
"one black, one white—separate unequal."

Violence is no stranger to American cities. Almost from the very beginning, cities have been the scenes of sporadic violence, of rioting and
disorders, and occasionally virtual rebellion against established authority. Many of these events resulted in only modest property damage and
a handful of arrests. Others were larger in scale with deaths running
into the scores and damages into the millions. This paper attempts to
survey briefly some of these outbreaks and to analyze their origins and
consequences. We confine ourselves, however, to the larger ones, and
omit any discussion of individual acts of violence or the general level
of crime. In addition, to keep these remarks relevant to the present
crisis, we have confined our analysis to disorders in urban areas.

There has been, in fact, a good deal more violence and disorder in
the American tradition than even historians have been willing to recognize. The violence on the frontier is, of course, well known, and in
writing, movies, and television it has been a persistent theme in our
culture. Indeed, one of America's favorite novelists, James Fenimore
Cooper, transformed the slaughter and mayhem of Indians into heroic,
almost patriotic, action. As the literary historian David Brion Davis
has observed: "Critics who interpret violence in contemporary literature as a symptom of a sick society may be reassured to know that
American writers have always been preoccupied with murder, rape, and
deadly combat." To be sure, violence is not "as American as cherry
pie," but it is no newcomer to the national scene.

Though serious scholarship on this dimension of the American past
is shamefully thin, it is already quite clear that disorder and violence
in our cities were not simply occasional aberrations, but rather a significant part of urban development and growth. From the Stamp Act

riots of the prerevolutionary age, to the assaults on immigrants and
Catholics in the decades before the Civil War, to the grim confrontation of labor and management at the end of the nineteenth century
and its sporadic reappearance after World War I and during the depression, through the long series of racial conflicts for two centuries,
American cities have known the physical clash of groups, widescale
breakdown of established authority, and bloody disorder.

Nor is it hard to see why this early history had more than its share
of chaos. American cities in the eighteenth and nineteenth centuries
were very young. They had not yet the time to develop a system of
orderly government; there was no tradition of habitual consent to local
authority; there was no established police system. In addition, these
cities grow at a spectacular rate. In the twentieth century, we have used
the term "exploding metropolis" to convey the rapid pace of urbanization. It is not often remembered that the first "urban explosion" took
place more than a century ago. Indeed, between 1820 and 1860 cities
grew proportionately faster than they had before or ever would again.
The very speed of this urban development was unsettling and made
the maintenance of internal tranquillity more difficult.

The problem was further compounded by the fact that nearly every
American city was born of commerce. This meant that there was always a large transient population—seamen engaged in overseas trade,
rivermen plying the inland waters, teamsters and wagonmen using the
overland routes, and a constant stream of merchants and salesmen
seeking customers. At any moment the number of newcomers was large
and their attachments to the community slight. Hence when they hit
town, there was always some liveliness. After exhausting the cities' mu-
seums and libraries, sailors and teamsters would find other things to do.
In the eighteenth and nineteenth century, transients comprised a significant portion of those who engaged in rioting and civil disorders.

In addition to being young, rapidly growing, and basically commercial, American cities also had very loose social structures. Unlike the
Old World, they had no traditional ruling group, class lines were constantly shifting, and new blood was persistently pumped into these
urban societies. One could say that up until the last part of the nineteenth century, mercantile leaders dominated municipal government;
but even that commercial leadership changed continually. Later, immigrant groups shared high offices in municipal affairs, thus under-

lining the shifting nature of the social structure of most cities. Within this looseness there was always a great deal of mobility, with people rising and falling in status not only from generation to generation but within a single lifetime.

This fluid social system contrasted sharply with other, older societies, yet it contained a high incidence of disorder. For it depended on the constant acceptance of new people and new groups to places of influence and importance, and their incorporation into the system on a basis of equality with others. This acceptance was only grudgingly conceded, and often only after some abrasive episodes. The American social structure thus had a large capacity to absorb revolutionary tensions and avoid convulsive upheavals. But it also bred minor social skirmishes which were not always orderly. It is significant that in the pre-Civil War South, where slavery created a more traditional social structure, there was less rioting and civil disorder than in the North (though one ought not underestimate the individual violence against the slave built into institutional bondage).

The American social structure was also unique because it was composed not only of conventional classes, but also of different ethnic, religious, and racial groups. They had at once an internal cohesion that came from a common background and a shared American experience and also a sense of sharp differences with other groups, especially with the country's older stock. These groups, the Negro excepted, were initially both part of the system and yet outside of it. The resultant friction, with the newcomers pressing for acceptance and older groups striving for continued supremacy, was a fruitful source of disorder and often violence. Since it was in the city that these groups were thrown together, became aware of their differences, and struggled for survival and advancement, it would be on the streets rather than on the countryside that the social guerrilla warfare would take place.

If the internal controls in the American social structure were loose, the external controls were weak. The cities inherited no system of police control adequate to the numbers or to the rapid increase of the urban centers. The modern police force is the creation of the twentieth century; the establishment of a genuinely professional system is historically a very recent thing. Throughout the eighteenth and nineteenth century, the force was small, untrained, poorly paid, and part of the political system. In case of any sizable disorder, it was hopelessly inadequate; and rioters sometimes routed the constabulary in the first confrontation. Josiah Quincy, for example, in Boston in the 1820's had to organize and arm the teamsters to re-establish the authority of the city in the streets. Many prudent officials simply kept out of the way until the worst was over. In New York's draft riots, to use another instance, the mayor wandered down to see what the disturbance was all about and nearly got trampled in the melee.

Moreover, since some of the rioting was political, the partisanship of the police led official force to be applied against one group, or protection to be withheld from another. And with every turnover in the mayor's office, a substantial and often a complete change occurred in the police. In Atlanta, for instance, even where there was only one party, each faction had its own men in blue ready to take over with the changes in political fortunes. In some places where the state played a role in local police appointments, the mayor might even be deprived of any control at all for the peace of the city. In New York in the 1850's there was an awkward moment when there were two police forces—the Municipals and the Metropolitans—each the instrument of opposing parties. At the point of the most massive confusion, one group tried to arrest the mayor and an armed struggle took place between the two competing forces.

The evolution toward more effective and professional forces was painfully slow. Separating the police from patronage proved difficult, the introduction of civil service qualifications and protection came only in this century, and the development of modern professional departments came even later. To be sure, after a crisis—rioting, widescale looting, or a crime wave—there would be a demand for reform, but the enthusiasm was seldom sustained and conditions returned quickly to normal. The ultimate safety of the city thus resided with outside forces that could be brought in when local police could not handle the mob.

These general considerations account in large part for the high level of disorder and violence in American cities over the past three centuries. The larger disorders, however, often stemmed from particular problems and specific conditions and resulted in widescale bloodshed and destruction. Though these situations varied from place to place and time to time, it is perhaps useful to divide them into a few categories. Some rioting was clearly political, surrounding party struggles

and often occasioned by legislation or an election. Some sprang from
group conflict, especially the resistance to the rising influence of immigrant groups. Still others stemmed from labor disputes. And the largest, then as now, came out of race conflict. A few examples of each
will convey some of their intensity and scale.

Politics has always been a fruitful source of disorders. Indeed, one of
the most significant groups of riots surrounded the colonial break with
Great Britain. In Boston, Samuel Adams and other radical leaders led
the otherwise directionless brawling and gang warfare around the docks
and wharfs into a political roughhouse against British policy. The
Stamp Tax Riots, the Townshend Duty Riots and, of course, the Boston Massacre were all part of an organized and concerted campaign by
colonial leaders. The urban middle classes initially tolerated the disorders because they too opposed certain aspects of British policy; they
later pulled back when they felt that radical leadership was carrying
resistance beyond their own limited objectives. Yet for nearly a decade,
rioting and organized physical force was a part of the politics of the
colonies.

This use of violence in politics was not as jarring to the eighteenth
century as it would be today. Rioting had been a common occurrence,
and not always among the underclasses. As early as 1721, Cotton
Mather, one of Boston's most prominent citizens, could bewail in his
diary the exploits of his "miserable, miserable, miserable son Increase.
The wretch has brought himself under public infamy and trouble by
bearing a part in a Night-riot, with some detestable rakes in town."
Two decades later, Philadelphia witnessed widespread disorder during
its "Bloody Election" in 1742. The widening of the franchise greatly
reduced the resort to violence in politics for the ballot provided an alternative to rock-throwing and physical force on important public questions. Yet historically the stakes of political victory have always been
high enough to induce some to employ force and mob action.

Attacks against immigrants comprise another theme in the story.
Often the assault by older, more established groups was against individuals or small groups. But in other cases it would be more general.
The string of riots against Catholic churches and convents in the nineteenth century, for example, represented an attack on the symbols of
the rise of the new groups. In the summer of 1834, for instance, a
Charlestown (Mass.) convent was sacked and burned to the ground;

scuffles against the Irish occurred in various parts of nearby Boston; some Irish houses were set afire. At the outset, the episode was carefully managed; then it got out of hand as teenage toughs got into action. Nor was this an isolated incident.

Characteristic of this period too was the resistance to the incorporation of immigrants into the public life of the city. "Bloody Monday" in Louisville in 1855 will perhaps serve as an illustration. Local politicians had become worried about the increase of the immigrant (German and Irish) vote. The Know-Nothings (a party built in part on anti-immigrant attitudes) determined to keep foreign-born residents away from the polls on election day. There was only a single voting place for every ward, thus numbering only eight in the entire city. Know-Nothing followers rose at dawn and occupied the booths early in the morning. They admitted their own reliables, but physically barred their opponents. The pre-election campaign had been tense and bitter with threats of force flying across party lines. By this time some on each side had armed themselves. Someone fired a shot, and the rioting commenced. When it was all through, "Quinn's Row," an Irish section, had been gutted, stores looted, and Catholic churches damaged. A newspaper which was accused of stirring up feeling only barely escaped destruction. The atrocities against the Irish were especially brutal with many being beaten and shot. Indeed, some of the wounded were thrown back into the flames of ignited buildings. Estimates of the dead range from 14 to 100, though historians have generally accepted (albeit with slim evidence) 22 as the number killed.

Labor disputes have also often spawned widescale disorder. Indeed, at the turn of the century, Winston Churchill, already a keen student of American affairs, observed that the United States had the most violent industrial relations of any western country. Most of this rioting started with a confrontation of labor and management over the right to organize, or wages and hours, or working conditions. A large portion of these strikes found the workers in a vulnerable if not helpless position, a fact which has led most historians to come down on the side of labor in these early disputes. Moreover, unlike the disorders we have previously discussed, these were nationwide in scope—occurring at widely scattered points. There was no question of their being directed since a union was usually involved and it had some control over local action throughout the country. Yet the violence was seldom uniform or confined to strikers. It might flare up in Chicago and Pittsburgh, while St. Louis, where the issues would be the same, might remain quiescent. Often, as in the case of the railroad strike of 1877, the damage to life and property was large. In the Homestead lockout alone, 35 were killed and the damage (in 1892 dollars) ran to $2,500.00. In the 1930's the organizing steel, auto, and rubber unions brought a recrudescence of this earlier grisly process.

The "Great Strike of 1877" conveys most of the elements of this kind of violent labor dispute. One historian of the episode observes that "frequently, law and order broke down in major rail centers across the land; what was regarded as 'domestic insurrection' and 'rebellion' took over." He calculated that "millions of dollars worth of property were destroyed, hundreds of persons were injured, and scores killed in rioting in pitched battles with law enforcement officials." The cities affected stretched across the country, including Baltimore, Pittsburgh, Philadelphia, Buffalo, Cleveland, Toledo, Columbus, Cincinnati, Louisville, Indianapolis, Chicago, St. Louis, Kansas City, Omaha, and San Francisco.

The strike began on July 16, 1877, in the midst of hard times when railroads tried to adapt to the depression by cutting wages 10 per cent. The workers' resistance began in Martinsburg, West Virginia, where the militia called to the strike scene soon fraternized with the workers. President Rutherford Hayes then dispatched troops to the town and no bloodshed occurred. But in Baltimore, the situation turned ugly and spilled over into violence on July 20. It is hard to know how many genuine strikers were involved and how much of the fighting and damage was done by others. At any rate, 11 people were killed and 20 wounded and the President again dispatched troops to the troubled area. After these eruptions, the riots spread elsewhere. One historian describes the subsequent disorders as "undirected, unplanned, and unmanaged save by impromptu leaders." "Everywhere," he continued, "but especially in Baltimore, Pittsburgh, and Chicago, the striking trainmen were promptly joined by throngs of excitement seeking adolescents, by the idle, the unemployed, the merely curious and the malicious."

Pittsburgh suffered the worst. As trouble first threatened, the governor called up the local militia whose members very quickly began to fraternize with the strikers as the latter took over the trains. The governor then called for troops from Philadelphia. In the furious clash that resulted, 16 soldiers and 50 rioters were killed. "For two days Pittsburgh was ruled by mobs," one account asserts, "which burned, looted and pillaged to their heart's content, and attacked savagely all who resisted them. Finally the riot died out; into harmlessness. The city was left in ruins." In the last stages, however, the same historian observed that "the rioting had little or no connection with the strike, and few strikers were included in the mobs." In addition to the lives lost, property destroyed included 500 freight cars, 104 locomotives, and 39 buildings.

The strike reached Chicago on July 23. Men left the job and large crowds began to collect. By nightfall, the city was paralyzed. Police were dispatched to disperse the throng and in the first clash they fired into the crowd, killing seven and wounding twenty. The militia arrived and citizens groups began to arm. The superintendent of police estimated that there were 20,000 armed men in Chicago by the second day. On the 26th the United States Army arrived. At 16th Street, 350 police faced a mob of about 6,000 and after an hour's battle at least twelve died and two score or more were seriously wounded. Like most riots, the point of origin and the purpose of the strike were soon forgotten. Indeed, an astute student of the event asserts that "practically none of the rioting may be fairly ascribed to the strikers." Rather, he asserts, "the disturbances were mainly caused by roughs, idlers, unemployed persons, and the criminal element. A surprisingly large percentage of the mobs was composed of women and young boys, and these elements were at the same time the most destructive and the hardest for the police to disperse." He adds, however, that the blame was not one-sided: "It seems also that a good deal of the disturbance was precipitated by the rough tactics of the police."

The Pullman strike in Chicago almost twenty years later also contained most of the familiar elements of a riot growing out of a labor dispute. It, too, stemmed from a wage reduction in the middle of a depression. On May 11, 1894, the strike began in a quiet and orderly fashion. As the gap between the workers and the Pullman Company deepened, the American Railway Union called for a general boycott of sleeping cars. A federal court, however, issued an injunction against the boycott to insure the movement of mail. On July 4 federal troops arrived in Chicago. Unitil that time a labor historian observed that "there had been little violence in Chicago proper. Some acts of sabotage had occurred and there had been occasional demonstrations but the police had effectively controlled the latter."

Now the temper of the episode changed. Crowds roamed over the tracks "pushing over freight cars, setting a few of them on fire, and otherwise blocking the movement of trains. Switches were thrown, signal lights changed, and trains stoned—much of the trouble caused by half-grown boys who seemed to welcome the opportunity for excitement and deviltry." Furthermore, "a large proportion of women and children" mingled in a crowd that reached 10,000. Adding to the incendiary possibilities was an "abnormally large group of hoodlums, tramps, and semicriminals, some of whom had been attracted to Chicago by the Columbian Exposition and left stranded by the depression." "In the movement of the mobs," the same historian continues, "there was seldom any purpose or leadership. Most of the destruction was done wantonly and without premeditation."

July 6 was the day of the greatest property destruction. A reporter from the *Inter Ocean* described the scene at the height of the frenzy. "From this moving mass of shouting rioters squads of a dozen or two departed, running towards the yards with fire brands in their hands. They looked in the gloaming like specters, their lighted torches bobbing about like will-o'-the-wisps. Soon from all parts of the yard flames shot up and billows of fire rolled over the cars, covering them with the red glow of destruction. The spectacle was a grand one. . . . Before the cars were fired those filled with any cargoes were looted. . . . The people were bold, shameless, and eager in their robbery. . . . It was pandemonium let loose, the fire leaping along for miles, and the men and women became drunk on their excess." By nightfall 700 cars had been destroyed. The next day clashes between the crowd and a hastily organized militia left 4 more dead and 20 wounded. In all, in three chaotic days, 13 people had been killed, 53 seriously wounded, several hundred more hurt and incalculable property damage, not to mention money lost in wages and railroad earnings. One estimate fixes the total at $80,000,000.

Of all the sources of civil disorder, however, none has been more persistent than race. Whether in the North or South, whether before or after the Civil War, whether nineteenth or twentieth century, this question has been at the root of more physical violence than any other. There had been some sporadic slave uprisings before emancipation, the largest being the Nat Turner rebellion in 1831. But most which moved from plot to action occurred on the countryside rather than in the cities. Yet even the fear of a slave insurrection took its toll; in 1822, for instance, Charleston, South Carolina, officials, acting on tips and rumors, hanged 37 Negroes and deported many more for an alleged plot to capture and burn the city. Seven years later, in a free state, whites invaded Cincinnati's "Little Africa" and burned and killed and ultimately drove half the colored residents from town. In the same period mobs also assaulted abolitionists, sometimes killing, otherwise sacking buildings and destroying printing presses.

Even the New York City riot against the draft in 1863 took an ugly racial twist before it had run its course. The events themselves arose out of the unpopularity of the draft and the federal government's call for more men as Lee headed into Pennsylvania. The situation was further complicated by a crisis in the police department as a result of the conflicting claims of command by a Republican mayor and a Democratic governor. The rioting broke out July 13 and the first target was the provost marshal's office. Within a short time 700 people ransacked the building and then set it afire. The crowd would not let the firemen into the area and soon the whole block lay gutted. Later the mob began to spill over into the Negro area where many blacks were attacked and some killed.

The police were helpless as the riot spread. The few clashes with the mob saw the police retreat; the crowd wandered about almost at will. Political leaders did not want to take the consequences for action against the mob, and soon it started to head toward the business district. Slowly the police reorganized, by Tuesday they began to win engagements with the rioters, and in a little while they were able to confine the action to the original area. The mobs were, however, better armed and organized and gave a good account of themselves in pitched battle. On the third day federal troops arrived and the control swung over to the authorities and quiet was restored. But in three days the casualties ran to at least 74 dead and many times that number wounded. The property damage was never accurately added up, but claims against the county exceeded $1,500,000 by 1865.

Emancipation freed the Negro from bondage, but it did not grant him either equality or immunity from white aggression. From the New Orleans riot of 1866, through the long list of racial disorders to the end of World War II with datelines running through Atlanta, Springfield, East St. Louis, Washington, Mobile, Beaumont, Chicago, Detroit, and Harlem, reveal something of the depth of the crisis and the vulnerability of American cities to racial disorders. These riots were on a large scale, involved many deaths, millions of dollars of property damage, and left behind deep scars which have never been fully erased. Most of these riots involved the resort to outside military help for containment; all exposed the thinness of the internal and external controls within our urban society.

In fact, the war had scarcely ended before racial violence erupted in New Orleans. The occasion of the outbreak was a Negro procession to an assembly hall where a debate over enfranchising the blacks was to take place. There was some jostling during the march and a shot fired; but it was only after the arrival at the convention that police and special troops charged the black crowd. In the ensuing struggle Negroes were finally routed, but guns, bricks, and stones were generously used. Many Negroes fell on the spot; others were pursued and killed on the streets trying to escape. Later General Sheridan reported that "at least nine-tenths of the casualties were perpetrated by the police and citizens by stabbing and smashing in the heads of many who had already been wounded or killed by policemen." Moreover, he added that it was not just a riot but "an absolute massacre by the police . . . a murder which the mayor and police . . . perpetrated without the shadow of necessity." Federal troops arrived in the afternoon, took possession of the city, and restored order. But 34 Negroes and 4 whites were already dead and over 200 injured.

Smaller places, even in the North, were also affected with racial disorder. In August 1908, for instance, a three-day riot took its toll in Springfield, Illinois. The Negro population in the capital had grown significantly in the years after the turn of the century, and some whites sensed a political and economic threat. On August 13th a white woman claimed she had been violated by a Negro. An arrest was made and the newspapers carried an inflammatory account of the episode. Crowds gathered around the jail demanding the imprisoned black, but the sheriff quickly transferred the accused and another Negro to a prison in a nearby town without letting the public know. "The crowd outside was in an ugly mood," writes an historian of the riot, "the sun had raised tempers; many of the crowd had missed their dinners, which added to their irritation; and the authorities seemed to be taking no heed of their presence. By sundown the crowd had become an ugly mob."

The first target of the rioters was a restaurant whose proprietor presumably had driven the prisoners from jail. Within a few minutes his place was a shambles. They then headed for the Negro section. Here they hit homes and businesses either owned by or catering to Negroes. White owners quickly put white handkerchiefs in their windows to show their race; their stores were left untouched. A Negro was found in his shop and was summarily lynched. Others were dragged from streetcars and beaten. On the 15th the first of 5,000 national guardsmen reached Springfield; very quickly the mob broke up and the town returned to normal. The death toll reached six (four whites and two blacks); the property damage was significant. As a result of the attack, Springfield's Negro population left the city in large numbers hoping to find better conditions elsewhere, especially in Chicago.

A decade later the depredations in East St. Louis were much larger, with the riot claiming the lives of 39 Negroes and 9 whites. The best student of this episode points out that the 1917 riot was not a sudden explosion but resulted from "threats to the security of whites brought on by the Negroes' gains in economic, political and social status; Negro resentment of the attempts to 'kick him back in his place'; and the weakness of the external forces of constraint—the city government, especially the police department." Tensions were raised when the Aluminum Ore Company replaced white strikers with Negro workers. In addition to these factors, race had become a political issue in the previous year when the Democrats accused Republicans of "colonizing" Negroes to swing the election in East St. Louis. The kindling seemed only to lack the match.

On May 28 came the fire. A Central Trades and Labor Union delegation formally requested the Mayor to stop the immigration of Negroes to East St. Louis. As the men were leaving City Hall they heard a story that a Negro robber had accidentally shot a white man during a holdup. In a few minutes the word spread; rumor replaced fact. Now it was said the shooting was intentional; that a white woman was insulted; that two white girls were shot. By this time 3,000 people had congregated and the cry for vengeance went up. Mobs ran downtown beating every Negro in sight. Some were dragged off the streetcars, others chased down. The police refused to act except to take the injured to hospitals and to disarm Negroes. The next day the National Guard arrived to restore order.

Two days later the governor withdrew troops although tension remained high. Scattered episodes broke the peace, but no sustained violence developed. The press, however, continued to emphasize Negro crimes and a skirmish broke out between white pickets and black workers at the Aluminum Company. Then on July 1 some whites drove through the main Negro neighborhood firing into homes. The colored residents armed themselves, and when a similar car, this time carrying a plainclothesman and reporter, went down the street the blacks riddled the passing auto with gunshot.

The next day was the worst. At about 10:00 A.M. a Negro was shot on the main street and a new riot was underway. An historian of the event asserted that the area along Collinsville Avenue between Broadway and Illinois Avenue became a "bloody half mile" for three or four hours. "Streetcars were stopped; Negroes, without regard to age or sex, were pulled off and stoned, clubbed and kicked. . . . By the early afternoon, when several Negroes were beaten and lay bloodied in the street, mob leaders calmly shot and killed them. After victims were placed in an ambulance, there was cheering and handclapping." Others headed for the Negro section and set fire to homes on the edge of the neighborhood. By midnight the South End was in flames and black residents began to flee the city. In addition to the dead, the injured were counted in the hundreds and over 300 buildings were destroyed.

Two summers later the racial virus felled Chicago. Once again, mounting tension had accompanied the migration of blacks to the city. The numbers jumped from 44,000 in 1910 to 109,000 ten years later. Though the job market remained good, housing was tight. Black neighborhoods could expand only at the expense of white ones, and everywhere the transition areas were filled with trouble. Between July 1, 1917, and March 1921, there had been 58 bombings of Negro houses. Recreational areas also witnessed continual racial conflict.

The riot itself began on Sunday, July 27, on the 29th Street Beach. There had been some stone-throwing and sporadic fighting. Then a Negro boy, who had been swimming in the Negro section, drifted into the white area and drowned. What happened is not certain, but the young blacks charged he had been hit by stones and demanded the arrest of a white. The police refused, but then arrested a Negro at a white request. When the Negroes attacked the police, the riot was on. News of the events on the beach spread to the rest of the city. Sunday's casualties were 2 dead and 50 wounded. On Monday, attacks were made on Negroes coming from work; in the evening cars drove through black neighborhoods with whites shooting from the windows. Negroes retaliated by sniping at any white who entered the Black Belt. Monday's accounting found 20 killed and hundreds wounded. Tuesday's list was shorter, a handful dead, 139 injured. Wednesday saw a further waning and a reduction in loses in life and property. Rain began to fall; the Mayor finally called in the state militia. After nearly a week a city which witnessed lawlessness and warfare, quieted down and began to assess the implications of the grisly week.

The Detroit riot of 1943 perhaps illustrates the range of racial disorders that broke out sporadically during World War II. There had been earlier conflicts in Mobile, Los Angeles, and Beaumont, Texas, and there would be some others later in the year. No doubt the war with its built-in anxieties and accelerated residential mobility accounted for the timing of these outbreaks. In Detroit, the wider problem was compounded by serious local questions. The Negro population in the city had risen sharply, with over 50,000 arriving in the 15 months before the riot; this followed a historical increase of substantial proportions which saw black residents increase from 40,000 to 120,000 in the single decade between 1920 and 1930. These newcomers put immense pressures on the housing market, and neighborhood turnover at the edge of the ghetto bred bitterness and sometimes violence; importantly, too, recreational areas became centers of racial abrasiveness.

On June 20 the riot broke out on Belle Isle, a recreational spot used by both races, but predominantly by Negroes. Fistfighting on a modest basis soon escalated, and quickly a rising level of violence spread across the city. The Negro ghetto—ironically called Paradise Valley—saw the first wave of looting and bloodshed. The area was, as its historians have described it, "spattered with blood and littered with broken glass and ruined merchandise. The black mob had spared a few shops owned by Negroes who had chalked COLORED on their windows. But almost every store in the ghetto owned by a white had been smashed open and ransacked." Other observers noted that "crudely organized gangs of Negro hoodlums began to operate more openly. Some looters destroyed property as if they had gone berserk."

The next morning saw the violence widen. The police declared the situation out of control and the mayor asked for state troops. Even this force was ineffective, and finally the Governor asked for federal help. Peace returned under the protection of 6,000 men; and the troops remained for more than a week. The dead numbered 34, 25 Negroes and 9 whites; property damage exceeded $2,000,000. And almost as costly was the bitterness, fear, and hate that became part of the city's legacy.

This survey covers only some of the larger and more important disorders. Others reached significant proportions but do not fall into convenient categories. For example, in the eighteenth century a protest against inoculation led to widespread rioting; mobs hit the streets to punish men who snatched bodies for medical training. In times of economic hardship, "bread riots" resulted in ransacking stores; crowds often physically drove away officials seeking to evict tenants who could not pay rent.

Two disorders perhaps best suggest the miscellaneous and unpredictable character of this process. One is so bizarre that only its bloody climax has kept it from being among the most amusing episodes of American history. It revolved around the rivalry between two prominent actors, the American Edwin Forrest, and William Macready, an Englishman. Both were appearing in "Macbeth" on the same night, May 7, 1849, in New York City. Some rowdies, mostly Irish, decided to break up the Macready performance, and when he appeared on the stage they set up such a din that he had to retire. After apologies and assurances, the English visitor agreed to try again on the 9th. This time, the police extracted the troublemakers and Macready finished the play. But a mob gathered outside after the final curtain and refused to disperse on police orders. Finally, the edgy guard fired into the crowd, killing 25 persons.

Another dimension is revealed in the events of March 1884, in Cincinnati. They came in the midst of what the city's best historian has dubbed "the decade of disorder." Two men were tried for the murder of a white livery man. Though one was Negro and the other German, race does not seem to be at issue. When the German was found guilty of only manslaughter, a public campaign developed to avenge the decision. A meeting at Music Hall, called by some leading citizens, attracted 10,000 people, mostly from the middle class, who were worried about a general breakdown of law and order and thought the light sentence would encourage criminals. The speakers attacked the jury and the administration of justice in the city. Afterward a crowd headed for the jail. In the first encounter with the police, casualties were light. But the next day the militia moved in and hostility climbed. Finally, a pitched battle ensued in which 54 died and over 200 were wounded. Thus, a meeting called to bring about law and order wound up ironically in disorder and violence.

This survey, which is only suggestive and not exhaustive, indicates that widescale violence and disorder have been man's companion in the American city from the outset. Some generalizations out of this experience might be useful in the light of the present crisis.

First, most of the rioting has usually been either limited in objective or essentially sporadic. This, of course, is not true of racial conflict, but it is characteristic of a large number of the others. In those, the event was discreet; there was no immediate violent sequel. After a labor dispute, especially if it involved union recognition, bitterness and hate persisted, but there was no annual recurrence of the violance. Attacks on immigrants seldom produced an encore, though they might have an analogue in some other city in the same month or year. In short, though there was enough disorder and mob action to create a persistent anxiety, the incidence of overt conflict was irregular enough to preclude predictions of the next "long hot summer."

Second, this sporadic quality meant that the postmortems were usually short and shallow. It was characteristic to note the large number of teenagers who got involved; to attribute the disruption to outsiders (especially anarchists and communists); to place a large responsibility on the newspapers for carrying inflammatory information and spreading unfounded rumors; to blame the local police for incompetence, for prejudice, for intervening too soon or too late, or at all. After any episode, the urge to fix blame led to all kinds of analyses. The historian of the 1877 railroad violence, for example, observes that "the riots were variously ascribed to avarice, the expulsion of the Bible from the schools, the protective tariff, the demonetization of silver, the absence of General Grant, the circulation of the *Chicago Times* and original sin." Others saw in it a labor conspiracy or a communist plot. And the *New York Times* could assert after the Chicago riot in 1919 that: "The outbreak of race riots in Chicago, following so closely on those reported from Washington, shows clearly enough that the thing is not sporadic (but has) . . . intelligent direction and management . . . (It seems probable) that the Bolshevist agitation has been extended among the Negroes."

There were a few exceptions. After the Chicago race riot, for example, an Illinois commission studied the event in some detail and also examined the deteriorating relations between the races which lay at the bottom. Others occasionally probed beneath the surface at the deeper causes of unrest. But most cities preferred to forget as soon as possible and hoped for an end to any further disorder. Indeed, even the trials that followed most riots show how rapidly popular interest faded. The number of people brought to trial was small and the number of convictions extremely small; and, most significantly, there was little clamor for sterner measures.

Third, if the analyses of the riots were shallow, the response of cities and legislatures was not every effective. After quiet was restored, there would almost certainly be a discussion of police reform. Customarily little came of it, though in Louisville the utter ineptness and obvious partisanship of the police in 1855 prompted a change from an elective to an appointive force. Legislation usually emphasized control. As early as 1721, Massachusetts responded to growing disorders with an anti-riot act. And Chicago's Commercial Club made land available for Fort Sheridan after the events of 1877 in order to have troops nearby for the protection of the city. But most cities rocked back to normal as soon as the tremors died down.

Fourth, there was a general tendency to rely increasingly on outside forces for containing riots. Partly, this resulted from the fact that in labor disorders local police and even state militia fraternized with strikers and could not be counted on to discipline the workers. Partly, it was due to inadequate numbers in the face of the magnitude of the problem. Partly, too, it stemmed from the fact that sometimes the police were involved in the fighting at the outset and seemed a part of the riot. The first resort was usually to state troops; but they were often unsatisfactory, and the call for federal assistance became more frequent.

Fifth, while it is hard to assess, it seems that the bitterness engendered by riots and disorders was not necesarily irreparable. Though the immigrant suffered a good deal at the hands of nativists, it did not slow down for long the process of their incorporation into American life. Ten years after Louisville's "Bloody Monday" the city had a German mayor. The trade unions survived the assaults of the nineteenth century and a reduction of tension characterized the period between 1900 and the depression (with the notable exception of the post-war flare-ups). And after the violence of the 1930's, labor and management learned to conduct their differences, indeed their strikes, with reduced bloodshed and violence. It is not susceptible of proof, but it seems that the fury of the defeated in these battles exacted a price on the victors that ultimately not only protected the group but won respect, however grudgingly, from the public.

At any rate the old sources of major disorders, race excepted, no longer physically agitate American society. It has been many years since violence has been a significant factor in city elections and no widespread disorders have even accompanied campaigning. Immigrant groups have now become so incorporated in American life that they are not easily visible and their election to high offices, indeed the highest, signals a muting of old hostilities. Even when people organized on a large scale against minority groups—such as the Americans' Protective Association in the 1890's or the Ku Klux Klan in the 1920's—they have seldom been able to create major riots or disorders. And though sporadic violence occasionally breaks out in a labor dispute, what is most remarkable is the continuance of the strike as a weapon of industrial relations with so little resort to force. Even the destruction of property during a conflict has ceased to be an expectation.

Sixth, race riots were almost always different from other kinds of disorders. Their roots went deeper; they broke out with increasing frequency; and their intensity mounted rather than declined. And between major disorders the incidence of small-scale violence was always high. Until recently, the Negro has largely been the object of the riot. This was true not only in northern cities where changing residential patterns bred violence, but also in the South where this question was less pervasive. In these riots the lines were sharply drawn against the Negroes, the force was applied heavily against them, and the casualties were always highest among blacks.

Finally, in historical perspective, if racial discord be removed, the level of large-scale disorder and violence is less ominous today than it has been during much of the past. As we have seen, those problems which have produced serious eruptions in the past no longer do so. In fact, if one were to plot a graph, omitting the racial dimension, violence and disorder over a long period have been reduced. Indeed, what makes the recent rioting so alarming is that it breaks so much with this historical trend and upsets common expectations.

Yet to leave out race is to omit the most important dimension of the present crisis. For it is race that is at the heart of the present discord. Some analysts, of course, have argued that the problem is class and they emphasize the numbers caught in widening poverty, and the frustration and envy of poor people in a society of growing affluence. Yet it is important to observe that though 68 per cent of the poor people in this country are white, the disorders stem almost wholly from black ghettos. The marginal participation of a few whites in Detroit and elsewhere scarcely dilutes the racial foundations of these disorders.

In fact, a historical survey of disorders only highlights the unique character of the present problem. For the experience of the Negro in American cities has been quite different from any other group. And it is in just this difference that the crisis lies. Because the black ghetto is unlike any ghettos that our cities have known before. Of course, other groups knew the ghetto experience too. As newcomers to the city they huddled in the downtown areas where they met unspeakably congested conditions, occupied the worst housing, got the poorest education, toiled, if fortunate enough to have a job, at the most menial tasks, endured high crime rates, and knew every facet of deprivation.

The urban slum had never been a very pleasant place, and it was tolerable only if the residents, or most of them, thought there was a way out. To American immigrants generally the ghetto was a temporary stage in their incorporation into American society. Even some of the first generation escaped, and the second and third generation moved out of the slums in very large numbers. Soon they were dispersed around the metropolitan area, in the suburbs as well as the pleasant residential city wards. Those who remained behind in the old neighborhoods did so because they chose to, not because they had to. By this process, millions of people from numberless countries, of different national and religious backgrounds made their way into the main current of American life.

It was expected that Negroes would undergo the same process when they came to the city. Thus, there was little surprise in the first generation when black newcomers did indeed find their way into the central city, the historic staging grounds for the last and poorest arrivals. But the ghetto proved to be not temporary. Instead of colored residents dispersing in the second generation, the ghetto simply expanded. Block by block it oozed out into the nearby white neighborhoods. Far from breaking up, the ghetto grew. In fact, housing became more segregated every year; and the walls around it appeared higher all the time. What had been temporary for other groups seemed permanent to Negroes.

The growth of the Negro ghetto created conditions which had not existed before and which generated the explosiveness of our present situation. In the first place, the middle-class Negroes became embittered at their exclusion from the decent white neighborhoods of the city and suburbs. These people, after all, had done what society expected of them; they got their education, training, jobs, and income. Yet even so they were deprived of that essential symbol of American success—the home in a neighborhood of their own choosing where conditions would be more pleasant and schools better for their children. For this group, now about a third of all urban Negroes, the exclusion seemed especially cruel and harsh.

As a result they comprise now a growingly alienated and embittered group. The middle-class blacks are now beginning to turn their attention to organizing among the poor in the worst parts of the ghetto. Their children make up the cadres of black militants in the colleges. And when the riots come, they tolerate the activity even though they usually do not themselves participate. In short, the fact of the ghetto forces them to identify with race, not class. When the riots break, they feel a bond with the rioters, not white society. This had not been true of the emerging middle class of any immigrant group before.

If the ghetto has new consequences for the middle class, it also creates a new situation among the poorer residents of the ghetto, especially for the young people. They feel increasingly that there is no hope for the future. For other groups growing up in the ghetto there had always been visible evidence that it was possible to escape. Many before had done it; and everyone knew it. This produced the expectation that hard work, proper behavior, some schooling, and a touch of luck would make it possible to get ahead. But the young Negro grows up in increasing despair. He asks himself—"What if I do all they say I should—stay in school, get my training, find a job, accumulate some money—I'll still be living here, still excluded from the outside world and its rewards." He asks himself, "What's the use?" Thus, the hopelessness, despair, and frustration mount, and the temperature of the ghetto rises. Nearly all of our poverty programs are stumbling on the problem of motivation. To climb out of the slum has always require more than average incentive. Yet this is precisely what is lacking in the ghetto youth.

The present riots stem from the peculiar problems of the ghetto. By confining Negroes to the ghetto we have deprived them of the chance to enter American society on the same terms as other groups before them. And they know increasingly that this exclusion is not a function of education, training, or income. Rather, it springs from the color of their skin. This is what makes race the explosive question of our time; this is what endangers the tranquillity of our cities. In the historian's perspective, until the ghetto begins to break, until the Negro middle class can move over this demeaning barrier, until the young people can see Negroes living where their resources will carry them and hence get credible evidence of equality, the summers will remain long and hot.

The Next Decade in American Foreign Policy

CHARLES MAECHLING, JR.

• The 1970's will mark a new era in foreign relations. Emerging nations in Asia, Africa, and Latin America will act more independently than they ever have in the past and will continue to move away from formal alliances with the superpowers. The number of nations possessing at least limited nuclear capability will increase, and as a result, the United States and the Soviet Union will no longer share the key to world survival.

How will the American government react to new limitations on its capacity to preserve order or to influence the policies of friendly nations? How will domestic concerns affect foreign commitments? Will the United States continue to commit its military forces to the defense of its allies? Charles Maechling is somewhat pessimistic about the possibility of an expanded arms race, the threat to global stability of additional nuclear powers, the specter of an aggressive China seeking to reduce American influence in Asia, and the decline in the relative strength and influence of the Western nations vis-à-vis the Third World. "The short range picture is therefore not encouraging," he concludes.

Many of Maechling's remarks are, of course, speculative; an unexpected revolution or war anywhere in the world might lead immediately to a new international balance. Moreover, domestic pressures in the United States, the Soviet Union, Communist China, or Great Britain might produce unexpected new policies.

In reading this selection try to determine whether Maechling's fears are justified. Compare his assessment of American foreign policies with the views expressed by Schiller in a

From *The Virginia Quarterly Review*. The University of Virginia, Summer 1969. Copyright © 1969 by The Virginia Quarterly Review. Reprinted by permission.

*previous selection. How would you disagree with the author
on the proper course of American foreign policy in the present decade?*

The world is entering a new and perilous era of international relations,
one already marked by the decline of Western influence in Asia and
Africa, extension of the Soviet military presence to the Mediterranean,
a deterioration in the postwar system of anti-Communist alliances, and
a relative rise in the political and military importance of the Third
World. It promises to be an era of turmoil and transition, posing
especially acute problems of readjustment in strategic thinking and
policy formulation for the United States, a country little used to
prolonged periods of frustration in international affairs and now un-
happily beset by deep-seated internal divisions.

That fluidity and polycentrism are likely to be the hallmark of the
next decade should come as no surprise to the trained observer. These
and other unwelcome realities are the inevitable product of the two
preceding decades—the Cold War period lasting from 1946 to the
end of the Eisenhower Administration, and the period of equilibrium
extending from that time until the present. The first period opened
with the overwhelming Allied victory over the Axis and closed with
the economic resurgence of Europe. From a politico-military standpoint it was dominated by the monopoly of the United States in
nuclear weapons and strategic air power, and the successful containment of Soviet and Chinese expansionist tendencies within the boundaries loosely delineated at Yalta and Potsdam. In the second period
the balance began to shift. A nuclear stalemate between the United
States and the Soviet Union for all purposes except overkill replaced
the formerly overwhelming superiority of the West. A de facto
accommodation between the two superpowers was reached on several
issues of vital national interest. At the same time, the wholesale liquidation of European colonial administrations and the withdrawal of
European garrisons and naval units from bases and strong points held
in many cases for nearly three hundred years, coupled with the
emergence of over fifty nationalistic new countries, mostly anti-West-

ern in orientation, sharply reduced Western influence in the Third World.

The United States sought to fill the power vacuum thus created by constructing a system of defensive alliances around the periphery of the Soviet Union and China. Later, it began to build up its neglected conventional forces to enable it to repel localized threats to the system without having to resort to nuclear weapons. This period was noteworthy for a series of crises—Cuba, Suez, Vietnam, the Dominican Republic, the Congo—in which the integrity of the alliance system was put to severe test by both Communist and local nationalist forces.

Each of these periods blends imperceptibly into the other, just as the second is now being metamorphosed into a third. Typically, the policies, strategic thinking, and national rhetoric characteristic of one period have tended to carry over into the next one, with the elements of future danger often being diagnosed incorrectly in terms of the factors that caused danger in the past.

Yet a sound comprehension of these factors is imperative if we are to understand the true significance of the age we are entering. Thus, the occurrence during the last decade of so many dramatic events—the Cuban missile crisis, the Czech crisis, the Israeli-Arab confrontations, the Vietnamese War—tends to obscure the real nature of the period, which was one of political and military equilibrium, at least between the United States and the Soviet Union. Its overriding feature was a realization on the part of both governments that any sudden move by one which transgressed the vital interests of the other could precipitate a nuclear confrontation and mutual extinction.

This negative community of interest, combined with the Sino-Soviet split, has given birth to a series of inchoate and sometimes ill-defined boundaries marking the security zones of the two superpowers and defining the limits beyond which neither power can step without risking a direct confrontation. The existence of these boundaries dictated both the genesis and the outcome of the Cuban missile crisis of 1962—and indeed shaped the manner in which the Kennedy Administration faced the crisis and overcame it. To a large extent it has also been responsible for the curious limitations under which the Vietnamese War has been fought—limitations that apply just as much to the floating sanctuary enjoyed by our cruisers and aircraft carriers in the South China Sea as to the freighters carrying munitions to Haiphong.

Even more significant is the fact that during a period characterized by constant hostile rivalry between the United States and the Soviet Union, and punctuated by dangerous crises, both countries were able first to negotiate and ratify the Nuclear Test Ban Treaty of 1962, and then to negotiate and carry through ratification the equally complex treaty on nonproliferation of nuclear weapons. Both of these treaties have national survival as their declared purpose. Both seek to preserve the existing equilibrium.

The key to these anomalies is that for some time relations between the two superpowers have been carried on at two different levels, an upper and a lower one. The upper level governs relations among the two superpowers and a handful of other countries. Here national survival is the sole stake. The joint interest of the superpowers in preventing non-vital collisions of interest from upsetting the power equilibrium and precipitating a nuclear confrontation overrides any subsidiary interest in which national existence is not at issue. At this level the rules of the game demand that neither power transgress the vital interests of the other to the point where the alternatives would be either mutual extinction or total capitulation.

International relations at the lower level are nothing more than the traditional norms of power politics. At this level the various factors influencing relations between states—geography, ideology, military power, economics—operate in much the same way as they have throughout history. It is only when a collision between national interests escalates to the threshold of limited war that the rules begin to change. At this point, national survival enters the picture and begins to impose constraints on the freedom of action of the protagonists. Fear of direct confrontation (and mutual extinction) circumscribes the implementation of orthodox political and military policy to the point where all the traditional norms of power politics, including the most hallowed precepts of military wisdom, are called into question. Such unassailable imperatives as overwhelming concentration of one's forces at the enemy's most vulnerable point, interdiction and, if possible, severance of the enemy's supply lines, and unremitting efforts to bring him to his knees as speedily as possible are forced to give way in the face of an apocalyptic menace that threatens to sweep into oblivion not only the pieces of the game, but also the board and players.

In this context, both the long agony of Vietnam and the brutal invasion of Czechoslovakia have a somber logic of their own. The Vietnamese War long ago reached the upper limits of military rationality. Since the inception of the Paris peace talks [in 1968] it has been a holding action aimed at influencing a political settlement—by definition a negative concept that postulates a settlement on the best terms one can get, not the best possible terms. The Czech crisis was significant not by reason of the Soviet action—entirely predictable in terms of Russian history and Soviet vital interests—but by reason of the pallid nature of the United States response. As with Hungary in 1956, the United States tacitly recognized the overriding interest of the Soviet Union in the integrity of its own security sphere and limited its reaction to a few denunciatory speeches in the United Nations.

II

Like the frozen surface of one of our Northern rivers in early spring, this phase of uneasy equilibrium is about to break up. Below the crust, titanic forces have been inexorably at work, dissolving the supporting structure and preparing the way for new combinations.

In the field of nuclear armaments, some proliferation of weapons and delivery systems seems to be inevitable. Sooner or later enough of these weapons will be distributed among countries of the second and third rank to impair the nuclear hegemony of the superpowers. Possession of atomic weapons will enable a country of the second rank to inflict so much damage on one of the superpowers in exchange for its own certain destruction that it will give that country a latitude of behavior difficult to reconcile with the old norms. It will greatly reduce that country's dependence on whichever of the two superpowers had been its protector in the past, and could potentially transform it into an unpredictable and intimidating neighbor. All the chauvinism, unrealistic aspirations, and suppressed rancor that had formerly been held in check by the realities of second-class ranking will return to the fore as credible ingredients of policy. At best, the addition of each new country to the roll of nuclear powers will add a new element of uncertainty—perhaps even volatility—to the world political scene.

The anarchical consequences of nuclear proliferation are bad enough in the case of countries that are part of the community of nations, like France and India. But the accession of China to the rank of a nuclear power—if not to that of a superpower—cannot help but alter the power balance in East Asia. China's exclusion from the United Nations and other forums of international intercourse, and the paranoid isolationism of her leadership, make it extremely difficult to integrate her into any sort of three-cornered *modus vivendi*, except at the extortionate price of total Western withdrawal from Asia. Once equipped with modern missile delivery systems and hydrogen warheads, she will pose an unremitting and unpredictable threat to India, Southeast Asia, Turkestan, and Siberia—all the more dangerous because of the still rudimentary and decentralized nature of her economy.

Another factor in breaking up the old equilibrium is the probability of a renewed arms race between the United States and the Soviet Union. Heretofore, the near nuclear monopoly enjoyed by the two superpowers and their joint interest in preventing military and space expenditures from exceeding their already hyperbolic levels have at least managed to slow down the development of new offensive weapons, if not to arrest the technology behind them. However, the threat of nuclear proliferation and the prospect of an outlaw China armed with intercontinental hydrogen missiles seem to have tipped the scales in favor of limited antiballistic missile systems—in our case the controversial ABM. A new generation of multiwarhead offensive missiles will be the inevitable sequel.

Moreover, the next phase of the arms race will not be confined to the earth's atmosphere. New weapons systems for the stratosphere on the one hand and the deep oceans and the seabed on the other are already on the drawing boards. The Soviets in particular are perfecting space vehicle and orbital platforms that need only be converted to war use to constitute a new arm of international blackmail. They have also built up a fleet of four hundred submarines, of which forty to fifty are nuclear-powered and an undisclosed number carry Polaris-type missiles. If they achieve a breakthrough in either area in the shape of an undetectable and indestructible second-strike capability, the current nuclear stalemate will be hopelessly broken and the United States will face a period of mortal peril.

On the political side, the chief factor undermining the old equilibrium is the growing political leverage and instability of the Third World. As the retreat of the United States and Western Europe from Asia, Africa, and Latin-America continues, the relative political importance of the less developed countries in the United Nations and other forums and their capacity to trigger international crises are bound to increase. Domestic pressures and the quasi-religious cult of anti-colonialism in many of these countries preclude the close economic and financial collaboration with the United States and Western Europe that is an essential prerequisite to their political evolution. Caught between the need for centralized administration and the counter pull of tribal, religious, and linguistic regionalism, plagued with economic difficulties and rising populations, many of these states are drifting into quasi-military dictatorships. In nearly all of them superstition, blind loyalty, and narrow local nationalism are being encouraged to inhere around the local government.

Some of these régimes will be incapable of playing a steady, constructive rôle in international affairs for years to come. As a group they will continue to oscillate in ideology and allegiance from left to right and back again as their dependence shifts from one superpower to the other. Whenever the local rivalries and animosities of the Third World reach the stage of actual warfare—as in the Middle East—they threaten to set in motion a train of events leading to precisely the kind of nuclear confrontation that the two superpowers have been at such pains to prevent.

Another drastic change from the preceding period of equilibrium is the mounting reluctance, and indeed incapacity, of the West to project its power decisively in distant areas beyond its immediate sphere of influence.

The complex array of bases, garrisons, naval squadrons, and colonial administrations through which Europe maintained an effective if often inequitable rule of order around the globe has disappeared. The United States possesses a naval, air, and airlift capability of global range but has never had the capacity or will to match it with a complementary political and administrative capability. Our inability to exercise direct control over the destinies of dependent areas for even the length of time necessary to tide them over periods of war and domestic upheaval imposes a crippling limitation on our capacity to preserve order. Moreover, at precisely the time when the military and economic assistance programs that constitute our only means of exercising indirect control should be expanded, our balance of payments has been allowed to reach the stage of hemorrhage, and our armed forces are locked into an extravagantly expensive war on the Asian mainland. Given the staggering complexity and cost of modern military operations, it is now virtually impossible for the United States to deal with more than one major crisis at a time without imposing wartime controls on manpower and the economy.

The reduction of our forces in Europe, the seizure of the *Pueblo* and shooting down of our reconnaissance plane in the Sea of Japan, the harassment and detention of our fishing vessels on the high seas, and the abandonment of any pretense of protecting our private economic and financial interests in less developed countries are also part of this pattern of weakness and withdrawal.

Meanwhile, the Soviet Union has assumed a new expansionist posture, now somewhat muted by the diversionary effect of the Chinese threat along her eastern frontier. Ever since Khrushchev's famous declaration of January, 1961, in support of national "wars of liberation" the fixed policy of the Soviet Union has been to exploit internal discontents and foster subversion wherever it will serve Soviet national aims. In Latin America, Cuba has been an enthusiastic ally and coadjutor of these policies, while in Asia and one or two African countries China pursues similar aims on a less ambitious scale. Recently, the Soviet Union has also been stretching out the fingers of its naval and maritime power in furtherance of its political objectives in the Third World. Since 1964 there have been a permanent Soviet naval force in the Eastern Mediterranean and task groups visiting the Red Sea and Indian Ocean. Since 1965 the Soviets have developed a corps of marine infantry, a fleet of amphibious landing ships, and new helicopter assault carriers; there has also been a sharp increase in the number of oilers, repair ships, and tenders necessary to sustain a fleet at sea and project Soviet naval power into distant areas. For the first time in its history the Soviet Union is on the verge of acquiring a capability that it never had before—strategic mobility beyond the confines of the Eurasian land mass.

As a result of these shifts, the old system of alliances, shaky at best, has lost nearly all of its credibility. CENTO and SEATO were artificial creations to begin with, while, since the French defection, NATO has been allowed to deteriorate into a planning organization and a forum for venting complaints about the proper apportionment of vehicle maintenance costs. All three alliances are now flimsy and contingent instruments, to be honored only at the convenience of each participant and requiring reconfirmation whenever a crisis arises that might give them meaning. In the event of a sudden nuclear confrontation between the two superpowers it seems improbable that those NATO members like Great Britain, the Netherlands, and Denmark, that have large populations crammed into a narrow living space, would risk total extinction except in the face of a direct threat to their own national existence.

Finally, the internal political and economic climate of the United States has become a more potent factor than ever before in determining the credibility of our foreign policy. Today, the United States is assailed by domestic afflictions that cannot help but impair the durability of its commitments and the applicability of its military strength. Neither our current social tensions nor the drain of our gold reserves can be cured or even mitigated without a careful husbanding of the national wealth and a diversion of a larger part of it into peaceful channels. In theory, the United States has the resources to embark simultaneously on large-scale domestic and foreign policy programs, with space and deep-sea exploitation thrown in—but the price would be a tax rate so high and government controls so stringent that the country would cease to be a democratic republic.

The short-range picture is therefore not encouraging. It necessarily portrays a decline in the relative strength and influence of the West vis-à-vis the Third World, and a progressive degeneration in the global system of public order that closely parallels a similar degeneration of public order at home. The preceding periods were hardly ideal, but at least they achieved a rough political accommodation on terms that allowed the economic revival of Western Europe and the orderly transition of many African and Asian countries from colonial to local rule. They also gave the ordinary citizen and his family some sense of security from the risk of instantaneous cremation—a boon not to be vouchsafed to the next generation unless the drift to international anarchy is arrested.

The world polity now emerging is likely to be an unstable and polycentric one, full of shifting alliances and doubtful commitments, in which more governments will possess arsenals of atomic weapons and more populations will live in fear and trembling of them. It will be a world of rising population levels and unresolved economic problems, where the insecure régimes of small states, unable to improve their economies without massive and unremitting assistance from outside, will often be ready to embrace extreme ideologies and unsavory allies in order to maintain themselves in power. It will be a world in which a third superpower—more like a rogue elephant than a domesticated animal—overshadows the Asian mainland. Within this uncomfortable planetary environment, living in uneasy symbiosis with its titanic Soviet adversary, the United States will have to grope for a new rôle—for the old one of conductor to an orchestra of pliant allies is gone forever.

III

If the foregoing analysis is correct, the United States already faces the "agonizing reappraisal" so long predicted by the late John Foster Dulles.

For the first time since World War II, the United States will have to come to terms with the limitation of its power and build a viable foreign policy to conform with it. In doing so, it will have a number of options. It can pretend to disregard the great alteration in the world power equation and carry on as if the conditions of the postwar period and nineteen-fifties were still operative. Or it can liquidate its more unrealistic commitments, on the theory that most of them are no longer reciprocal, and stand behind its oceanic moat. Or it can seek some sort of transient politico-military accommodation with the Soviet Union or China, the choice to be determined by which one is most in need of containment at the moment. Or it can combine two or more courses in some rational permutation and set about creating a new security system.

None of these choices alone would be satisfactory, but the first would be disastrous. Any policy the United States adopts must be tailored to the realities of the world situation. It must also take into account enormous popular pressure for achievement of overdue domestic reforms.

Thus, the first task of the new administration should be to make an objective assessment of the position of the United States in the world and the rôle that it aspires to play. This must necessarily begin with a careful exposition of United States strategic interests, graded in order of priority.

A next step must be an evaluation of our national resources to determine what proportion of them we can afford to spend on the machinery designed to protect these interests—i.e., our defense, space, and foreign aid programs—taking into account all the other competing demands on these resources.

Next we must decide what kind of defense establishment we need in light of altered requirements, and how far distant from the mainland and Hawaii to maintain our floating picket lines and outposts—without having them converted into hostages for our good behavior.

In making this assessment we must liberate ourselves from the delusion that the beloved cliché of the last administration—that all the United States seeks is a free community of independent nations, each pursuing its own destiny—represents a policy or even a statement of the national interest. There are no longer any independent nations in the world—only interdependent ones—and only a tiny minority of the world's peoples have ever been free. Science, technology, and modern communications have brought all the nations of the world into uneasy bondage with each other, and our security now depends on the viability of our relationships with others.

It would be impossible for anyone outside the national security establishment to detail all the factors and considerations which would need to go into the making of such an assessment, much less to predict the specific recommendations that might emerge from it. All that an observer can do is to point out some of its more probable conclusions.

First, the range of United States commitments overseas will be drastically reduced. President Nixon has already said we have a "full plate" of them. Artificial alliances like SEATO which cannot be formally dismantled without loss of "face" will be allowed to lapse or fall into desuetude. There will be increasing reluctance to construe mutual defense treaties in ways that would obligate the United States to automatic political or military responses, or which would necessitate stationing large contingents of men and equipment in remote areas. The fear of becoming "bogged down" in expensive and inconclusive military operations in regions only marginally important to American security will exert a cautionary influence over United States policy-making.

Second, our foreign policy will become more restrained in both word and deed. In some respects, it will revert to what it was in the period between the two world wars—as used to be said of Britain in the old days, we will have no permanent allies, only permanent interests. Consistency and certainty will be at a premium, however, in order to preclude accidental confrontations and war by miscalculation.

We may also discover that our gratuitous and doctrinaire espousal of certain African and Asian "liberation movements" at the expense of good relations with European governments in these areas is a luxury we can no longer afford. The strident nationalism of many of the countries of the Third World may lead to combinations and policies totally antagonistic to American ideals and interests. Conversely, we are likely to rediscover that blood is thicker than water—that our community of interest with the English-speaking countries of Europe, Africa, North America, and the Pacific, who share with us a common heritage, culture, and language, constitutes a bond of stronger and more endearing value than associations with alien peoples, based on false analogies and a distorted interpretation of history.

Our strategy will conform to our foreign policy. It will be essentially an oceanic strategy, placing much stronger emphasis than heretofore on our most priceless assets, command of the sea and strategic mobility. It will require further modernization of our defense establishment, particularly the strategic airlift capability of the United States Army. It will also necessitate a reversal of the depreciation of the navy and the scandalous neglect of the merchant marine that characterized the MacNamara era in the Pentagon.

Indeed, the next decade is likely to tax our naval capabilities to the utmost. Not only is the arena of future limited war or temporary military intervention likely to be Africa, Latin-America, Asia, or the Middle East, but the unpredictable nationalism rampant in these areas, and their trend toward disengagement and even hostility, may often preclude the use of key land areas for staging areas and bases. Our projection of military power in the future may thus become absolutely dependent on the existence of large, self-sufficient naval, air, and amphibious forces.

Moreover, the oceans are not only a protective moat for the United States and a highway to distant regions, but also an avenue of access to North America. We have no way of knowing when a prospective enemy may achieve breakthroughs in underwater technology that will enable him to use the deep oceans and seabed for offensive devices of one sort or another that will threaten the safety of the entire North American mainland—at this advanced stage of technology it all depends on the resources he is willing to invest. Even if the enemy threat remained confined to missile-carrying submarines, it would still have to be countered by vast arrays of underwater detection devices and a strong anti-submarine capability.

On the plane of nuclear stategy, the future gives us little choice. We will have to match as best we can the technological advances of the Soviet Union in weapons systems, space vehicles, and electronic guidance and detection devices. The dismal feature of this imperative is that given the dynamic character of modern science there is virtually no ceiling to the amount of funds that can be expended on an arms race in this area. If the next stage of this sinister marathon extends to space vehicles, orbital platforms, and other elements of space technology capable of conversion to offensive purposes the sky will literally be the limit. The most one can hope for is that its own domestic needs and a comprehension of the futility of adding further to the arsenal of overkill will finally persuade the Soviet Union to co-operate in stopping the arms race.

Even though the United States will probably remain the world's leading military power for some time, in the sense of possessing modern naval, air, and ground forces capable of being deployed and sustained over vast distances, this "flexible response" capability will in the future be much less usable as an instrument of policy, and therefore less credible as a deterrent, because of the growing political complications attendant on its use. The political influence of the underdeveloped countries, the force of world public opinion, and the continuing danger of confrontations with the Soviet Union and China are increasingly likely to blunt and deflect the peremptory employment of preventive or retaliatory military measures. Consequently, the United States will probably rely more on politico-military modes of joint action similar to the OAS cover accorded to the Dominican intervention of 1964 (and for that matter to the Warsaw, Pact mantle thrown over the Soviet invasion of Czechoslovakia) or on multinational forces mustered and deployed by the United Nations.

As a result, the United States will have to place far more reliance on economic, technological, educational, and scientific assistance as an instrument of policy than it has in the past. There is a long overdue need to correct the overly militaristic and chauvinistic image of the United States in much of the world and to publicize the extraordinary dynamism of our private economy and civilian technology. With contracted security commitments, and the diminished efficacy of naked military intervention unaccompanied by political measures, the United States should be able to take advantage of its unique capabilities in these fields to render selective assistance to countries of the Third World that are prepared to play a constructive rôle in the community of nations.

The new conservative posture of the United States foreign policy will also put a premium on skillful diplomacy. This was not a vital factor during the postwar era when our nuclear monopoly and vast economic aid programs spoke for themselves. But with the trumps more evenly distributed, the skill of the players counts for more. Experience in negotiation, rapport with foreign political figures, and a sensitive appreciation of domestic political forces are likely to be more valuable qualities in an American ambassador than the bland reportorial gifts of the career diplomat.

Finally, in the dangerous age ahead, extraordinary skill will be needed at the top levels of government to preserve inflexibility of purpose and imperturbability of demeanor. The United States may often find itself in a position similar to that of Britain in the nineteenth century, but with every move reflected and illuminated in the enveloping glare of the mass media. Such a rôle cannot be played successfully unless the reaction time of our government is greatly slowed down, and there is a drastic reduction in the confusing torrent of speeches, statements, explanations, and clarifications of explanations that poured out of Washington during the Kennedy and Johnson years. (It is not, for example, either necessary or desirable to produce an instant rebuttal to every statement by an adversary or an immediate counterproposal to every demand in the United Nations.) A calculated display of calm and deliberation is a more effective way to defuse a dangerously inflammatory situation or promote a quiet transition of policy than frantic activity.

The supreme problem of the next decade will be how to achieve viable co-existence with the two Marxist superpowers without, on the one hand, contracting our defense posture to the point of abandoning those parts of the free world crucial to our security and, on the other, jeopardizing the achievement of essential domestic goals. A policy of either extreme would further imperil national unity and make both goals impossible of achievement. Yet these goals now compete with each other to an unprecedented extent. They each make monumental demands on our national resources. Somehow they must be reconciled by a foreign policy that defines and grades our strategic interests in light of the resources available, and then makes a skillful and judicious choice of the courses of action necessary to protect those interests. Since the resources themselves define the practical limits of our interests, while the nature and character of each course of action determines its feasibility, the options are far narrower than we realize. Our survival as a nation depends on whether we make the right choice.